Theatrical Space and Historical Place in Sophocles' *Oedipus at Colonus*

Greek Studies: Interdisciplinary Approaches
General Editor: Gregory Nagy, Harvard University

On the front cover: A calendar frieze representing the Athenian months, reused in the Byzantine Church of the Little Metropolis in Athens. The cross is superimposed, obliterating Taurus of the Zodiac. The choice of this frieze for books in *Greek Studies: Interdisciplinary Approaches* reflects this series' emphasis on the blending of the diverse heritages—Near Eastern, Classical, and Christian—in the Greek tradition. Drawing by Laurie Kain Hart, based on a photograph. Recent titles in the series are:

The Transformation of Hera: A Study of Ritual, Hero, and the Goddess in the Iliad, Joan V. O'Brien, Southern Illinois University
Hegemony and Greek Historians, John Wickersham, Ursinus College
The Scepter and the Spear: Studies on Forms of Repetition in the Homeric Poems, Steven Lowenstam, University of Oregon
The Origins and Development of Ancient Greek Democracy, James L. O'Neil, The University of Sydney
Heat and Lust: Hesiod's Midsummer Festival Scene Revisited, J. D. B. Petropoulos, Democritean University of Thrace
The Pastoral Narcissus: A Study of the First Idyll of Theocritus, Clayton Zimmerman, Carleton College
An Archaeology of Ancestors: Tomb Cult and Hero Cult in Early Greece, Carla M. Antonaccio, Wesleyan University
The Seal of Orestes: Self-Reference and Authority in Sophocles' Electra, Ann G. Batchelder, College of the Holy Cross
The Shield of Achilles and the Poetics of Ekphrasis, Andrew Sprague Becker, Virginia Polytechnic Institute
The Blinded Eye: Thucydides and the New Written Word, Gregory Crane, Tufts University
The Wrath of Athena: Gods and Men in the Odyssey, Jenny Strauss Clay, University of Virginia
Talking Trojan: Speech and Community in the Iliad, Hilary Mackie, Rice University
Poet and Audience in the Argonautica *of Apollonius,* Robert V. Albis, The Hotchkiss School
Theatrical Space and Historical Place in Sophocles' Oedipus at Colonus, Lowell Edmunds, Rutgers University

Theatrical Space and Historical Place in Sophocles' *Oedipus at Colonus*

LOWELL EDMUNDS

ROWMAN & LITTLEFIELD PUBLISHERS, INC.
Lanham • Boulder • New York • London

ROWMAN & LITTLEFIELD PUBLISHERS, INC.

Published in the United States of America
by Rowman & Littlefield Publishers, Inc.
4720 Boston Way, Lanham, Maryland 20706

3 Henrietta Street
London WC2E 8LU, England

Copyright © 1996 by Rowman & Littlefield Publishers, Inc.

All rights reserved. No part of this publication may be reproduced, stored in a retrieval system, or transmitted in any form or by any means, electronic, mechanical, photocopying, recording, or otherwise, without the prior permission of the publisher.

British Cataloging in Publication Information Available

Library of Congress Cataloging-in-Publication Data

Edmunds, Lowell.
 Theatrical space and historical place in Sophocles' Oedipus at Colonus
/ Lowell Edmunds.
  p. cm.
 Includes bibliographical references and index.
 ISBN 0–8476–8319–2 (cloth : alk. paper). — ISBN 0–8476–8320–6
(paper : alk. paper)
  1. Sophocles. Oedipus at Colonus. 2. Political plays, Greek—History and criticism.
3. Greek drama (Tragedy)—History and criticism. 4. Oedipus (Greek mythology) in
literature. 5. Sophocles—Political and social views. 6. Politics and literature—Greece.
7. Sophocles—Dramatic production. 8. Space and time in literature. 9. Theater—
Semiotics.
PR4413.053E36   1996
882'.01—dc20   96–23870
                                                                                CIP

ISBN 0–8476–8319–2 (cloth : alk. paper)
ISBN 0–8476–8320–6 (pbk. : alk. paper)

Printed in the United States of America

♾™ The paper used in this publication meets the minimum requirements of American National Standard for Information Sciences—Permanence of Paper for Printed Library Materials, ANSI Z39.48–1984.

Contents

Foreword	vii
Preface	ix
Introduction	1
Part I	13
1 Theorizing Theatrical Space	15
2 Theatrical Space in *Oedipus at Colonus*	39
Part II	85
3 Historical Place in *Oedipus at Colonus*	87

Historical background and apologetic tendency. Mythical background and apologetic tendency. Code of place. Exile and ἔγκτησις. ἀτιμία. Philia (1). Philia (2). Livelihood and Curse. Xenia. Self-exoneration and Draco homicide law. Eumenides. Soteria. Oedipus in Pindar, *Pyth.* 4.236–69.

Conclusion	149
Appendix	
Life of Sophocles and Reception of *Oedipus at Colonus*	163
Works Cited	169
Indexes	181
About the Author	191

Greek Studies:
Interdisciplinary Approaches

Foreword
by Gregory Nagy, General Editor

Building on the foundations of scholarship within the disciplines of philology, philosophy, history, and archaeology, this series spans the continuum of Greek traditions extending from the second millennium B.C.E. to the present, not just the Archaic and Classical periods. The aim is to enhance perspectives by applying various different disciplines to problems that have in the past been treated as the exclusive concern of a single given discipline. Besides the crossing-over of the older disciplines, as in the case of historical and literary studies, the series encourages the application of such newer ones as linguistics, sociology, anthropology, and comparative literature. It also encourages encounters with current trends in methodology, especially in the realm of literary theory.

Theatrical Space and Historical Place in Sophocles' "Oedipus at Colonus," by Lowell Edmunds, re-examines the historical context of this drama in light of its political impact as a theatrical—not just poetic—masterpiece. The semiotic world of Sophocles' *Oedipus at Colonus,* Edmunds argues, is built from its very essence as *theater.* Even Colonus, the outlying Athenian district that serves as a dramatic setting for Oedipus at Colonus, turns out to be a most significant landmark of this world, and it is no coincidence that Colonus happens to be the birthplace of that premier dramatist of his era, Sophocles himself. Nor can we forget that Sophocles had been a premier statesman of Athens as we begin to contemplate the political implications of this last drama of his, this poetic *and* theatrical *and* political swansong composed toward the very end of his long life of over ninety years, in the turbulent times that engulfed the city-state of Athens in the wake of the oligarchical revolution of 411 B.C.E. Sophocles died before his *Oedipus at Colonus* was released, and we can only begin to imagine the theatrical and political excitement of this posthumous drama on the awaited day of its première, as the audience of citizens at long last quieted down to hear the poet's final words, as if spoken from the dead.

Preface

If I give a brief record of the writing of this book, which went on for several years, it is not for the sake of autobiography but to express thanks for the various events and encounters (many face to face, some through e-mail, some epistolary in the old sense) without which the result would look different. The origin of Part II was Charles Segal's seminar on Sophocles at Princeton, at which, in December, 1988, I presented the outline of the historical reading and the substance of Chapter 3§3 (on the theme of place). In the fall of 1989, *Oedipus at Colonus* was one of the tragedies I read with students in a seminar at Rutgers. In April, 1990, I gave five seminars on this tragedy at the University of Venice and a lecture at the University of Urbino. In July, I gave a paper, based mainly on Chapter 3§1 (on horses, Knights, and Poseidon) at a conference at the University of Nottingham organized by Alan Sommerstein, where I had the good fortune to meet P. E. Easterling, who later read Chapter Three and sent me detailed comments. I also met Mary Whitlock Blundell at this conference and she, too, read this chapter. In September, I gave a new version of the Nottingham paper at the University of Toronto and, in December, yet another version at the University of Pennsylvania. I am most grateful to interlocutors at Nottingham and at the universities I have named. In the footnotes, I have thanked still others who have given me help.

    I was fortunate to be able, in May and June 1991, to take a Rutgers University "Course for Faculty" taught by Elin Diamond (Department of English), a specialist in theory of drama. She has been generous with comment on Chapter One despite qualms about several of my arguments. A shorter version of Chapter One was presented at a conference ("Antike Dramatheorien und ihre Rezeption") in Zurich, September 23, 1991. I am grateful to Bernhard Zimmermann for the invitation to participate and to several other participants for their comments. Fellow-*convegnisti* Angela Andrisano, Lutz Käppel, and Bernd Seidensticker later sent me useful references. Stephen Halliwell and David Wiles generously sent written comments on Chapter One, which caused me to rethink several points, though probably not to the point of agreement. Michael Issacharoff, whose course in semiotics of comedy I audited at Johns Hopkins in the mid-1980s and whose divisions of theatrical space I have appropriated in Chapter One, kindly sent me extensive bibliographical information and advice. Victor Bers, Richard Hamilton, Jeffrey Henderson, Donald Mastronarde, Robert Renehan, and Niall Slater responded to my calls of *boêthia* while I was writing Chapter Two. The last-named kindly allowed me to read his "From Ancient Performance to New Historicism," then forthcoming in *DRAMA* 2 (Slater 1993). Kurt Raaflaub sent me the galley proofs of his "Politisches Denken und Krise der Polis: Athen im Verfassungskonflikt des späten 5. Jahrhunderts v. Chr." (Raaflaub 1992), an article that masterfully describes the situation to which I believe that *Oedipus at Colonus* was *pro tanto* a response. Elli Mylonas sent me a photograph from Athens that helped clear up a point (in Chapter Two) concerning the Theater of Dionysus.

In the spring of 1992, I took another Rutgers "Course for Faculty," this time on Jacques Derrida, taught by Derek Attridge. This course helped me as much with rethinking the conclusion of my book as Elin Diamond's had helped with the beginning. (The relation between the beginning, on the theatrical sign in theatrical space, and the end, on the sign in the vector of différance, is adumbrated further on in this preface.) During the summer, I received very useful sets of detailed comments on the manuscript from Victor Bers, to whom I again express my gratitude, and from Gregory Nagy, whom I also thank. In January 1993, I had the opportunity of reading the first chapter ("Approaches to Theatrical Space") of a book in progress by David Wiles, which, in effect, continued the dialogue begun over a year earlier and led to further rethinking of my own opening chapter.

One of the reactions I received from a reader was the question: "have you justified adequately your choice of Antonin Artaud?" I had in fact taken my statement about Artaud and Brecht at the beginning of Chapter One, that they are the two principal mid-twentieth-century theorists of drama, as axiomatic. If it is necessary, however, to justify my use of Artaud as a pivotal figure in the history of the theory of drama, I can refer to the relevant articles in, say, The *Encyclopaedia Britannica*, or I can cite the introduction to the special 1992 issue of *PMLA* on theater (Benston 1992), in which Artaud and Brecht are fundamental influences and stand for fundamental alternatives. This citational gesture would satisfy the expectations of many and would constitute a certain kind of justification of my use of Artaud. But a more fundamental issue would remain. What is the standing of a book on an ancient tragedy and on the historical context of that tragedy that takes twentieth-century theory as its starting point? For now, I offer the following brief reflections.

It seems to me that any work of classical scholarship on a Greek tragedy as a whole or on a whole Greek tragedy (thus even a textual edition, thus certainly a commentary) is also a work about how one reads a tragedy. Even if one has maintained a strict silence about one's theoretical commitments, they are still there, and someone else will be able to say what they are. (Indeed this process of exposure goes on in the branch of classical scholarship called the history of classical scholarship.) So all classical scholarship is equally based in theory. The theoretical component differs from one work of scholarship to another only in the degree to which it is exposed. In calm periods, when unanimity on how poetry should be read prevails, and when, in consequence, methodology is secure and there is a standard for correctness, it is unnecessary to state or even to reflect on theory and method. As nearly as I can tell, this is not one of those periods. Thus, the book here offered to fellow-classicists and to others, while somewhat monographic in content, focusing on a single tragedy, is polygraphic in approach, registering the changes that this tragedy caused in the theoretical orientation of a certain reader and scholar at the end of the twentieth century.

The project began, as said, with an interest in historical place, in Colonus, in Colonus as a place where the Knights congregated. Thus an interest directly in line with work of mine on Aristophanes' *Knights* completed not long before and in line with my focus on ideology in that work. The historical research on *Oedipus at Colonus* yielded the results seen in the many sections of Chapter Three, which I then wanted to coordinate with a reading of the play as a whole. Since the meaning of the historical place had come, for the original audience, from its representation in a theatrical space, the question arose of how to read the play in this specifically theatrical dimension. The approach to theatrical space was going to be semiotic; its theoretical basis is set out in Chapter One.

Was the theory, in the form in which I reasoned it out, already unconsciously determined by the body of Oedipus, that central object of contention in the tragedy? In any case, my fascination with the body of the actor as the primary semiotic-theatrical fact no doubt betrays the modern nostalgia for ritual that goes back to Nietzsche's *Birth of Tragedy* and to the Cambridge School, that inhabits Artaud, and that is played out again and again in scholarship (witness the revival of interest in ritual and sacrifice in classical scholarship inspired by Walter Burkert) and in theatrical theory and practice (Benston 1992:442 col. 1). But the concentration on the sign or signifier had a predictable and perhaps inevitable result, leading on to a characteristic twentieth-century problematics, the so-called "crisis of representation," and in fact—this is what might have been predictable—discovering that this problematics was already foreseen in the tragedy (Johnson 1988:xii). The ontogeny of this book, as it moves from semiotics to différance, thus retraces the broad outline of the phylogeny of twentieth-century critical theory.

I wish to display three disclaimers as prominently as possible. First, this is a book about theatrical space, not about space in general. Therefore I have nothing to say about space in the history of philosophy, and I have not cited two books widely discussed in recent years, those of Gaston Bachelard (1969) and Henri Lefebvre (1986). (Neither discusses theatrical space.) Nor have I discussed Derrida's *Khôra* (Derrida 1993a), a book that would have required me to read my conclusions concerning *Oedipus at Colonus* against Plato's *Timaeus* and thus to depart from the space of this book. Second, while my book offers a theory of theatrical space and an application thereof that are semiotic, I have deliberately refrained from discussion of the relation between semiotics of theater on the one hand and general theories of semiotics on the other—that would have required another book. Third, because my book reached its present shape by January, 1992 and has been little changed since then, the bibliography on its proper concerns is in arrears. The bibiliography may already have appeared deficient in 1992. My failure to cite such-and-such does not, however, always mean (though it often means) that I have not read it, nor does it mean, if I have read it, that I think it is valueless.

The text of *Oedipus at Colonus* that I have used is mainly the new OCT of Lloyd-Jones and Wilson. The transliteration of Greek names and words is inconsistent. An earlier version of Chapter One appeared in *DRAMA* 1. I am grateful to the editors for permission to reprint.

Finally, I am grateful to Susan Edmunds for reading and discussing with me the drafts of this book.

L.E.
Highland Park, NJ
October, 1995

Introduction

The importance of historical place—of Colonus, of the grove of the Eumenides, of Athens—in *Oedipus at Colonus* has been a theme of scholarship on this play. In a performance, historical place first appears as theatrical space. For this reason, a reading like mine, again concerned with the meaning of the places just named, might want to begin with theatrical space. This approach via the perception of a spectator or reader/virtual spectator would conform to Hans Robert Jauss' hermeneutic premise that the esthetic is primary in interpretation. On this premise, the possible meanings of place originate only within esthetic perception. How, then, to read the play with a view to the esthetics of space? The first chapter of this book attempts to lay the theoretical foundation for such a reading. As it happens, both theatrical practice and theory of drama in the twentieth century have been preoccupied with problems of space, and thus the materials for a theory of theatrical space are ready to hand. The first task of that chapter, however, is to relativize the Aristotelian primacy of the verbal text as distinguished from the performance text or script. Semiotics of theater, the body of theory most promising for a critique of the tradition deriving from Aristotle's *Poetics*, provides the basis for a theory of theatrical space developed in the rest of Chapter One.

This starting point might appear more radical than necessary, as anyone can read *Oedipus at Colonus* or any other ancient play as a script, looking for imbedded stage directions (in the absence of any other), "blocking" the performance, and, in general, planning the mis en scène. Such a directorial reading, however, whether historical or contemporary, whether dedicated to study of ancient theatrical production or to a present-day performance, does nothing to qualify the primacy of the verbal or dramatic text, which remains an item in a genre of Greek literature and can still be read and studied like any item in any other genre. The play remains in an either-or status: either a script or a text. The focus on stagecraft thus leaves non-theatrical interpretation of the dramatic text untouched, and the preparation of a performance does not entail the specifically theatrical interpretation that a theory of theatrical space intends to provide.[1] The stage that is left empty at the end of the fourth episode of *Oedipus at Colonus* is an example of the dilemma of the dramatic text. A directorial reading of the play as a script cannot fail to have everyone on stage exit at the end of this episode, with Oedipus leading; but such a reading has completed its task with the stage directions and says nothing about the significance of the empty stage. A nontheatrical reading of the play as a dramatic text, for its part, has nothing to say about the empty stage, because this emptiness is not verbal, is not "in" the text. And yet, as perhaps will be intuitively conceded, this emptiness is as significant as anything that any character says in the play.

The first chapter, then, attempts to secure the theoretical foundation for a specifically theatrical interpretation of space. In order to foreground the Aristotelian basis of the persistent either-or status of the dramatic text, I begin with a comparison of Aristotle and Antonin Artaud, one of the principal mid-twentieth-century theorists of drama. Artaud represents a new horizon of expectation concerning the theater within which mis en scène and, in particular, theatrical space loom large. Semiotics of theater is a theoretical reflex of this historical change of horizons from Aristotle's to Artaud's concept of theater. The field of classics has experienced this change in the form of an interest in ancient stagecraft and theatrical production. The studies of Oliver Taplin and Wolf Steidle come immediately to mind,[2] and others are cited in the notes of Chapter One. The reconquest of the space of ancient tragedy and comedy proceeds, one senses, on many fronts. Thus the semiotic approach is only a heretofore lost or unknown relative of much well-known work in the general area of the theatrical space of Greek tragedy. But, as said, theatrical semiotics provides the basis for systematic analysis of mis en scène and thus for a specifically theatrical hermeneutics that dissolves the either-or antinomy of the dramatic text. Reading based on theatrical semiotics would be especially attentive to "instances of discourse," demonstrative

---

1. The split persists in Aston and Savona 1991. They have two chapters on stage directions. In the introduction to the second, they say: "Whereas that analysis [the first of the two chapters just mentioned] was pitched at the level of text, we propose now to examine the implications of the directions, as a sign-system operative in parallel to the dialogue, for stage practice" (123).
2. And see the bibliography in Schwinge 1990:5 n. 9.

pronouns, particles, paralinguistic signs (interjections), the relation of utterance to physical position, and the like, and, on another scale of magnitude, to the relation of stage space to space off stage. The reader would ask how, in addition to the entrances, exits, and other actions explicitly required by the text, these other aspects of discourse may already presuppose a theatrical space, how, indeed, the whole written dramatic text is already motivated by the physical conditions of performance. The reading may be only a virtual performance or it may be intended as preparation for a real performance. It does not matter. Reading and performance can now legitimately be used as mutual metaphors. Reading is performance,[3] and performance is reading.[4]

The practitioner of theater, director or actor or whoever, might wonder: why all this reference to reading? An answer, for present purposes: Greek tragedy can and will be read far more often than it is performed. It is appropriate, then, and in the spirit of the practitioner, to attempt the most theatrical reading.

Within the theorizing of theatrical space that goes on in Chapter One, the self-referentiality of the theatrical sign begins to emerge as the primacy of the written text fades. Whereas, in life, language is the primary human sign system, in theater, language is relativized as it is thrown into relation with other sign systems that cause its status as a sign system to lose its naturalness and self-evidence and to become an aspect of the spectacle. Theater provides "the spectacle of discourse," to use Michael Issacharoff's phrase. Discourse itself is on display. And whereas a semiotics of non-dramatic poetry is the study of how language is encoded in a text, semiotics of theater is the study of how a multiplicity of codes, of which language is only one, affect and refer to one another. Since theatrical signs have this capacity for cross-reference, they are also, within the system of the performance or the virtual performance of reading, autoreflexive and thus potentially metatheatrical. The reader or spectator may at some point become the spectator of an actor turned spectator or may somehow perceive theater in theater. This possibility is often denied in the case of Greek tragedy, where metatheatricality has seemed to be precluded because it would break the spell that tragedy must cast if it is to have its proper effect.[5] Metatheater has come into discussion mainly apropos of

---

3. Jauss 1982:142.
4. Wiles 1987:141. Cf. Goldhill 1989:180-81. As for spectating as reading, cf. my critique of Ubersfelder at the end of Ch. 1.
5. Taplin 1986. See the critique of Wiles 1987:143.

Euripidean allusions to Aeschylus and of Dionysus in the *Bacchae*.[6] The second chapter of this book, which applies to *Oedipus at Colonus* the semiotic principles established in Chapter One, in fact discovers a pervasive metatheatricality; and a comment on the supposed spell-breaking effect of this dramatic device can be offered in advance. I shall take an example from *Oedipus at Colonus* not discussed in Chapter Two, which I preface with "evidence" from my own experience of self-reference in another, related medium. On December 1, 1991, at the Museum of Natural History in New York, I attended the performance of a series of ritual dances, which are part of a larger potlatch ritual, by the Wewanagila Dance Company of Vancouver, British Columbia. These dancers are a Kwakiutl family. In one episode, the hero Siwidi has to encounter a succession of monsters on the ocean floor. As each of these monsters appears on stage, the magnificence of its mask and costume inevitably draws attention and appreciation, as aspects of the chief's display of his munificence; but this self-reference to the material of the performance in no way detracts from the cultural significance of the myth of Siwidi that is represented in the dance nor does it contradict the predominant seriousness of the feelings and ideas conveyed to the audience. In *Oedipus at Colonus*, the many references to the eyes and face of Oedipus are inevitably references to a mask, which would have been a new mask, outside the canon of theatrical masks, the curiosity and excellence of which would have been appreciated as such but would not have diminished the over-all seriousness of the scenes in which Oedipus himself, Theseus, or Polyneices describe Oedipus' face.[7]

To sum up the relation of the first two chapters, Chapter One establishes a semiotic theory of theoretical space that serves in Chapter Two as the foundation for a hermeneutics of space in *Oedipus at Colonus*. The reading of the tragedy is, however, a historical one. The virtual performance at which the reading aims is one that took place in the Theater of Dionysus in Athens, and the reading is oriented to what an ancient spectator might have seen, without any bias toward or concession to the

---

6. Whereas in Aristophanes it is a standard comic device. Taplin 1986 takes metatheatricality as a distinguishing characteristic between comedy and tragedy.
7. Segal 1982:248-49 argues that *prosôpon* at Eur. *Bacch*. 1277 is metatheatrical. Contra: Taplin 1986:170. The discussion of the mask by Foley 1980:126-33 does not address the question of metatheatricality, but much of her article demonstrates this aspect of *Bacch*. "The language of the play refers with remarkable frequency to the visual and musical experience on stage and emphasizes that both honoring and comprehending the god are essentially theatrical acts." (108). Cf. Foley 1985:217-28 and 246-54 for the mask.

historical situation of the reading itself. Thus I might seem not only to have avoided the fundamental hermeneutical problem of the meaning of a historically remote work for a present interpreter but even to have moved toward the situation somewhat playfully imagined by Terry Eagleton:

> Let us imagine that by dint of some deft archaeological research we discovered a great deal more about what ancient Greek tragedy actually meant to its original audiences, recognized that these concerns were utterly remote from our own, and began to read the plays again in the light of this deepened knowledge. One result might be that we stopped enjoying them. We might come to see that we had enjoyed them previously because we were unwittingly reading them in the light of our own preoccupations; once this became less possible, the drama might cease to speak at all significantly to us.[8]

If my historical reading were as good as I hope it is, then might I not be bringing *Oedipus at Colonus* closer to the dead end that Eagleton conjectures? A hermeneutic answer to this question would come from the notion of the esthetic as the bridge between the historical "otherness" of the text, on the one hand, and its reading in the present, on the other. Jauss speaks of the esthetic character of poetry as a "hermeneutic bridge" between past and present. It is "that which makes possible the historical understanding of art across the distance in time in the first place, and which therefore must be integrated into the execution of the interpretation as a hermeneutic premise."[9] This hermeneutic bridge, it should be added, does not entail some transhistorical esthetics; on the contrary, esthethic perception originates within and is conditioned by the present horizon of expectation. My historical reading, I could argue, would never have come to pass if it had not been preceded by a first esthetic reading or readings that motivated the further work represented in Chapter Two. Further, Oedipus is already historically mediated to us because he is a special case among the Greek heroes, one who has been received already, who has found his own bridge to the present. The exiled Theban king, after he was buried in Colonus, was to establish a new kingdom of thought in the twentieth century.[10] He is a theme for us, a focus of concern, and we can become engaged with the interpretation of *Oedipus at Colonus* even in spite of what many readers now consider its esthetic deficiencies.

8. Eagleton 1983:12.
9. Jauss 1982:146.
10. Edmunds 1991.

6   Introduction

The kinds of response to Eagleton's paradox that have just been suggested might account for the motivation of my historical reading of the tragedy but they would still leave unanswered the question of the present value or meaning of the ancient work as historically interpreted. This question is one that I shall approach from a distance, starting with what I believe is the current understanding of the matter in the field of classics. In short, classicists deny that Eagleton's radical historicism is either their aim or their result. Consider this opening of a book review by Oliver Taplin:

> There used to be Greek Tragedy, which presented eternal issues of morality and religion in a poetry that lent itself to the autonomous, context-free critical approach of the not-so-New Criticism. The trend of the 1980s has been displacing this with *Athenian* tragedy, which exposed and exercised the deepest selves and self-images of its citizen audience, that is, the free-born men who as a mass (the *demos*) held on to political power during the great age of democracy in the fifth century BC. In rejecting the appropriation of their dramas by our present prejudices, and restoring them to the alien conceptual and social systems of that remote world, this approach, at its best, manages to keep them none the less alive. Nicole Loraux, for example, distances Euripides' *Ion* by interpreting it in terms of autochthony and patrilineal filiation; yet her thesis is that the play exposes the imbalance of the nuclear family, that the "fiction" of the parental couple is "a civic way of masking the inevitable disjunction between paternal and maternal roles". She would presumably not want this lesson to be lost on her contemporary readers.[11]

I am concerned not with Taplin's point about Nicole Loraux's article but with the general strategy that he diagnoses: the abandonment of transhistorical claims for Greek tragedy in the name of an unprejudiced historical contextualization in which, however, the transhistorical claims reappear in a new guise ("none the less alive"). For the classicist interpreter of Greek tragedy, the problem of the bridge between the present and the past does not arise. But the notion of "rejecting the appropriation of [the ancient Greeks'] dramas by our present prejudices" directly confronts one of the largest concerns of contemporary critical theory. In this notion of objectivity, of an unconditional, unprejudiced starting-point of research, one finds indeed the central difference between classics and the rest of the humanities, and, for that matter, the sciences. In virtually

---

11. Oliver Taplin, "Drastic Celebrations" (review of Winkler and Zeitlin, edd. 1990), *TLS* July 13-19, 1990, p. 759.

every other field, the prejudices of the reader or observer are assumed and problematized.

It would be very unfair to the field of classics, however, to suggest that the standpoint of the historically remote reader has never presented itself as a problem. H. D. F. Kitto, for example, proposed: "Perhaps there are two separate questions: What does the play mean to this generation? and, What did it mean to the dramatist and his generation?"[12] This notion of changing questions appears also in the conclusion of R. G. A. Buxton's survey of the state of interpretation of Sophocles in 1984:

> I am well aware that my approach might be taken to imply that 'the problems' are isolable and finite, and that in order to solve them one has simply to choose between the alternatives which critics have already put forward. In fact, of course, 'the problems' alter as scholarship itself develops, and my account of the state of play is necessarily a provisional one. It is certain that in thirty years' time those who think about Sophocles will be asking different questions from those we ourselves are disposed to ask. It is impossible to predict whether those questions will be generated by new movements in literary studies, in anthropology, in history, or in some quite different branch of enquiry.[13]

Kitto spoke of the difference in the questions put to a play by its original audience and by the present generation. Similarly, Buxton speaks of changes in the questions put to Sophocles by successive generations of scholars. This notion of changing questions is perfectly reconcilable with Gadamer's notion that a text is an answer to a question. Gadamer took the further step, however, of arguing that the reconstructed historical question is already included within the horizon of the present. Therefore, understanding is a "fusion of horizons," of the horizon of the past and the horizon of the present.

It might seem, then, that hermeneutics goes to an extreme opposite of classical scholarship: instead of a purportedly unprejudiced, unconditional view of the past, it offers a fusion of present and past that would amount to a hopeless confusion. We would never know if we were talking about ourselves or the Greeks. Even if we had contemporary records of response to *Oedipus at Colonus*, they could not establish a historical horizon because they themselves could be understood only with the same kind of fusion as the tragedy and thus would be no more transparent than it. This dilemma can to some extent be overcome, however,

12. Kitto 1956:91.
13. Buxton 1984:34.

by the further application of semiotics in Chapter Three, where a historical contextualization of the tragedy is attempted. The premise is the same as the one to be argued in Chapter One: theatrical signs are signs of signs.[14] The semiotic codes of theater are taken from life (and also from the given, contemporary conventions of theater) and are remade in performance. For the purposes of my discussion, the standard definition of code suffices: a code is a set of signs together with the rules for their combinations. In the case of theatrical signs, their semantic value is a transaction between their pregiven meaning in their historical cultural context and their new meaning in the context of theater, which rebuilds codes and resemanticizes signs, which thus become signs of signs. This is the process that is studied in Chapter Three. The stage space of *Oedipus at Colonus* represents Colonus and, in particular, the edge of the grove of the Eumenides. Nearby, off stage, is the altar of Poseidon, and other items of the landscape are indicated. This place and these geographical points acquire a particular new meaning in the tragedy as their pregiven meaning is resemanticized. The geographical code is perhaps the predominant one in the tragedy (Ch. 3§3). But several other codes are undergoing the same process of remaking in the course of Oedipus' reception at Colonus and in Attica, beginning with the narrative code of the Oedipus myth itself (Ch. 3§2). Various legal and social mechanisms are recodified (mostly in quite abbreviated, subtle forms and not always consistently with one another): the grant of *enktêsis* (Ch. 3§4), the removal of *atîmia* (Ch. 3§5), xenia (Ch. 3§9), the Draco homicide law (Ch. 3§10), and others.

In their remaking, the signs that become signs of signs do not disappear in the heroic age in which *Oedipus at Colonus* is set but preserve some degree of contemporary reference. If they did not, they could not contribute to the apologetic tendency that I shall hypothesize and argue in Chapter Three. They are, then, anachronisms in the heroic setting. While anachronism is generally considered normal in Greek tragedy, its pervasiveness in *Oedipus at Colonus* has not, to judge from the standard commentaries, been completely appreciated. In Ch. 3§10, I speak of the legal coloring of Oedipus' speech of self-defense against Kreon. Here I point out that the whole of the second episode has this coloring, and I introduce a set of examples from that episode, not discussed in

---

14. This formula unifies the apparently opposed positions of Taplin and Goldhill. Cf. Goldhill 1989:174ff., where it is argued that the grammar of theatrical devices desiderated by Taplin (and by Wiles 1987, to which Goldhill 1989 is a reply) must be supplemented by a semantics.

Chapter Three, as a basis for preliminary reflection on the function of anachronism in the tragedy. Kreon uses a legal term to justify his seizure of Antigone and Ismene (ἐφάψομαι 859; cf. LSJ s.v. II.1.c). Theseus uses another one to reprove this action (ἕλκω 927; cf. LSJ s.v. II.3). Kreon considers Oedipus a surety owing to the city of Thebes (ῥύσιον 858; cf. LSJ s.v. I.1).[15] Using the verb πημαίνειν, Kreon states that any injury to him is tantamount to an act of war against Thebes (837). When Theseus appears as the rescuer, he uses the same verb to ask Oedipus who is injuring him (893; cf. Sappho frag. 1.19-20 L-P). In the context of international conflict that has now been established in several ways, Theseus' question would also suggest a hostile incursion into his city's territory, a sense that the verb πημαίνειν has in inscriptions and in Herodotus.[16]

The question arises of how such anachronisms are accommodated to the heroic age setting. P. E. Easterling has shown that anachronism must be considered a poetic device like any of the others that the tragedians have at their disposal and must therefore be interpreted as such.[17] In Chapter Two, I shall in fact treat anachronism in this way, twice noticing its semiotic effect in defining relations amongst stage, orchestra, and audience, and once noticing its contribution to a metatheatrical effect. While I agree with Easterling that the tendency of the tragedians is to minimize the inconcinnity of anachronism and to present a stylistically self-consistent picture of the heroic age, I believe that anachronism can also and at the same time, as in the examples to be seen in Chapter Two, have other functions that do not conflict with the over-all stylistic effect, just as metatheater does not undercut seriousness. The several examples discussed in Chapter Three must be softened and blurred in the ways that, on the basis of other examples, Easterling has well demonstrated; if not, they become a mass of jarring, distracting contradictions. (To return to the examples in the preceding paragraph, the context has the effect of blurring them: the verb that Kreon uses in 859 has been anticipated by the non-legal simplex in 830; the verb that Theseus uses in 927 is anticipated by Antigone's use of the non-legal compound in 844.) At the same time, they maintain an indirect reference to the contemporary situation

---

15. These and other terms are discussed, in a comparative legal context, in Schulze 1918:483 nn. 2 and 4; 502.
16. *IGI*³38.8. This inscription is dated to 460-440 B.C.E. by Figueira 1991:123-24, who discusses it with *IGI*³83.4-5 (restored from Thuc. 5.47.2), *IGII*²105.25-26, 29-30 (368/7 B.C.E.), and Hdt. 9.13.1.
17. Easterling 1985.

whence they were drawn; and the ever-varying synthesis of old and new invites the audience to draw conclusions about its own situation.[18]

The meaning for the historical audience that emerges from the semiotic analysis in Chapter Three is a political one. While this tragedy has usually been regarded as patriotic, I argue that it can be understood as bearing a particular, apologetic relation to the events that began at Colonus in 411 B. C. E. and that included the bitter recriminations of the restored democracy during the period in which I assume this tragedy was written (Ch. 3§1 is on the historical background). Furthermore, I suggest that, in the reception of Oedipus in Attica, Sophocles provided a model or, better, models of the attitudes that he wished Athenians would adopt toward their fellow-citizens. In the ideal Athens of Theseus' day, where he finds his final resting place, Oedipus can say that "of all men only among you have I found piety and fairness and truthtelling" (1125-27). An interpretation of this sort would immediately invite the suspicion that it sought to reduce a highly complex dramatic work to a single meaning if another kind of reading, as in Chapter Two, had not already suggested another large area of significance. And even within the area of possible historical meanings, I do not at all regard the apologetic tendency that I find in this tragedy as a "key" or a master significance. On the contrary, it seems to me only one of several articulations of historical meaning.[19]

In short, the semiotic approach in Chapter Three is a way of compensating for the lack of a fully attested historical response that might be compared with the virtual performance of Chapter Two. The relationship between the given historical codes and their re- or encoding in the tragedy can be quite clearly established, and, on this basis, at least a partial answer to the question "What did the text say?" can be found.[20]

---

18. Easterling 1985:9 says of Eur. *Suppl.*: "The idea of yearly magistrates sits oddly with that of heroic kingship; one cannot help feeling that Euripides is going beyond the traditional presentation of Theseus as champion of democracy and is inviting his audience to notice the mixture of old and new and perhaps to think critically about the city's institutions." While *OC* has nothing as patently anachronistic as yearly magistracies, I believe that a similar process is at work.

19. My interpretation of the tragedy is, I believe, compatible with the most recent major historical reading of the tragedy, that of Segal 1981, and also with those of Slatkin 1986 and Lardinois 1992.

20. "The reconstruction of the original horizon of expectations would .... fall back into historicism if the historical interpretation could not in turn serve to transform the question, 'What did the text say?' into the question, 'What does the text say to me, and what do I say to it?'": Jauss 1982:146.

Introduction   11

The closest thing to contemporary response oddly seems to be the ancient testimonia for the life of Sophocles, which are discussed in the Appendix. No matter what their deficiency for a biography of Sophocles conforming to our standards of factuality, these testimonia might, I thought, provide facts about the reception of this tragedy, at least for generations subsequent to Sophocles'. I was encouraged in this hypothesis by the widely held view that the testimonia tend to derive from the poet's own works. On this view, by a rather naive literary-critical procedure the author(s) of the testimonia read the tragedies for information about the tragedian. How, then, did he or they understand *Oedipus at Colonus* in particular? How did he or they "read" the tragedy? In a nutshell, whereas, as the receiver in his own lifetime of a new hero or god, Asclepius, Sophocles corresponded to Theseus in *Oedipus at Colonus*, he then, after this death, being received by the orgeones of Amynos and Asclepius as himself a hero (Dexion), corresponds to Oedipus in that tragedy. This ancient "reading" of the tragedy, which is already established by the mid-fourth century, then, expands the ancient horizon of expectations to a point at which it meets some of our own contemporary responses, for example, *The Gospel at Colonus*, which thematizes the redemption and exaltation of the hero.[21]

---

21. *The Gospel at Colonus*, adapted (mainly from Robert Fitzgerald trans. of *Oedipus at Colonus*) and directed by Lee Breuer, with music by Bob Telson, sung by the Five Blind Boys of Alabama and three other gospel groups, at the Brooklyn Academy of Music (first performance 1983).

PART I

1

Theorizing Theatrical Space

Both of the two principal mid-twentieth-century theorists of drama, Antonin Artaud and Berthold Brecht, met the Aristotelian tradition head-on. Of the two, Brecht is the more explicitly anti-Aristotelian, but Artaud is perhaps the more radical and is the one who will be compared with Aristotle in what follows. Artaud overturns the Aristotelian ranking of the parts of tragedy, putting the spectacle on top. Whereas Aristotle had said that tragedy could have its effect through reading or recitation,[1] without performance, Artaud would largely do away with a written text and, to the extent possible, with an author. Comparison of Aristotle and Artaud brings out, in the first place, the subordinate, and somewhat ambiguous, position of spectacle in the former and its overwhelming importance in the latter. One would not need Artaud, however, in order to be aware of the problematic nature of the spectacle in the *Poetics*: For this subject, classical scholarship would be a sufficient starting-point and guide. Artaud becomes useful at the point at which he introduces into theory of drama problems with which, for whatever reason, Aristotle was completely unconcerned. One such problem is space. For Aristotle is so far from concern with theatrical space that, even when he speaks of *opsis*, he means only the visual aspects of the actors.[2] It is fair to say that such concepts as theater space, stage space, and dramatic space—to invoke some dis-

---

1. 26.62a11-13: "Tragedy does its work even without motion, just like epic. For through reading it is apparent of what sort it is"; cf. 6.50b15-20. For what Aristotle means by reading see Halliwell 1986:341; cf. 68.
2. 6.50b15-20. Else 1967:233-34. Lucas 1968 on 50b20: "Pollux 4.115 suggests that masks and costumes were the main, if not the only, concern of" the *skeuopoios*. Halliwell 1986:339: Aristotle "is thinking of the various visual aspects of the actors, rather than the stage setting as a whole."

tinctions that will become important later in this chapter—could hardly be derived from the *Poetics*.

The comparison of Aristotle and Artaud proceeds from quite extensive common ground. The *Poetics*, as the title says, is a treatise on the "making" of tragedy. Artaud, whatever else he did in his voluminous writings on the theater, provided, as Aristotle had done for the theater of his day, prescriptions for the making of his "theater of cruelty."[3] And, despite his radical difference from the Aristotelian tradition, Artaud is still (unlike post-modern theory of drama) squarely within that tradition in his assumption of a fundamental binarism: drama and reality outside the drama.[4] For Artaud, the theater has a Double, which, in one of its various meanings, is a "reality" that is transmitted in the theatrical experience.[5] (Unlike Aristotle, Artaud would like to convey that reality directly and "cruelly," overleaping the intermediacy of character and action in what would now be called the "referential" dimension of the Aristotelian plot.[6]) The corresponding notion in Aristotle is mimesis, another multifarious concept that, in all of its meanings in the *Poetics*, assumes this same binarism. One could go even further: Artaud is still in an Aristotelian tradition of philosophical realism according to which the universals behind their dramatic or theatrical imitation or doubling are realer and truer than what the audience sees on stage.[7] Thus Derrida, perhaps Artaud's most

---

3. For example, in "The Theater of Cruelty (First Manifesto)," *TD* 89–100.

4. On Aristotle, cf. Jones 1962:26 on the distinction between *muthos* and *praxis*: "the *a priori*, metaphysical principle of action and the dramaturgic principle of plot"; "the felt ontological discontinuity, very near the heart of the *Poetics*, between the visionary form, lucid and necessarily beautiful, and mere aspiring stage-event."

5. *TD* 49; cf. 65 on the Balinese theater: "There is an absolute in these constructed perspectives, a real physical absolute which only Orientals are capable of envisioning." Ch. 5 of *TD* ("Oriental and Occidental Theater") is a short, "theoretical" synkrisis, which could be tested by Smethurst 1989.

6. *TD* 48: "[T]he theater must ... be considered as the Double not of this direct, everyday reality of which it is gradually being reduced to a mere inert replica ... but of another archetypal and dangerous reality." The metaphysics of Artaud is of course anything but Aristotelian. As against the vision of an orderly, intelligible universe moved by the Unmoved Mover, Artaud's "dangerous reality" seems to have much in common with the play of forces described in the last entry of *The Will to Power*.

7. Artaud's writings are full of expressions like "forms of art ... in confrontation with the absolute" (*TD* 69). The theater is "analogical" (*TD* 109). For Aristotle, cf. Jones (n. 4 above) and consider Ch. 9 of the *Poetics*, with Halliwell 1986:135–37. If not "realer and truer" at least more knowable, as Halliwell has cautioned me (*per litteras*).

sympathetic interpreter, speaks of "the classical ontotheology or metaphysics ... to which Artaud still belongs."[8]

A curious index of the similarity of Aristotle and Artaud in this respect is their relation to Greek mythology. Artaud speaks, in the context of the poetics mentioned above, of "the metaphysical ideas of certain Fables whose very atrocity and energy suffice to show their origin and continuity in essential principles."[9] That Artaud has Greek myths in mind is shown by a proclamation uttered elsewhere: "Either we will be capable of returning ... to this superior idea of poetry and poetry-through-theater which underlies the Myths told by the great ancient tragedians, ... or ...."[10] Though Aristotle lived two millennia before Artaud was born and in a period in which the Theater of Dionysus was still flourishing in Athens, he, too, already called for adherence to those myths that the practice of the tragedians had discovered to be the most suitable for tragic plots (13.53b17-23). These myths, through an empirical process, in the history of the genre's development, had attained a special status: they produced the best tragedies. To Artaud's "metaphysical ideas" (let us leave open the question of what these are) corresponds Aristotle's notion of the universality of the tragic plot (Ch. 9).

Another similarity follows close on the one just observed. In the *Poetics*, the tragic plot, through the mimesis of certain actions, produces pity and fear, and these result in a catharsis of such emotions (6.49b27-28). The clause on catharis is probably the most commented upon in Greek literature.[11] For present purposes, a minimal general interpretation suffices: catharsis is a beneficial psychological effect experienced by the audience. In terms of the Aristotelian causes, catharsis is the final cause of tragedy, the one for the sake of which the others exist. In Artaud (not so much the plot—for reasons to be given below—but) the theatrical experience has a purpose and an effect similar to catharsis. An analogy

---

8. Derrida 1978:326 n. 29.
9. *TD* 93.
10. *TD* 80. Cf. "the dark hour of certain ancient tragedies which all true theater must recover," *TD* 30 (he has just mentioned the Mysteries of Eleusis). Of course the Greek myths were not the only sources of the new theater desiderated by Artaud. Cf.: "[W]e shall try to concentrate ... a drama which, without resorting to the defunct images of the old Myths, shows that it can extract the forces which struggle within them" (85). Cf. the reference to Aeschylus and Sophocles (*TD* 108).
11. Halliwell 1986: Ch. 6 and app. 5. He cites and discusses earlier literature.

or image that Artaud uses for his theater is alchemy. As the operations of alchemy turn base metal into gold, so the theater should purify the mind of the spectator.[12] Artaud even believes that his theater of cruelty can prevent war, riot, and murder.[13] This notion of purification is astonishingly similar to Aristotelian catharsis in one of its major interpretations.[14] Again, Artaud believes that his theater can instill a heroic attitude in men, a notion that matches Aristotelian catharsis understood as the acquisition of emotional fortitude.[15]

This rather extensive common ground of similarity between Aristotle and Artaud reaches a boundary in their views of the theatrical spectacle. Artaud's call for a new theater can be summed up in the phrase "mise en scène." In order to meet his requirements, this new theater would have to free itself from the domination of texts and to seek "expression in space."[16] In this respect, Aristotle is so remote, conceptually, from Artaud that he does not even require the theater: tragedy can have its proper effect without benefit of actors and performance (6.50b15-20). In ways to be studied below, Aristotle's theory of tragedy leads on not only to the predominance of text as script, the sense of text that Artaud almost always assumes when he denounces the text, but even further to the predominance of text *over* script, so that drama becomes something only for reading, a genre of literature. Artaud's position on this phenomenon is in the nature of an obvious a fortiori, and he does not have to spend much time denouncing the scholarly reading of dramatic texts.[17]

The relation of text to theater is simple, however, in neither Artaud nor Aristotle. To begin with the latter, his disparagement of *opsis* and his explicit reference to reading might seem to presuppose a clear concept of the written dramatic text (26.62a11-13), especially when his own research necessarily depended upon a collection of such texts. On the contrary, in the *Poetics* Aristotle never uses γράφω or its compounds in the sense of "to write," nor does any word referring to a written text appear (except once, at 16.55a19, apropos of the letter sent by Iphigeneia in Eur. *IT* 577-83[18]). The standard words for composing poetry (*poiein*

---

12. *TD* 48-52.
13. *TD* 82.
14. Halliwell 1986:351 on the neo-classical understanding of catharsis: "we learn through *katharsis* to avoid those passions which can lead to suffering and tragedy."
15. *TD* 32 Cf. Halliwell 1986:351-52.
16. *TD* 89.
17. Perhaps the only passage is in "No More Masterpieces": "Let us leave textual criticism to graduate students, formal criticism to esthetes" (*TD* 75).
18. Schwinge 1990 has shown, in a series of examples from Greek tragedy, how

and deverbatives) are problematical for Aristotle[19] and he introduces a technical term, *sunistanai*, which he uses of the plot in particular. The poet (*poiêtês*) should be the poet of plots, he says, rather than of verses (9.51b27-28), implicitly removing the traditional notion of poet even further from line-by-line composition whether oral or written. When Aristotle speaks of this "putting together" of the plot, he is referring to a mental operation. And yet, as Diego Lanza has said, "Separated from its creator, freed from the circumstances of production, indifferent to modes of transmission, the poetic product now truly appears to be something that is the autoguarantor of its own identity. We would say: a text,"[20] i.e., a written work that presupposes a reader, as distinguished from a script for performance. If the situation of the text in the *Poetics* is projected onto the history of writing in ancient Greece, Aristotle appears to be poised at a moment at which it has become possible to speak of reading tragedy but not yet possible to speak of it as composed in writing.[21] Similarly, the extant works of Aristotle himself, while they are too fully shaped to be merely lecture notes, are not yet finished texts and were not in fact published as such in his lifetime.[22] His own works have the same ambiguous status as the dramatic text in the *Poetics*. They were not conceived of in the form of written, publishable works any more than Aristotle conceives theoretically of Greek tragedies as written, published texts, even if, to repeat, his research depended upon such material texts.

---

anagnorisis requires not only words but action on stage. One of his examples is the anagnorisis in Euripides' *Iphigenia Taurica*. Aristotle approved of this scene (16.55a18ff.), even though he elsewhere said that a tragedy could have its proper effect without actors and performance.

19. Note especially 1.47b2ff. Aristotle tends to use *poiein* of the early poets (1.47b14, 6.50a35, cf. 6.50b7, 14.53b28) and of epic (18.56a11, 24.59b27, 24.60a3, cf. 25.60b23, 25.61a28). Homer is "the poet (*poiêtês*)." Aristotle uses *poiein* once of Euripides (14.53b29) and once of Aeschylus (22.58b22).

20. Lanza 1987:95.

21. The concept of a written text is clearly presupposed already in Thucydides and Plato, who antedate Aristotle, who is thus, in terms of the history of writing, a conservative or who, for reasons of his own, chose not to adopt this technology of communication. On writing as integral to Thucydidean historiography, see Edmunds 1993. Aristotle's relation to writing is epitomized in a remark in *Rhet*. 1409a20: the end of the period should be made clear "not by the scribe nor by the paragraphos [mark in the margin of the text] but by the rhythm." He presupposes writing; but the writing should be nothing but a transcription of the oral delivery of the period.

22. W. D. Ross, "Aristotle," in *OCD*, 2nd ed., p. 116/1: "The extant works were not prepared for publication, but they are for the most part too full and elaborate to be mere notes for lecture purposes."

Chapter 17, which has more to do with mise en scène than any other in the *Poetics*, provides a nice example of how commentary on Aristotle assumes the notion of written text that is still only latent. In this chapter, Aristotle says that the poet should, amongst other things, work out the plot in gestures (17.55a29-30), here coming closer to Artaud than anywhere else, whether he means the poet's own gestures or his visualization of the characters' or the actors'.[23] Gerald F. Else, who wanted "gestures" (*schêmata*) to refer to figures of speech, scornfully conjures up a picture of the poet "leaping alternately to his feet and back to his writing table" and explains: "The poet's task is to *write a text*, on the basis of which a good actor can then project gestures, voice-effects, and the like."[24] Else thus imports back into the *Poetics* the text-dominated theater and the independence of the actor that Artaud would later abominate as the "classical theater," meaning the traditional theater that had taken shape in the Renaissance largely under Aristotelian influence. Aristotle, for his part, repudiates spectacle not in the name of script or written dramatic text, but in the name of plot, which he considered the "soul" of tragedy (6.50a38). And yet, even within the argument that maintains the primacy of plot, spectacle will not disappear but occasionally reasserts itself in what seems like equivocation on Aristotle's part.[25] It will be worthwhile later in this chapter to see how, why, and to what degree the spectacle can obtrude itself in the *Poetics*.

23. Lucas 1968 ad loc; Halliwell 1986:40.
24. Else 1967:489-90 (his emphasis). Else later (1967: 643), referring to the troublesome Ch. 17 (in particular to the visualization called for at 17.55a22ff. [the Karkinos example]), says of the vividness in which tragedy surpasses epic that it "will communicate itself even to a reader, because it is written into the text, i.e., into the actions, feelings, etc., directly implied by the text. This is something the epic, as a narrative art, does not have inherently, although a poet like Homer may achieve it." See, on 17.55a29-30, Dupont-Roc and Lallot 1980:283-84. It is interesting that, in reconciling this passage with 19.56b8ff., where Aristotle associates *schêmata* with the actor, Dupont-Roc and Lallot invoke the notion of the text: "[D]onner à l'oeuvre du fini par l'expression, c'est, tâche éminemment poétique, imprimer dans le texte même, selon un code qui lui est propre, les formes expressives, les 'figures', qui, transposant les mouvements émotifs d'où elles sont issues, se prêteront à leur tour à la retraduction gestuelle et vocale qui définit la fonction interprétative de l'acteur." What they have in mind differs, I believe, from Else's notion of "projection" in that the *schêmata* that originated in the poet are transmitted via the text to the actor. If so, the dramatic text is, as I propose at the end of this chapter, already gesturally, i.e., spatially, informed.
25. "Equivocation": Halliwell 1986:343. Cf. Lanza 1987:35: "Lo spettacolo, la vista, possiede ... in Aristotele questo ambiguo statuto marginale: è uno dei sei elementi della tragedia e insieme pare sfuggire al dominio proprio dell'arte poetica, necessario e insidioso complemento di cui la tragedia pare a tratti poter fare a meno."

Artaud calls for a "concrete language, intended for the sense and independent of speech," a "solidified, materialized language," "a language of signs, gestures, and attitudes having an ideographic value," "a new physical language, based upon signs and no longer upon words." The mise en scène itself is to be "considered as a language in space and in movement." The Balinese theater is taken as a model for "inventing a language of gesture to be developed in space, a language without meaning except in the circumstances of the stage."[26] It might seem that words, and thus the traditional script, and thus the playwright, would have to be abandoned. Artaud does not go that far. In a letter to Jean Paulhan (September 28, 1932), who had apparently called upon him to clarify his position, Artaud states:

> I am adding another language to the spoken language, and I am trying to restore to the language of speech its old magic, its essential spellbinding power, for its mysterious possibilities have been forgotten. When I say I will perform no written play, I mean that I will perform no play based on writing and speech, that in the spectacles I produce there will be a preponderant physical share which could not be captured and written down in the customary language of words, and that even the spoken and written portions will be spoken and written in a new sense.[27]

Artaud seems here to be seeking a compromise with the harder anti-text position of the essays in *The Theater and Its Double*. In the realm of practice, as distinguished from theory, *The Cenci*, the only full-length play that Artaud wrote and produced, has a conventional script; and it can be observed in passing that, in the history of twentieth-century drama, Artaud's "new sense" has come from the defamiliarizing of linguistic codes.[28]

Though the relation of dramatic text to theater is complex in both Aristotle and Artaud, the distance between the two is still, in more than one sense, millennial.[29] Even in the passage just quoted, Artaud affirms the new physicality of language that can be achieved only in the mise en scène, precisely the aspect of tragedy that Aristotle repudiated. One of the consequences of the difference between their attitude toward spectacle is their valuation of the producer or director. This valuation is, of course, implicit in Aristotle, but it seems fairly certain that part of the

---

26. *TD* 37-39, 45, 54, 61.
27. *TD* 111. Cf. *TD* 98: "We shall not act a written play."
28. Aston and Savona 1991:65-70.
29. As observed in passing by Donadi 1970-71:422 n.23.

background of what might be called the textualization of tragedy in Aristotle is the contemporary separation of the functions of tragedian and producer.—The *Poetics* has been seen as, in addition to everything else, a pamphlet directed against contemporary theatrical practice.[30]—Whereas in the fifth century, the tragedian had always produced his own plays, this practice began to break down in Aristotle's time, and this separation must of course be assumed for the restaging of older tragedies in the fourth century. Concurrently, the actors, who were also the ones responsible for the re-productions, altered the received dramatic texts, especially by interpolations. The Athenian statesman Lycurgus (ca. 390–ca. 325 B.C.E.) passed a law against this practice.[31] This law, rendering the tragedian's text immune to tampering, is the legal analogue of Aristotle's theory of tragedy, which, in effect, restores absolute authority to the tragedian by making him immune to performance. When Artaud, for his part, speaks of the "absurd duality" of author and director, denounces the slavery of the director to the author,[32] and demands that the author become a director, he is returning, in effect, to the pre-Aristotelian conditions of Greek tragedy. If, *per absurdum*, one were to divide the history of Western theater into two phases, one stretching from the beginning to Aristotle, the other from Aristotle to Artaud, one could say that, at the end of each phase, the relation of text to performance becomes problematical; that the theoretical responses are opposite; that Aristotle's response was to try to rescue the text from performance; that he succeeded, thus founding the distinction between script and dramatic text and the preeminence of the latter; that Artaud's response was then to try to reverse the Aristotelian inheritance and to rescue performance from text, thus reverting to the pre-Aristotelian origins of theater.

In this fantastically abbreviated historical schema, the success of Aristotle is clear. What of Artaud? At the level of practice, the success of Artaud is assured. Certainly the practical effects of Artaud's theory of theater of cruelty (and also of his own activities in the theater) have been felt on all the stages in the Western world, and it is now impossible to attend a theatrical performance that has not felt his influence, whether positively or reactively. In theory of drama, too, Artaud's influence has been strong. Semiotics of theater is an example.[33] Even if precise lines of filiation cannot be established in every case, it is clear that Artaud stands

---

30. Marzullo 1980. Cf. Flashar 1984:7–12.
31. Pickard-Cambridge 1968:84, 100, 155–56.
32. *TD* 112, 119.
33. On the term "semiotics" see Pavis 1982:14–15.

behind the French semiotics of theater of the 60s and 70s.[34] A clear echo of Artaud can be heard in the statement of Patrice Pavis that "theatrical semiology has arisen in reaction to textual 'imperialism' and the habit of regarding theater as nothing but a literary genre."[35] Artaud was the one who reestablished the stage as the locus of signification, of the theatrical sign[36]; and semiotics of theater is true to Artaud's priority of mise en scène precisely in its principle of the theater's uniqueness, which consists in its peculiar ontological status: performance,[37] *whether or not semiotics of theater is true to any other aspect of Artaud's radical project.* In taking performance as its starting point, semiotics parts company with Aristotle, who regards tragedy as a species of the genus poetic art, along with epic, dithyramb, comedy, and "most of" the art of the aulos and the kithara, all of which are equally imitations (1.47a13–16). Of these, epic is especially close to tragedy, and Homer is never far from Aristotle's mind. The analysis in terms of genus and species undoubtedly influences the textualization of tragedy in Aristotle observed above. Semiotics of theater provides a corpus of theory that, against Aristotle, legitimates the priority of spectacle or performance.

Spectacle and performance entail the even more fundamental requirement of a theatrical space. If, with Erika Fischer-Lichte, theater is: "A represents or plays the role of X while S watches,"[38] then this minimal definition entails a theatrical space as one necessary condition. (Compare the opening words of Peter Brook's *The Empty Space:* "I can take any empty space and call it a bare stage. A man walks across this empty space whilst someone else is watching him, and this is all that is needed for an act of theatre to be engaged."[39]) S cannot watch or cannot know

---

34. For a brief history of semiotics of theater, see Fischer-Lichte 1983:250 n. 392. (Unless otherwise noted, references to Fischer-Lichte 1983 are to vol. 1.) She distinguishes two main phases: (1) the Prague School of the 30s; (2) parallel French and Polish developments in the 60s and 70s. In the 70s, Italians were also active in semiotics of theater. Only in the 70s, through translations from the Czech, did the works of the Prague school come into the discussion. See also Pavis 1982:13 and 21 n. 3 for references to the history of Prague School semiotics of theater; Matejka 1976 (a short history of the Prague School); postface by Salvestroni in Lotman 1981:30–45.
35. Pavis 1982:28–29. Cf. reference to Artaud by Übersfeld 1978:147.
36. Though Artaud is not an absolute starting-point. He had predecessors in Max Hermann (see Veltrusky 1985), Erwin Piscator (see the quotation in Kowzan 1985:5), Gordon Craig and Adolph Appia. See also Braun 1982:chs. 8–11.
37. Fischer-Lichte 1983:180.
38. Fischer-Lichte 1983:16 and passim. After the time in which I wrote this chapter, an abridged English translation of Fischer-Lichte's work appeared: Fischer-Lichte 1992.
39. Brook 1978:9.

that he/she is watching a performance except within a determinate space. This space may be the open-air amphitheater of the Greeks and Romans, the enclosed indoor theater of the Renaissance and modern times, or the space defined by a procession, as in the Shi'ite *ta'ziyah* or the medieval passion play. Or it can be a space ordinarily dedicated to some other purpose that now, designated as the place in which A represents X, becomes a theatrical space.[40] Though performances and thus "acting" are always going on, they do not, without a definition of space, constitute theater. Aware of a performance (in some sense) outside a theatrical space, I do not feel that I am S and the performer is A, an actor representing X, a character. If my colleague Elin, whom I encounter in my day-to-day haunts and who I thought was a professor, proves to be the agent of a foreign government, I shall not, upon this realization, conclude that she was A playing the role of X (foreign agent) nor will my experience have been a theatrical one. A semiotics of theater can, then, begin with theatrical space.

In an essay published in 1981, Michael Issacharoff provides a semiotic theory of theatrical space based on modern French theater.[41] He distinguishes three kinds of space: theater space, stage space, and dramatic space. The first is determined by the architectural design of the theater, which imposes certain unalterable conditions. The second is the stage and set design and includes, in addition to decor and properties, the costumes and the body of the actor. These various aspects of stage space can be broken down into separate codes (e.g., the body of the actor into make-up or mask, hair-style, etc.),[42] and the question will arise

---

40. Fischer-Lichte 1983:18: "Wenn A hier agiert, *um X darzustellen*, dann denotiert dieser Raum nicht seine ursprüngliche Gebrauchsfunktion, sondere die besondere des Aufführungsortes, als jeder beliebige andere Raum zu gelten, in dem X sich aufhält" (my emphasis). It is notable that, at the end of her taxonomy, Fischer-Lichte reduces all theatrical signs to two categories, one of which is space: "Als solche irreduziblen Faktoren haben ... unsere Ausführungen in Kapitel 1-4 mindestens zwei Kategorien ausgewiesen: die der Rollenfigur *und* dies des Raumes" (187; her emphasis). Cf. Übersfeld 1991:52-55; 60-63.

41. Issacharoff 1981. Scolnicov 1987 has a similar but less rigorous analysis of theatrical space.

42. The concept of code is a necessary evil in the semiotics of theater, evil in the sense that it is so complex, since "virtually *all* the codes operative in society are potential factors in the theatre" (Elam 1980:50). Or, in other words, theatrical codes consist of "signs of signs," to put the matter in the terms that guide the analysis of Fischer-Lichte 1983 (see below in the text of this chapter). A recent discussion of the problem is Issacharoff 1988. Cf. Übersfeld 1991:67: "*Ce qui est donné dans l'espace théâtral, ce n'est jamais un image du monde, mais l'image d'une image. Ce qui est 'imité' n'est pas le monde,*

of the interrelationship of these codes with speech. Dramatic space, the third kind, is space as created by dramatic discourse, which can be further divided into diegetic space, when dramatic discourse is focused on space off stage, and mimetic space, when dramatic discourse is focused on the visible space of the stage. To refine upon Issacharoff's concept of diegetic space, it can be divided into space represented as visible to the characters on stage (but not visible to the spectators) and space invisible to both the characters on stage and the spectators.[43] Diegetic space is continuous with the mimetic space of the stage and is not infinite but is determined by the limits of actions and events or possible actions and events that affect what happens or may happen on stage. Time, i.e., the unit of time presupposed and represented by the dramatic action, establishes the coordinates of diegetic space, which is, in effect, a space-time.[44] Characters may, of course, refer to places that do not fall within the diegetic range of the play, as, for example, the chorus in Aeschylus' *Agamemnon* refers to the sacrifice of Iphigeneia at Aulis. (Paradoxically, Troy, which is farther away from Argos, the setting of the play, than is Aulis, *is* within the play's diegetic range.) Any given play can be characterized by the relative importance it assigns to the two spaces, the diegetic and the mimetic.[45] In the case of the rather bare stage of the ancient Theater of Dionysus, even after scene-painting came into use, most of the burden of creating the dramatic space fell upon mimetic discourse, which had to be completed by the audience's imagination. Diegetic space can be reinforced by sound effects that, invading the inner mimetic space, help to create an outer space that is invisible.[46] The storm in *King Lear*, even in the absence of sound effects, belongs to both mimetic and to diegetic space, because it takes place both on and off stage.

Two elements of Issacharoff's theory call for further discussion. One is the hierarchy of theatrical codes that he proposes. The other is the theatrical autoreflexivity engendered by the reference of codes to one

---

mais le monde repensé selon la fiction et dans le cadre d'une culture et d'un code" (her emphasis).

43. Post-illusionist theater can of course introduce the division between mimetic and diegetic into the stage-setting itself. For example, in Alice Childress' *Wedding Band*, the stage is divided by the wall of Julia Augustine's house: on one side is her bedroom, on the other the street. The bedroom is diegetic space for characters in the street; the street for characters in the bedroom. These, then, are a third kind of diegetic space, one that is invisible to (some) characters but visible to the audience.

44. Übersfeld 1991:52.

45. Scolnicov 1987:15.

46. Issacharoff 1981:218.

26 Chapter 1

another. The hierarchy of codes comes into Issacharoff's theory at the point at which speech or dramatic discourse refers to an element of stage space, i.e., at the intersection of mimetic space and stage space. Here, says Issacharoff, discourse has an indexical function: "the verbal is centered on ... the visible; ... In this process of reference between codes, there is, of course, a hierarchy: language is the dominant code. Nonverbal codes obviously cannot acquire the function of referring ... Thus in the process to which I allude, language points to some other sign system and in so doing establishes its own semiotic preeminence."[47] At this, Artaud would turn over in his grave. Within a semiotics of space, the classical theater with its primacy of the text has returned, because the linguistic code is presumably identical with the written dramatic text. It is possible, however, to challenge Issacharoff's hierarchy of codes while preserving the main categories of his theory (as in the preceding paragraph), and, in what follows, various arguments will be offered that seek, not to establish a new hierarchy, but to relativize the dominance of the linguistic. Thereafter, I shall turn to the matter of autoreflexivity.

One can begin by using Aristotle himself against the Aristotelian tradition whose hierarchy Issacharoff has reinstated. In Chapter 17 of the *Poetics*, which has already come into this discussion as a somewhat anomalous statement on mise en scène, Aristotle refers to the audience's perception of the action on stage: "One must watch out for these things [the rules for character-portrayal and the principle of the probable and the necessary],[48] and, in addition, for whatever is in violation of the perceptions that of necessity attend on the art of poetry. For it is often possible to err with respect to perceptions. Enough has been said about them in the published discussions (*logoi*)" (17.54b15–18). Aristotle's cross-reference, the only one in the *Poetics* to a published work, is usually taken to be to his dialogue *On Poets*. In the *Poetics* itself, however, Aristotle will provide an example of this kind of error, and he continues: "One should compose plots and work them out with diction setting them before one's eyes as much as possible. For in this way, seeing most clearly, as if he were present at the deeds themselves as they come be, he would discover what is fitting and would least overlook inconsistencies. An example is the blame assigned Karkinos. For Amphiaraos was coming back from the temple, [a mistake] that escaped one who did not visualize [the action],[49] but on stage it failed as the spectators were annoyed at it"

---

47. Issacharoff 1981:216.
48. Else 1967:483.
49. Lucas 1968:174: "i.e., those who read it."

(17.55a23-29).[50] Though the tragedy to which Aristotle refers is not extant and his remark is all that is known of it, clearly Amphiaraos' last exit had made it practically and thus visually impossible for him to enter from the temple.

Aristotle's example shows how, on stage, when it is a matter of the audience's perception of a play, the visual code of the stage space qualifies the verbal code of the script. Though a non-verbal code seems to lack the capacity to refer to anything, the audience instinctively uses this code as a control on the discourse of the play and thus endows the non-verbal with a power that it lacks in the inert script or in the play as a text for reading. The examples that Issacharoff gives from Ionesco's *Les Chaises*, in which ostensibly mimetic discourse makes reference to objects not in fact present on the stage, depend for their effect on the audience's presupposition that the mimetic discourse will be founded on visible things. These examples thus presuppose an efficacy of the visual code equal to that of the linguistic. Even Aristotle implicitly concedes this equality. To return to the passage from Chapter 17 quoted in the preceding paragraph, while it is perhaps possible to reconcile the precept (plot should be visualized) with the principle that tragedy is independent of performance (6.50b15-20), the fact remains that the need for visualization is demonstrated by the results of an actual performance.

The contradiction observed by Aristotle emerged not from anything that Amphiaraos said but from something that this character did on stage. The mute action of the character is thus, Aristotle seems at least for a moment to concede, the most telling ingredient of the drama, the dominant semiotic code. Here Charles R. Lyons' notion of the dramatic character in space and time, i.e., in performance, as "an irreducible esthetic unit" can be usefully applied.[51] Lyons' principle is that "it is impossible to separate the image of theatrical space from the image of character."[52] Like Issacharoff, however, Lyons, despite his apparent orientation to spatial codes, remains within the classical primacy of the dramatic text: "The imagination of the audience transforms the actual physical dimensions of the stage into an assimilated image of scene derived from observing the behavior of characters within that space, *behavior that is, predomi-*

---

50. "If he came back out of a temple, the anomaly must have been that he had not previously gone into it, so that the audience expected to see him return by one of the *parodoi*" (Else 1967:488). For other interpretations of the anomaly, see Craik 1980; Green 1990.
51. Lyons 1987:30.
52. Lyons 1987:28.

nately, verbal".[53] While verbal behavior might predominate in the sense that there is more of it than of non-verbal behavior, it is difficult to see how to quantify and compare the two, and, in any case, it is undoubtedly not quantity that Lyons has in mind. He is assuming the same hierarchy of codes as Issacharoff; and the same objection to the semiotic preeminence of language can be made, again on the basis of an example already provided by the author. Lyons' prime case is the woman rocking in a chair in Samuel Beckett's *Rockaby*. An anonymous voice tells the story of her life as she rocks. She thrice commands the voice to continue when it falters. Then the voice is heard no more, she gives no further command, and she stops rocking. Against Lyons, it can be argued that the action of stopping with which the play concludes, this purely visual gesture, has, at the very least, semiotic parity with anything the voice has said. Furthermore, neither the actual stage space beyond the confines of the rocking chair nor a mimetic space created by the character is of any importance in this play, and thus, contrary to Lyons' own thesis, scene has little or nothing to do with the creation of character.[54] But, with these qualifications, Lyons' notion of the irreducibility of the character on stage as a dramatic sign (a notion with strong resonance of Artaud) must form part of a semiotics of theatrical space.[55]

In order to decide on the priority of theatrical codes, it is useful to apply the test of replacability. The one theatrical code that could replace all other theatrical codes would be dominant, and, intuitively, the linguistic code seems to be the one. In general, S will see whatever A/X says is there on stage. But the intuitive dominance of the linguistic must be qualified. If a purely auditory play (e.g., the radio broadcast of a play) is ex-

---

53. Lyons 1987:35. My emphasis.

54. Cf. 36: "The space that surrounds the character, the site itself and the objects and other characters it contains, provide the fictional mind of that figure with material that will generate substantive images that inform his consciousness. The character will perceive objects, spaces, and other characters and will mediate these objectivities into the images that constitute his conscious awareness of himself in the world. Scene in that sense is crucial to the development of an image of character since the objectivities of the scene provide the consciousness of the character with the immediate images with which it constitutes itself." The example of *Rockaby* seems to go against this statement and to show that character is indeed independent and irreducible while scene, for its part, is irreducible to character. The two are irreducible, heterogeneous elements: cf. Fischer-Lichte n. 40 above.

55. Lyons' main argument has apparently also been made by Stefania Skwarcynska: see Fischer-Lichte 1983:212 n. 67. For a discussion of the actor, with further bibliography, see Aston and Savona 1991:102–105.

cepted,[56] A, who speaks, is present. This presence necessarily implies gestic and proxemic signs.[57] Even if A does not move, this motionlessness is received as a gestic sign. Gestic and proxemic signs, at least, cannot be replaced by linguistic ones, even if all other codes can.[58] Theater proceeds from, in Fischer-Lichte's phrase, "the apriori of the body." She says:

> The body of the actor represents, so to speak, the condition of the possibility of theater. The body, for its part, cannot, however, be thought of as anything but a body that appears. Theater can therefore happen only when we are confronted with the appearance of the actor. The external appearance of the actor is normally the first thing we perceive about the actor. This first perception allows us to undertake an identification of the character, just as we confer on the outward appearance of a person a definite identity as its meaning. With this preliminary attestation of identity, the spectator connects the other signs brought forth by the actor, the linguistic and paralinguistic, the mimic, gestic, and proxemic.[59]

The physical presence of the actor in a determinate physical space is thus prior to the linguistic code.

This conclusion goes directly against the hierarchical superiority of the word maintained by the Prague School and now by its epigones. A half-century ago, Jindřich Honzl in "The Hierarchy of Dramatic Devices" took the ancient Greek theater as a case in point and established the law that "actions and deeds are realized visibly on the ancient stage only by means of verbal reference to them." Honzl believed that the rather incessant reference by actors in Greek tragedy to their own and to others' actions was owing to the origin of tragedy in dithyramb, in which action had to be narrated. Whatever the truth of this historical explanation, Honzl's law certainly corresponds to a peculiarity of Greek tragedy that everyone senses. Honzl does not, however, regard the actors' verbal self-reference

---

56. Though even the radio play may not be an exception: see Issacharoff 1988:66ff., who shows how sound can represent space.
57. The term "proxemic" was apparently introduced by Edward T. Hall: see Elam 1980:62. In discussion of theater, the term usually applies to relations of proximity or distance between A and A or between A and S. Cf. Aston and Savona 1991:153-55.
58. I have summarized the argument of Fischer-Lichte 1983:34-35. Consider the priority of the gestic in the example discussed by Ubersfeld 1978:240.
59. Fischer-Lichte 1983:98; cf. Ubersfeld 1978:123-24;300 and Ubersfeld 1991:78-81 on theatrical space as a field of force of which the bodies of the actors are the origin. Cf. also Ch. 4 of Ubersfeld 1991 on the actor and in particular section 4.7 on the body of the actor ("source de joie"!).

as a simple narrative doubling of their action but as the creating of an opposition between word and action that is perceptually canceled through the spectators' synthesis of these two codes. "Theatrical perception comes about by virtue of this opposition being overcome, by virtue of the fact that the opposition between mental representation [stemming from the verbal] and reality [stemming from the visual] is synthesized in the spectator's act of interpretation which transforms both the representation and the reality in a flash of emotionally charged 'seeing'."[60] But if this is the case, the verbal is not dominant. The blame of Karkinos can again serve as a counter-example. No matter how excellent the poetry of the linguistic code, it cannot transfigure a completely inconsistent action. Such an action would block the synthesis of which Honzl speaks. In passing, it can be observed that Honzl's law is corroborated by the normal fifth-century expectation that a tragedy would be performed only once.[61] If a tragedy was composed for a single performance and if the poet participated in the production as actor and/or director, then stage directions imbedded in the text would have been unnecessary and what look to us like imbedded stage directions must have been something else. These supposed "intra-dialogic modes of direction" are not the equivalent of stage directions in "bourgeois" or illusionistic drama.[62]

To conclude this critique of the Aristotelian hierarchy that places the linguistic code at the top, I shall discuss paralinguistic signs. These are vocally created signs that are neither linguistic nor musical nor iconic vocal signs (e.g., the imitation of the baying of a hound or of the twittering of a bird).[63] The paralinguistic sign differs from the word in that there is no stable relation between sound and meaning. For this reason, the paralinguistic sign is accompanied by a gesture or in itself constitutes a gesturalizing of speech, e.g., through a tone of voice that conveys scorn or irony. Indeed, in performance the linguistic as spoken is imbedded in the paralinguistic, in signs, like those just mentioned, that convey a certain tone or a characteristic of X or X's belonging to a certain group (the sign is accent) or the emphatic point in a statement (the sign is stress). The non-phonetic auditive dimension of speech not only gives speech a certain quality and plasticity but also implicitly or explicitly gesturalizes

60. Honzl 1976:121, 123.
61. Cf. Pickard-Cambridge 1968:99; Newiger 1979:443.
62. *Pace* Aston and Savona 1991:93–94, to cite the most recent proponents of this common view.
63. Fischer-Lichte 1983:38. My argumentation concerning the relation of the paralinguistic to the spatial builds on Fischer-Lichte's analysis of the paralinguistic sign.

speech and thus deploys it in space. If two characters are standing close to each other on stage, the paralinguistic signs of one character's speech may charge the space between her and the other with a hostility or a desire that the linguistic signs alone fail to convey or even conceal. In the case of laughing, weeping, or screaming, paralinguistic signs that are not combined with linguistic ones, gesture or movement are always entailed or, if absent, are perceived as suppressed. Such signs, then, presuppose theatrical space. In sum, beginning with the paralinguistic dimension of the linguistic, it is possible to show that the spatial is already coinvolved in the linguistic and thus once again to relativize the hierarchical superiority of the linguistic found in Aristotle's *Poetics* and still found even in semiotics of theater.[64]

In the same context in which he argued the hierarchical supremacy of the linguistic code, Issacharoff observed that, when speech or dramatic discourse refers to an element of stage space, i.e., at the intersection of mimetic space and stage space, theater becomes autoreflexive. This is the second of the two elements of Issacharoff's theory requiring further discussion. In keeping with the hierarchy that he posited, Issacharoff also observed that "non-verbal codes obviously cannot acquire the function of referring." The example of *Rockaby* is again applicable. The action of stopping in this play shows that a mute action by itself can have theatrical autoreflexivity. For this stopping both ends the play and is the end of the drama that was presented in that play. The stopping means, in addition to whatever it means within the drama (probably the woman's death), that the play is over, and thus the action is a self-reference on the part of the play. Another example is Brecht's mise en scène of the conclusion of *Mother Courage*: the woman continues to circle the stage with her wagon, giving the impression that she will do so forever.[65] One can argue further that, because theater is an autoreflexive medium, it is always also potentially metatheatrical, always on the verge of calling attention to itself as a theater.[66] To return to Issacharoff's point concerning the autoreflexivity of mimetic discourse, one can observe that it is in particular the enunciative property of this discourse that carries the potential for metatheatricality.

---

64. From one historical period of theater to another, of course, and between one kind of theater and another, the relative semiotic value of dialogue and action will differ: cf. Aston and Savona 1991:58–59. But dialogue will never be absolutely prior to action.
65. Fischer-Lichte 1983:222 n. 138; cf. Ubersfeld 1978:232.
66. As suggested rather tersely by Grande 1989; cf. Ubersfeld 1978:276-77.

32   Chapter 1

The now standard distinction between "enunciation" (*énonciation*) and "utterance" (*énoncé*)[67] goes back to a short essay on the nature of pronouns by Émil Benveniste.[68] Pronouns, he argued, do not constitute a unitary class, as they appear to do in descriptive grammars, but differ according to linguistic mode. Some belong to syntax, others to what he called *instances de discours,* which he defines as "the discrete and always unique acts by which language (*langue*) is actualized in speech (*parole*) by a speaker (*locuteur*)."[69] The first person singular is the prime example of a pronoun as an instance of discourse. It refers to no other "reality" but that of discourse. A group of markers belonging to other linguistic classes have an aptitude for combining with the first person: certain demonstrative pronouns, adverbs, and adverbial expressions. Benveniste emphasizes the temporal aspect of these markers: they constitute the *present* instance of discourse.[70]

In the theater, it is the peculiar relation of instances of discourse to an already given stage space and an already given theatrical fiction that creates the metatheatrical potential. When an actor says "I," referring to him- or herself, the reference is to the actor's character, and thus the instance of discourse not only reinforces an already given visual presence but articulates the difference between the presentation, the performance, and that which is being performed, the theatrical fiction. The instance of discourse on stage is in the nature of a repetition. The actor's "I" that avows itself in discourse is the manifestation of the implicit "I" of the character who has already appeared before the spectators. In this repetition, there is, then, a distinction between the two "I's", and in virtue of this distinction, the spoken "I" already implicitly comments on the theatricality of the character.[71] André Gide exposed the metatheatricality

---

67. Ducrot and Todorov 1972, s.v. ÉNONCIATION; Greimas and Cortés 1982, s.v. ENUNCIATION, with cross-references at the end of the article; Greimas and Cortés 1986 s.vv. ÉNONCIATION and ÉNONCÉ.
68. Benveniste 1966. Cf. Ubersfeld 1991:47.
69. Benveniste 1966:251.
70. This paragraph has been adapted from two paragraphs in Edmunds 1993, where the distinction between enunciation and utterance is applied to the two systems of self-reference in Thucydides (first-person and third-person). Cf. Compagnon 1979:346: "Toute énonciation produit concurrement un énoncé et un sujet. Il n'y a pas un sujet préalable à l'énonciation ou à l'écriture, et ensuite une énonciation, à la façon d'un attribut ou d'une modalité existentielle de ce sujet; mais l'énonciation est constitutive du sujet, *le sujet advient dans l'énonciation*" (my emphasis). Cf. Elam 1980:72–73, 139.
71. Ubersfeld 1991:45: "Le Je-1 (le comédien) montre (par le jeu) que le Je-2 (personnage) fait ou dit telle chose. Par cette refente du *je*, le théâtre s'exhibe lui-même, affirmant la division de la scène et de la fiction, de la voix du comédien et celle du

of the instance of discourse in the opening flourish of his *Œdipe*, in which Oedipus says: "Me voici tout présent, complet en cet instant de la durée éternelle; pareil à quelqu'un qui s'avancerait sur le devant d'un théâtre et qui dirait: Je suis Œdipe."[72] To say "Me voici" and to call attention to one's presence on stage in the present instant, i.e., to employ an instance of discourse, is indeed the typical function of the dramatic character.[73]

The linguistic code is not the only one that has this metatheatrical potential. All theatrical signs and codes have it.[74] If theatrical signs are signs of signs, what distinguishes them from signs in other art forms, which are also signs of signs, is their transposition in their very materiality onto the stage. While a rose must become language to appear in a poem and paint to appear in a painting, a rose can appear as such on stage, where it is now the theatrical sign of something that it signifies in the cultural-historical context from which it was drawn. The play may or may not qualify the given cultural-historical meaning of the rose as sign. Even if, however, the role, so to speak, of the rose is rather insignificant, it will still call attention to its cultural sign-character and thus implicitly to its status as a theatrical sign. This self-conscious "loosening" of the theatrical sign from its cultural moorings, even in its material transposition, results in the semiotic mobility peculiar to theater: a sign can replace another sign that belongs to another code. Words can replace scenery, gestures props, sound-effects gestures, props lighting, etc. This mobility of the sign thus entails semiotic polyfunctionality: the rose can become an edible plant, a dagger, a comb, etc.; it can take on whatever meanings the play is able to endow it with.[75]

The mask carries theatrical self-consciousness to a further degree, because it in effect replaces the face of A as the sign of the face of X. (I

---

personnage, de Je-1 et Je-2, irréconciliables mais présentes ensembles dans le même bouche."

72. Gide 1942:253.

73. It is interesting that an analysis proceeding from ideology and relations of power reaches the same conclusion concerning theatrical autoreflexivity. Übersfeld 1978:290 concludes her discussion of Act 2, Scene 2 of Musset's *Lorenzaccio* thus: "Scène extraordinaire montrant comment la *référence* n'est pas tant à chercher dans le référent socio-historique des énoncés, que dans la situation même de production du dialogue" (her emphasis). Elam 1980:86: "The actor is always to some degree *opaque*, putting his very histrionic strategies on show as an index of his own virtuosity."

74. Übersfeld 1991:161: "En un certain sens, l'objet scénique est toujours *métaphore du théâtre*; ce qu'il dit, c'est toujours, outre le reste: je suis objet de théâtre."

75. In this paragraph, I have summarized and somewhat extended the argument of Fischer-Lichte 1983:180-83. Cf. Übersfeld 1978:31-35;194;202; Übersfeld 1991:127-33.

am speaking of the stiff mask used in the ancient Greek and in other theaters.) The mask is not the material transposition of a cultural sign into the theater (though it may be the transposition of the cultural *function* of the mask into the theater). Rather, the mask is, one might say, a meta-sign, a sign of theatricality:

> The actor who wears a mask is identified by the spectator not as actor A but as the character X indicated by the mask, without, however, being interchangeable with X. The wearing of the mask appears in this sense as precisely the theatrical process par excellence: whoever puts on a mask shows the public, through this act alone, that he no longer wants to be identified as himself but as the one meant by the mask, without, however, wanting to be equated as a real social subject with the subject meant by the mask. In this way the difference between the two subjects is neither effaced nor ignored. A does not become X but represents X. To this extent, the mask functions not simply as the sign for the face of the character X but at the same time as the sign of the realization of the fundamental theatrical phenomenon that here one (A) plays another (X). In this context, the mask can be conceived as one of the theater's foremost constitutive signs.[76]

The theatrical self-consciousness of the mask is continued in the practical consequence that the mask permits the same actor to play two or more roles at different times in the same play. The result is that the body of the actor becomes polyfunctional: it can represent the body of Y, etc. as well as of X.

Issacharoff's divisions of theatrical space provide, then, the basis for a semiotics of spectacle that can serve as a corrective or as an alternative to the Aristotelian hierarchy of the parts of the tragedy. Indeed, the semiotics here adumbrated would require that space, which is not even one of Aristotle's parts of tragedy, be assigned equal importance. On the basis of this semiotics, one can propose a non-Aristotelian rereading of a dramatic text, whether for its own sake, i.e., for the mental creation of a virtual production, or in preparation for an actual production. Such a reading would hardly be unprecedented: semioticians of theater have naturally wanted to apply their theories to actual plays.[77] A non-Aristote-

---

76. Fischer-Lichte 1983:108-109. Cf. Übersfeld 1991:231.
77. E.g. Elam 1980:184-207; Pavis 1982:165-77 on Richard Demarcy's *Disparitions*; Fischer-Lichte 1983, vols. 2 and 3.

lian rereading of a Greek tragedy starting from the semiotics of space would have as its goal the discovery of the spatial in the linguistic. The hypothesis of such a reading is that the language of the text, as a script, is not only spatially oriented, by, e.g., didascalia inferable from the dialogue, but more fundamentally spatially informed, that "[t]he written text ... is determined by its very need for stage contextualization, and indicates throughout its allegiance to the physical conditions of performance, above all to the actor's body and its ability to materialize discourse within the space of the stage."[78] A tragedy would be read as "a linguistic transcription of stage potentiality which is the motive force of the written text."[79] Thus the text of, say, a choral passage of Aeschylus, who is spoken of, no doubt properly, as a profound religious thinker, would be approached from the point of view that Aeschylus was a dancer, a choreographer, and a metteur en scène as well as a poet. Or, to put the case more strongly, to be a poet was to be the other things, too.

This approach offers a hermeneutic circle that moves from (1) the dramatic text to the text as script in large, obligatory features (entrances, exits, and other such changes of position); to (2) a subtler level of director and metteur en scène, to the putative uses of space by means of the costumes, masks, gestures, motions of the actor's body, etc., i.e., from script to the stage space of a virtual performance; to (3) the interplay of script and stage space in the creation of dramatic space, and thus also to theatrical autoreflexivity; (4) and finally back to the text, now gesturally and spatially conceived. Two sequential virtual performances can be imagined. The first is one that might have taken place in the ancient Theater of Dionysus; the reading of the dramatic text is thus historical.[80] On the basis of the text as recovered in this first virtual performance, a second one can then be undertaken, one that could be the basis of an actual performance. The second reading, whether it yields a virtual or an actual performance, will be oriented within the reader's contemporary horizon, as regards both theatrical practice and the questions of meaning to which the dramatic text should provide an answer. As for this second aspect of the contemporary horizon, it is nothing but the fundamen-

---

78. Elam 1980:209. Note resonance of Artaud.
79. Pugliatti quoted by Elam 1980:209. Cf. Übersfeld 1991:15, 67-68, 85 for the notion of a geno-text anterior both to the written text or script and to the first performance.
80. For a related procedure, see Kindermann 1979, who moves from the ancient spectators and the material conditions of theatrical production to the texts. For the historical context of Kindermann's approach, i.e., the growth of semiotics and reception theory in the 1970s, see Angela Andrisano's introduction to the Italian translation: Kindermann 1990:7-11.

tal hermeneutic assumption that the text is not now an answer to the same questions to which it was an answer in its own time. In this hermeneutic circle, the written dramatic text and the dramatic space are 180 degrees apart, and the ineluctable circularity of the procedure follows from the fact that the text to be interpreted in terms of space must provide the foreknowledge that will lead to that interpretation. Moving around this circle may lead to new insights into old, textual problems and may thus implicitly reinstate the "written poetry" that Artaud despised,[81] and provide new work for those lowly creatures, graduate students,[82] not to mention professors. In so doing, one would go against Artaud but would do so perhaps in his own spirit, for this kind of reading would seek to maintain a sense of the spatial in the dramatic text.

The circle here proposed can be further defined in contrast to the principles of reading found in Anne Ubersfeld's *Lire le théâtre*. Her title is designedly ambiguous: it refers both to the reading of plays and also to the spectator's reading of a performance.[83] Whereas the second reference of "reading" might seem to be metaphorical, for her it is not. One reason for this notion of the reading of a performance is that the author of the play is, on her understanding, present in the performance and the spectator is engaged with the author. In the "theatrical work," author or writer, practitioner (metteur en scène, actor), and spectator are all equally involved.[84] In the hermeneutic circle that I have proposed in the preceding paragraph, however, the author counts for little or nothing in a performance, even if, as in fact both in antiquity and in modern times, he or she participated in the production. It is a matter of common sense that the spectator's experience is not focused on the garnering of some focal, authorial consciousness in the performance. Whereas the distinction between author and actor/role may well become the preoccupation of the reading of a play, especially one that wants to determine some central meaning, this distinction does not present itself as such to a spectator. Though Ubersfeld brands as "reductive" the refusal to see the connection

---

81. *TD* 78: "Written poetry is worth reading once, and then should be destroyed."
82. Reference to graduate students in same context with scorn of "textual criticism": *TD* 75 (quoted in n. 17 above).
83. E.g. "Le spectateur lit et/ou construit" (Ubersfeld 1978:96); "les réseaux de signification qui . . . ont étés lus et ordonnés par le spectateur" (166). "L'espace scénique étant devenue objet poétique ... la lecture qui en est faite par le spectateur ..."(179). Like the script from which it began, the performance is also writing: e.g., 91: "l'écriture du théâtre."
84. Ubersfeld 1978:97. N.b. n. 45.

between author and spectator,[85] a semiotics of theater can assume an unconscious, habitual "reduction" on the part of the spectator. (Indeed, as she herself well observes, any performance will express only some small percentage of a dramatic text's fund of meaning.) It seems that Ubersfeld has transposed a typical interpretative concern of the reading of a dramatic text onto its reception in performance despite her own recognition of the fundamental difference between diachronic, linear reading and the synchronic semiotic thickness of the theatrical experience.[86] Ubersfeld's second book, *L'école du spectateur*, although it has the subtitle *Lire le théâtre 2*, departs from the first book in the matter of the spectator's "reading" of the performance. In the chapter called "Le travail du spectateur," there are only four references to spectatorial "reading," and Ubersfeld distinguishes in fact between spectator and reader.[87] Her study of the spectator is in terms of seeing and of cognitive psychology.

The relation of text to performance in Ubersfeld can be called Aristotelian in the sense that the text is not just pragmatically but also absolutely prior. There is the "textual level" and the "domain of representation."[88] A performance is the transposition of the text into another medium. For this reason, the theatrical text, as in Aristotle, can be considered a species of a genus that includes non-theatrical species and is open to the same kind of analysis as these other species. In Ubersfeld's case, this analysis is based on Greimas' actantial model, and though she claims that the deep structure of text and performance are the same,[89] she can do so only on the premises criticized above. The theatrical text proves to differ from other kinds of texts only in that it always has at least two possible actantial models. Here one could argue that this trait of the theatrical text is owing to its potentiality for performance and that this text is therefore not a species of a genus but in a class by itself. Ubersfeld verges on recognizing this point when she says, "le ou les modèles actantiels, dans leur concurrence ou leur conflit ne peuvent se comprendre que si

---

85. Ubersfeld 1978:251.
86. Ubersfeld 1978:153. Cf. Lotman 1981:18–21 for the notion of performance as text and Kowzan 1985:8–10 for a critique of the application of the word "text" to performance.
87. Ubersfeld 1991:321 (bis), 327, 328; 305 (distinction between spectator and reader).
88. Ubersfeld 1978:133. Cf. "[l]a faille entre les images textuelles et les signes de la représentation" (138), etc. And thus semiology of theatrical discourse and semiology of representation (267).
89. Ubersfeld 1978:66.

l'on fait intervenir la notion de la spatialité."[90] The hermeneutic circle that I have proposed, for its part, takes the text as primary only pragmatically. A circle has no beginning. Given a spatially, dramatically conceived "stage potentiality," the text is intermediary between this potentiality and its realization in a performance. Since the text is not primary, neither, as argued above, is the linguistic code dominant in performance. (Curiously, despite her orientation to the text and thus to reading as opposed to seeing, Ubersfeld herself several times avows the equal importance of the non-linguistic.[91])

Ubersfeld's second book, despite numerous corroboratory references to the first, has a profoundly different character. It is by turns a history of Western European theatrical practice over three decades, a poetics for the metteur-en-scène, a display of connoisseurship and criticism, and, perhaps more than the first book, a contribution to semiotics of theater. Its wealth of concrete observation is overwhelming; something of it could have been cited in every paragraph of this chapter; I have had to limit myself to the most salient points of agreement and disagreement. As for theatrical space, the notion of text, though etiolated in the second book as compared with the first, persists: "l'espace est véritablement un texte"![92] In my reading of *Oedipus at Colonus* in the next chapter, I try to reverse Ubersfeld's metaphor.

---

90. Ubersfeld 1978:104.
91. Ubersfeld 1978:116, 182, 258.
92. Ubersfeld 1991:102.

2

Theatrical Space in *Oedipus at Colonus*

An old man and a young woman enter from the spectators' left,[1] and slowly traverse the 100 feet or more from the corner of the Long Hall (if the beginning of their entrance is measured from this point) to the place on the stage where they will stop, short of the center. The stage is slightly raised[2] above the orchestra, where the chorus will later enter, and, at the edge of the stage, there are two rocks, one closer to the left, the other closer to the right, which will be Oedipus' seats.[3] The façade of the wooden stage building (*skênê*) in front of the Long Hall may or may not have had painted scenery representing the grove of the Eumenides;[4] it had an opening into the interior of the grove.[5] The slowness and difficulty of the man's gait indicate his age. His mask shows that he is blind (286; 551–56); his hair is wild and unkempt (1261). The two wear the tattered clothes of

---

1. By convention, an entrance from the left is from the territory outside Athens and an entrance from the right is from Athens. The main evidence is Pollux 4.126. See Klaus 1971:409–10.
2. Pickard-Cambridge 1946:21–23, 70; Taplin 1977:441–42.
3. Seale 1982:114. The rocks make us think of the outcrop of rock on the east side of the orchestra, i.e., on the spectators' left, that Hammond 1972 argued was still there in the Aeschylean theater. Contra: Taplin 1977:448–49; at 198 he says "it is likely that there was some permanent mound of some sort, probably outside the circle of the orchestra."
4. Arnott 1962:99: no scenery is needed. Pickard-Cambridge 1946:51: "[T]he background must have represented a grove of trees (by means, perhaps, of painted panels attached to the façade), with a way in and out among the trees—in other words through the background—and corresponding to the ordinary door." Critique of Arnott's views on scenery: Newiger 1979:472–74. Surveys of evidence for painted scenery in Dingel 1971 and in Padel 1990:346–54.
5. Pickard-Cambridge 1946:51.

beggars (555, 747-51, 1258-60, 1597), and the old man carries a beggar's pouch (1262-63).[6] The young woman leads him; he is so feeble that he cannot walk without support.[7] It is a highly conventional scene: a child or an attendant leads a blind person on stage. As they proceed along the stage, the old man begins to speak, naming the young woman: "Child of a blind old man, Antigone, what region have we reached or what city of men?" (1-2). The old man's question breaks the convention by which the attendant is mute: this one is a named character who will be able to speak.[8] He concludes by asking her to stop his movement and sit him down (11). She identifies the place as best she can, and then complies with his desire to be seated (14-20). The old man is so feeble that his sitting down is difficult and protracted (consider 19-22).

Oedipus' opening speech contains more than one kind of mimetic discourse. At the simplest level, "blind old man" refers to the figure seen by the spectators from the moment of its entrance and already identified as such visually; and "Antigone" (1) and "the wanderer Oedipus" (3) attach names to the two characters. But only in these matters of "factual" information can Oedipus' discourse be mimetic. Since he cannot see the stage space and the other characters, his discourse cannot refer to them, at least not as things perceived. Thus his discourse can never participate in the dramatic autoreflexivity of the other characters' discourse, which can always refer to the stage space that they and the spectators can see (cf. Chapter 1). Oedipus cannot, for example, use a demonstrative pronoun of someone or something on stage, unless the referent has been supplied to him (as, for the first time apropos of the stage space, at 45). His discourse can be mimetic only at a second remove, as mimetic of someone else's mimetic discourse. To return to the opening lines (1-2), the interrogative form of the sentence represents not only the character's desire for information but, more fundamentally, the fact that he is blind. His disjunction between "region" and "city of men" arises from his inability to make the perceptual distinction that would have simplified the question or rendered it unnecessary. Thus the interrogative form itself mimetizes the speaker's blindness and, in effect, announces Oedipus' whole relation to the stage space. His discourse can never be commensurate, in this respect, with that of the other characters. He can only refer to his own

---

6. See L-J-W 1990b:253 on 1262.
7. 501-502. The young woman is practically as well as metaphorically a "prop": cf. 848-49, 1109. The old man may also carry a staff: see Kaimio 1988:12 n. 3 for references in Greek tragedy to a character's carrying a staff.
8. Kaimio 1988:14-15, 85.

actions, and, since he depends upon others for guidance and support, these will tend to be stated in the form of questions, commands, refusals, and entreaties.

The plight of age and blindness is expressed in both of Oedipus' opening questions in the shift from third to first person (1-2: "blind old man ... we"; 3-6: "the wanderer Oedipus ... me"). The shift of persons is undoubtedly related to the necessity of titling the work or of identifying the subject-matter, at least in Oedipus' second sentence, and is an example of the two-level discourse normal in Greek tragedy.[9] (One can compare the opening sentence of Hecataeus [FGrH 1 F1]). In the mouth of Oedipus, this shift has the further function of a self-representation in which the speaker is an object before he is a subject: he is dependent on others (as he speaks the first two lines of the play, he is being led by Antigone). He is passive (note "sufferings," which will be thematic, in 7) and disposed to do the bidding of others (13). In terms of stage space, not only is he the object of others' mimetic discourse, which, as blind, he cannot reciprocate, but he is also the object of their actions. In their use of his body, he becomes, until the moment of his final exit, part of a stage space that they control. His own physical reaction can only be gesture or the refusal to comply. Thus the incommensurability of the dramatic discourse of Oedipus and the others, is played out at the level of the physical stage space, at the level of the often contested disposition of the body of Oedipus. In the opposition, then, between third and first persons, as in the interrogative form of the opening sentences, the spatial conception of the dramatic action is already inscribed. Even when Oedipus initiates an action, it is within a fundamental passivity. He says to Antigone: "Seat [imperative] me [first person pronoun in the accusative], and watch over [imperative] the blind man [self-reference in the third person; cf. "the blind old man" (1)]." Here he shifts from the first to the third person. The authority of the first of the two imperatives (followed by the first person) is modulated into the passivity implicit in the next (followed by the third person).

Antigone's reply to her father's opening speech is richly mimetic. She begins, no doubt with a gesture: "Father, wretched Oedipus, off in the distance, to judge by sight [*ommata* "eyes"], are towers that crown a city" (14-15).[10] If she gestures toward the buildings atop the Acropolis,

---

9. The actor communicates both with other actors and with the audience: Poe 1992:146. The opposition between third and first person is developed into an historiographical strategy in Thucydides: see Ch. 1 n. 70.

10. On the reading in 15, see L-J-W 1990a ad loc.

behind the spectators, then objects at the boundary of the theater space are brought into the dramatic space, and she creates an axis between those objects and the stage space.[11] She refers to the stage space as "this place," using the demonstrative adjective, and names the laurel, olive, and vine that she, but not her father, can see (16-17). Her discourse, with its mimetic specificity, is in complete contrast to her father's. Only when she refers to the many nightingales inside the grove, does she "notice an indication which her blind father can recognize."[12] Unless there were the sound effects of the nightingales' song, the reference to sound is, however, a complex form of dramatic discourse. Antigone refers to a diegetic space, visible to her, off stage, beyond the opening in the façade. Her discourse is also mimetic: she refers to a sound coming from this diegetic space, in fact inaudible to the audience, but "dramatically" perceptible within, and thus able to take the form of mimetic discourse within, the stage space. The effect of this sound is to establish the existence of an "inside" (*eisô* 18), of an inner dimension of the grove. Thus the axis already posited continues into this inner grove (from the *prosô* [15] of the "towers" on the Acropolis to the *eisô* within the façade). Having completed her answer to her father's question concerning the place in which they find themselves, she says, now in response to his bidding that she sit him down (11): "Sit here on this unwrought stone," where again the demonstrative refers to something that she and the spectators, but not Oedipus, can see. The contrast between her discourse and her father's is complete.

For Oedipus, the stone becomes "this stone" only when he can feel it and when he sits down upon it. Only his action brings it into existence for him, whereas, for Antigone and the spectators, it already lies within the dramatic space and is a straightforward referent in the mimetic discourse of Antigone. The contrast between her mimetic discourse and her father's non-mimetic discourse thus entails two distinct creations of dramatic space, one lagging behind the other. The primary dramatic space is the visually given stage space, to which Antigone refers and which the spectators can see. The dramatic autoreflexivity of her discourse, which refers to other characters and to things on stage, is standard and conventional. A secondary dramatic space emerges in Antigone's and later in others' translation for Oedipus of the primary space into another dramatic space that is specifically his. He himself can to some extent partici-

---

11. The top of the Parthenon can be seen from the stage area of the Theater of Dionysus. I am grateful to Elli Mylonas for a photograph that confirms this point.
12. Jebb 1928 ad loc.

pate in this process in ways already mentioned. In this distinct, secondary process focused on Oedipus, the spectators witness and hear not the "natural" relation of a character to dramatic space but a frustrated, delayed, groping towards its realization. Further, to the standard auto-reflexivity of the primary dramatic space there corresponds another kind of autoreflexivity in this secondary creation for and by Oedipus: the spectators become aware of the very process of the creation of dramatic space. The difference between the mimetic discourse of Antigone and the other characters, on the one hand, and the non-mimetic discourse of Oedipus, on the other, as this difference unfolds in the stage space, amounts to the play's comment on itself as a play. The secondary process, autoreflexive in the sense that it is self-conscious on the part of the characters, exposes the first.

After Antigone's opening speech in reply to her father, there ensues a brief series of exchanges between the two, leading up to the appearance of the stranger of Colonus (21-35). The series begins with Oedipus' command that she sit him down and tend to him. This undoubtedly labored action is in Brecht's term a Gestus: it is the basic action in which the whole incident, and, in the case of this play, the whole play, is epitomized.[13] It is the relationship between father and daughter: when Antigone refers, with the demonstrative *tode* (22), to what she is doing (i.e., not, as *tode* is usually understood, to the statement that her father has just made), it is in the context of a generalization about what she has always done during their wanderings, which is what she will continue to do in the rest of the play. The Gestus is at the same time the most emphatic form of stopping (cf. 11); it is Oedipus' occupying a particular place of his own—this stone—in this new place that they have reached, which is thus all the more in need of identification. With the action of sitting down, Oedipus has arrived, he has ceased his wanderings, and he has found his place: this action, in which the body of Oedipus changes position in space, is the essential action of the play. Appropriately, his first question, once he is seated, is: "Can you tell me where we have arrived?" (23). His need, as a stranger, to know where he is and the audience's need to have the dramatic space named coincide, and, to some extent, Antigone will be the one who will arrange the communication between Oedipus and the stranger that will lead to the identification. She will thus do explicitly on

---

13. Brecht 1964:200; cf. translator's notes 42. As Seale 1982:139 observes, "The seated, oracular figure of the blind Oedipus is the dominant visual impression." Cf. Segal 1981:365.

stage what the tragedian usually does implicitly, without calling attention to the fact that the dramatic space is being identified.

It now turns out that both Oedipus and Antigone knew that they were in the proximity of Athens (24-25).[14] Oedipus is therefore unimpressed by her identification of the city whose towers she has referred to (24-25, cf. 15) and sends her off to get information about the place in which they find themselves (26-27). But before she leaves him, she sees someone approaching: "I think there is no need for me to go, for I see this man hard by us" (28-29). The man had made his entrance and was approaching them while they talked. The demonstrative "this" (*tonde*) suggests that she gestures toward him, a gesture lost on the blind Oedipus, who asks "Coming hither and setting out?" (30). The manuscripts offer variants for the first of the two verbs. No matter how the textual question is resolved, a hysteron proteron remains: Oedipus has reversed the logical sequence of the actions, which is also the perceptual sequence. While the figure of speech may express his surprise and eagerness, it arises more fundamentally from the fact that he is blind: to him the relation of the two actions is a matter of indifference. The dramatic space, except for his rock and the description he has been given by Antigone, remains a blank for him. Antigone's "this" in the phrase "this man" has its normal theatrical autoreflexivity for the spectators, referring to something that they can see on stage. For Oedipus, however, her demonstrative is at best an invitation to imagine or visualize the man in his mind's eye. The spectators are thus aware not only of the dramatic space created for them by Antigone and also to some extent by the actions of Oedipus, but also of the secondary creation by Antigone of a meaningful space for Oedipus, a creation that depends upon the same kinds of mimetic discourse as their primary and normal experience of dramatic space. In this way, that discourse is exposed to them *as* mimetic discourse.[15]

Antigone's "staging" for Oedipus of the stranger's entrance continues as she replies to Oedipus' question: "No, here he is now right beside us" (31). The four particles that introduce her reply convey no new information to the spectators, who can see that the man is there, who, indeed, have seen the man before Antigone did. These particles are for the purpose of making present to Oedipus the presence of the man. The first

---

14. I have always felt a slight inconcinnity between lines 24-25 and 1-2.
15. Dunn 1992 well observes that the opening of *OC* is about the problem of beginning a tragedy.

two are often used to announce the arrival of a new character on stage,[16] and the second two show that Antigone is substituting a stronger form of expression ("present") for her father's ("coming" and "setting out").[17] She continues by urging her father to speak, since "the man is here (*hode*)" (31-32). She uses the same demonstrative as before (16, 19), in effect repeating her statement that the man is present. In short, Antigone's task is to represent to her father the presence of the stranger beside them, just as it is the tragedian's task to represent a dramatic action to the spectators, and she uses the same means as the tragedian. In response to Antigone's imperative ("speak")—an even more pronounced "directorial" gesture—Oedipus makes an elaborate overture, which the stranger will interrupt.[18] Referring to Antigone, Oedipus uses the same demonstrative that she has used (*têsde* 33), but this usage depends upon physical proximity. The demonstrative either accompanies his touching her, or, if not, it can be used because she is so close to him that he knows from the sound of her voice or by a sixth sense exactly where she is. Oedipus' usage is thus asymmetrical with, of a different order from, Antigone's: it issues from his negative dramatic space to the positive visual dramatic space inhabited by the stranger. Antigone's demonstratives—this grove, this rock, this man—moved in the opposite direction, attempting to cross the boundary of her father's blindness and to create for him a mental version of the dramatic space. (There is tendance of her father at every level of her discourse.) As the entrance of the stranger shows, the stage on which the blind Oedipus appears will be criss-crossed by the boundaries, ever changing, between his negative and the other's positive dramatic space.

The situation is epitomized in the verb (*adêleô* 35) that Oedipus uses just before the stranger interrupts him. The verb forms part of a set of contrasts in Oedipus' elaborate overture: the sightedness of Antigone and his own blindness (33-34); the stranger and "us" (34); the stranger's function, expressed in visual terms by the word *skopos*,[19] and the igno-

---

16. Denniston 1966:251, though he puts this example in a related category in which the sense is close to that of ἤδη (252).
17. Denniston 1966:475, citing this place.
18. See Mastronarde 1979:65: "The interruption immediately throws an effective emphasis on the sacredness of the ground upon which Oedipus surprisingly insists he will remain." In other words, the interruption itself is a textual reflex of the spatial conception.
19. "A scout [i.e., one who sees] of those things with respect to which we ..." I follow the interpretation of Jebb ad loc. Kamerbeek 1984 ad loc. is wrong, I think.

rance of Oedipus and Antigone, expressed by the verb. It is a hapax in classical Greek and means "to be *adêlos*," i.e., "to be obscure." Oedipus' statement is thus neatly ambiguous: the stranger has come as a scout to inquire into the obscure matter of the presence of two new-comers; the stranger has come as the scout for Oedipus and Antigone of the matter with respect to which they are subjectively obscure, i.e. in the dark, namely, the identity of the place in which they find themselves. The two aspects of this ambiguity correspond to the two kinds of dramatic space, negative and positive. The stranger may provide, and in fact does provide, precise information concerning the place, thus expanding the possibilities of mimetic discourse (cf. Ch. 3§3); but Oedipus as blind will remain in the dark; and his discourse can never become mimetic. At the same time, Oedipus, if not Antigone, though he may form part of the visual field of the other characters and of the dramatic space shared by them and the audience, will remain obscure to them in the sense that his growing knowledge of the place as the site of his grave can only be shared by them on faith and that the climactic action of the play will take place outside their sight and thus outside their mimetic discourse, outside, in fact, even the sight of the messenger whose diegetic discourse reports the death of Oedipus. Thus the stranger's information increases and renders more significant the negative dramatic space of Oedipus, though, as negative, it cannot easily become significant for anyone else.

In the rest of the prologue, after the stranger's interruption of Oedipus (38-116), the incommensurability of the two dramatic spaces is intensified. The stranger is standing; Oedipus is seated, and will not move, despite the stranger's injunction (36-37). This spatial relationship subtends everything they say to one another. After Oedipus learns that he has reached a grove of the Eumenides (39-43), he explicitly refuses to obey the stranger, putting himself in the relation of suppliancy to the Eumenides (44-45). In a pattern already observed, he refers to himself in the third and then in the first person (44-45; cf. 49-50 [first and then third]; 109-110 [third]); but now he is a third person vis-à-vis not other characters whom he may or does encounter but vis-à-vis the divinities of the place. This special relationship will guide everything else Oedipus says and does, i.e., it will be the basis of the dramatic space that he perceives and, to the extent possible, creates, though the others on stage will be slow to understand. When Oedipus says, in refusal, "I would never depart from my seat in this land" (45),[20] neither the stranger nor Antigone

---

20. L-J-W 1990a ad loc. have accepted Musgrave's emendation, which goes against the spatial conception of the scene and of the whole play, for that matter.

has any way of knowing, but Oedipus already has in mind his special destiny, the future benefit that he will confer on his final resting place (72, 92-93). It is more precisely a "seat [in the precinct] of the awful goddesses" (89-90, where the same partitive construction as in 45 occurs; cf. the similar phrase in 84-85). His and the others' repeated references to his "seat" (36, 45, 84-85, 90, 112; consider also Oedipus' curious emphasis on the unhewn stone at 101, to the condition of which Antigone had already called attention at 19) are the verbal reflex of the Gestus of sitting and of the spatial conception of the seated Oedipus opposite the standing stranger.

The use of demonstratives in the exchanges between Oedipus and the stranger is an index of the difference between the two dramatic spaces that they inhabit. Though he knows from the outset that Oedipus is blind, he speaks to him, for the most part, as if he were sighted, somewhat less considerately than Antigone, though even she had to use mimetic discourse, with the metatheatrical effects discussed above. In particular, the stranger thrice refers to "this" horseman, a statue on stage or one that he can see from the stage. If it is on stage, it would not have to be a "real" equestrian statue. The stranger could gesture toward the altar in the center of the orchestra,[21] which would thus lie on the axis already described, and his mimetic-constative discourse would serve to complete the dramatic identification of this object. Oedipus can use the same demonstrative but as discourse it has a different value, since Oedipus cannot call attention to the presence of something in the same modality as the others can. What for the stranger is "this place" (54, cf. 16) is for Oedipus "the place we have entered" (52).[22] On the contrary, as the example just given suggests, Oedipus' "this" will as an instance of discourse be either physical or general (for example, "this region" [64], "this land" [84-85], "this journey" [96], "this grove" [98]). What I have called the physical instances of discourse are almost tautological.[23] They simply restate verbally what Oedipus has done physically or indicate something with which Oedipus is in physical contact, like the stone or like Antigone herself, as pointed out above. They do not add to the other characters' or the spectators' knowledge of the positive, shared dramatic space, though they

---

21. Pickard-Cambridge 1946:9-10. Wiles 1990-91:158-160 demonstrates the opposing significations of statue and grove.
22. With the stranger's "this seat" (36) cf. Oedipus' "seat" (45) without demonstrative. The stranger uses a metonym and a metaphor to designate the place: "bronze-stepped way of this land" (cf. 1591) and "bulwark of Athens" (55b-58). On these, see Ch. 3§3.
23. For the concept of instance of discourse, see Ch. 1 above.

have other effects, as Oedipus' negative dramatic space acquires its own dimension and value. Indeed, there is a tendency, again already noted, for Oedipus to refer to himself in the third person, as if the first-person instance of discourse, the self-presentation of the dramatic self, were drastically inhibited. Thus at the end of his prayer to the Eumenides, he refers to himself as "this wretched phantasm" (109), where the demonstrative looks to the body of the actor. Likewise, in the same context, "this" stone (101) can be thus referred to because Oedipus is physically sitting upon it. Such physical instances of discourse have a zero degree of referentiality: limited to the physical compass of the speaker's body, their reference is dramatically tautological. Because of his blindness, Oedipus is left with only his own body, as distinguished from dialogue, as a means of dramatic discourse: only within the scope of his own body can he endow the dramatic space with significance. The non-referential or non-dramatic discourse of Oedipus must then carry unusual weight: "Whatever I say, it will all be sighted" (74).

The exchanges between Oedipus and the stranger, in addition to their development of the spectators' sense of the positive and negative dramatic spaces, also create a new, broader space. Pursuing his line of questioning about the place in which he finds himself, Oedipus learns that the people of Colonus are ruled from Athens by king Theseus (66-69). Athens, then, is not only on the periphery of the dramatic space, the boundary of the dramatic space, as established in Antigone's opening speech; it is also a continuous part of that space, accessible, Oedipus has inferred, by a messenger (70), so that an implicit diegetic space comes into existence. In terms of the stage action, characters' entrances from and exits to this diegetic space will be from the parodoi or wings, thus at a right angle to the axis already mentioned several times. If I was correct in placing Athens at one end of that axis, in virtue of Antigone's supposed gesture toward the buildings atop the Acropolis behind the spectators, then this new diegetic space moves this point and describes an arc: Athens is not simply a point at the end of the axis defined by Antigone; Athens surrounds Colonus. For now, Athens and the space implied by the references to the journey of Oedipus and Antigone (20, 96), are the farthest reaches of any possible diegetic discourse.

As against these reaches, within the dramatic space, Antigone appears to be, and believes that she is, the nearest thing to Oedipus. When, in response to her father's question, she confirms that the stranger has gone, she adds that only she is near (83). Instead of replying to her, Oedipus bursts into a prayer to the Eumenides, thus implicitly contradicting her. The Eumenides, too, are near, perhaps nearer than Antigone.[24] The prayer reveals that this grove is the destined place of Oedipus' death and that his grave will be a gain to "those who receive him" (92). Since one of the concluding petitions of his prayer is addressed to the city of Athens, by "those who receive him" Oedipus must mean all of the Athenians, not just the Colonans. The proportion of the dramatic to the diegetic space has thus, as was already suggested, begun to change, even if the stranger has said that the decision as to Oedipus' disposition will be referred to the Colonans, not to those in the city (78-79). Oedipus is thus near to divinities who cannot be seen (and whose grove should not even be looked at: 130) and are unrepresentable within dramatic discourse. His grave is for all of Athens, which lies in the now expanding diegetic space off stage. How, then, can Oedipus represent to the other characters the negative space as known to him? How can Sophocles represent to the audience Oedipus' struggle to cross the boundary of his negative space to the others' positive space? The parodos will provide a test.

The parodos begins visually when Antigone sees and points out old men approaching, "inspectors of your seat" (112), she tells her father. These are the locals who the stranger said would judge whether Oedipus could remain (79-80). They are *episkopoi* (cf. *skopos* above): their function is based on seeing and observing. Oedipus' reaction is to leave his seat and retreat into the grove. "Hide me in the grove" (114), he says to Antigone.[25] The chorus enters from the spectators' right, grouped or grouping themselves in three rows of five, moving into the orchestra in front of the stage, energetic in proportion to their age, and purposeful.[26] They carry staffs.[27] Fifteen pairs of eyes look for Oedipus, who has disappeared. The chorus' or chorus leader's first word is "look!" (*hora* 117), and they scan the whole grove (135-36) with their hands in the "peering"

---

24. Dawe 1978:138, wanting to delete line 83, says: "The superfluous reassurance that she alone is near, so that Oedipus can say what he likes without fear of interruption, might be justified if Oedipus were then to enter into a confidential conversation with her; but as it is he launches into a grand invocation of immortal powers." But if lines 83ff. are read with a view to dramatic space, the contradiction pointed out by Dawe becomes meaningful.

25. On the text of 113-14, see Renehan 1992:372-73.

26. For the evidence concerning the chorus, see Pickard-Cambridge 1968:234-41. The entrance of this chorus may not be in the standard formation: see Taplin 1977:379-80.

27. Lawlor 1964:38.

schema,[28] but they, who are sighted, cannot see Oedipus. He, who is blind but knows their location from their voice, reveals his location to them. "For I see (*horô* 138) by voice."[29] Briefly, the negative and positive spaces have been reversed. He presents himself by means of the demonstrative (*hode* 138) by which a character announces the arrival of a new character on stage (cf. above and 723, 1249). His gesture and/or action must reinforce this sense of arrival, as he comes forth out of his hiding place, perhaps reemerging into the stage space from the opening in the stage building.[30] He is new in the sense that he is "that one" (138), i.e., the one the chorus was looking for. He is not new to the spectators, for whom this is a second, different self-presentation, indeed the imitation of a new character's arrival on stage. The stage becomes a stage in relation to the orchestra. The situation is epitomized in the enunciative properties of Oedipus' statement. "This is that one," he says, and he adds, "I." The whole sentence is: "This is that one—I."[31] On the one hand, he, who "sees by voice," shares the visual field of the chorus and presents himself from their point of view. On the other, in the same statement, he refers to himself from his own point of view as "I." Oedipus' "this" with its two predicates thus encompasses the two principal positions in the dramatic space, which are further defined by the chorus' action or gesture as it reacts with horror at the sight of Oedipus (140).

Oedipus' self-referential discourse does not end with the statement just analyzed. He continues to call attention to what he is doing: "I make it plain" (*dêlô* 146), he says, as he refers to his leaning on his guide Antigone ("thus" *hôde* 146) in order to prove how unfortunate he is. For its part, the chorus tries to "direct" Oedipus, in effect to reverse the advantage that Oedipus had established by means of his self-presentation. As he and Antigone continue to move along the grove (n.b. 155–56), the chorus tries to stop him. The mimetic-constative discourse of their description of the grove (156–60) contains a warning for Oedipus, who is entering the even more sacrosanct inner grove. The chorus soon wins the contest for control of the dramatic space and for the disposition of characters within that space. The stage soon ceases to be a place on

---

28. Lawlor 1964:44. For comparison of this searching-scene with the similar one at Aesch. *Eum.*, see Kaimio 1970:134–37. She doubts a division of the chorus into groups.
29. An entry within a lyric structure would in itself have been striking: cf. Taplin 1977:174; 248; 283.
30. "Oedipus hides in the grove (i.e., probably, leaves by the door in the background)": Pickard-Cambridge 1946:51; cf. Arnott 1962:99; Taplin 1977:455 n. 2.
31. "This is that" would become Aristotle's formula for mimesis: *Poetics* 3.48b17. Cf. Nagy 1990b:44.

which Oedipus acts autonomously and becomes instead a place on which the chorus deploys him. This process begins when Oedipus decides to assent to the chorus' condition for negotiation, which is that he move to a position where it is lawful to speak (166-69: end of the first antistrophe). As Oedipus makes his decision, taking counsel with his daughter, the physical contact between them (cf. 146-48) is broken, and he must then call upon her to take his hand, and she says that she is already doing so, drawing attention to her action (173).[32] As they begin to move toward the chorus, Oedipus asks that he not be wronged, having trusted them and having "changed position." (175). The remarkably dense autoreflexivity of the parodos continues in the second strophe, in which the chorus coaxes Oedipus and Antigone forward, and the latter instructs her father, again referring to her action ("thus" *hôde* 182). The demonstrative adverb that she uses refers to something that Oedipus feels and that the others can see. (The relationship of negative and positive spaces has been reestablished.) At the beginning of the second antistrophe, the chorus bids Oedipus to stop and not to move his foot outside "this platform of living rock" (192). "Platform," the standard term for the raised place where a speaker stood in a public assembly or in a lawcourt, may be here a metaphor for the raised stage on which Oedipus and Antigone are seen or it may even be a theatrical term.[33] In any case, it can be assumed that the chorus halts Oedipus at the edge of the stage, precisely the place at which, by the conventions of the theater, he could go no farther anyway. Their directions, which include rather precise details concerning Oedipus' seated posture (195-96), in the context of what has developed as competitive stagings of the action, reestablish the stage as the stage in relation to the orchestra, where the chorus is, but now the chorus is the director, not Oedipus. His slow, painful sitting down, impossible without Antigone's aid (195-202; note the exclamations and also what the chorus says at 203) has been seen by the audience once before (21-22), where it was a matter of Oedipus' own volition. This time, the sitting down is "staged" by the chorus for itself.

The parodos ends with Antigone's supplication of the chorus on behalf of her and her father, who have been banished from the land upon

---

32. Her καὶ δή means "now, already." Jebb and Kamerbeek compare 31; L-J-W 1990b give other examples of this meaning of the phrase. Neumann 1965:49: "Die Handreichung, der Händedruck, ist für den Griechen nicht eine gewöhnliche und abgenutzte Geste, sondern ein Zeichen der Zueignung und Liebe. Sie ist sichtbarer Ausdruck der Verbundenheit, die vor allem in bedeutsamen Augenblicken des Lebens zum Sprechen kommt."

33. See LSJ s.v. βῆμα II and note II.3, with which compare LSJ s.v. θυμέλη II.c.

the chorus' realization that it is the execrable Oedipus with whom they are dealing. Her speech is replete with reference to her own action. She announces her supplication (241). She repeatedly refers to herself as "approaching the chorus with prayers" (243, 244, 250). She describes herself as looking into the eyes of the chorus leader (note the shift to the second person singular at 245).[34] When she says, "we depend on you as on a god" (248), she could be referring to the suppliant's typical embracing of the knees,[35] provided that physical communication across the division between stage and orchestra was possible, as later action in the play seems to indicate.[36] She tells the chorus how to indicate acceptance of her prayer: "signify by a nod" your granting this favor (248). Antigone even makes explicit the contrast between her father's negative space and the positive dramatic space shared by her and the chorus. "Not with blind eyes" does she look the chorus leader in the eye (244-45). Unlike her father, she has at least visual equality with the chorus. As sighted, she can appeal to them within the same dramatic space. She can perform the supplicatory actions to which she refers; she can "direct" the response that she hopes for from the chorus, which is a visual sign, a nod.

So ends the parodos, with a tableau of supplication. The chorus rejects Antigone's plea, and now Oedipus, still crouching on the rock (263-64), becomes the suppliant (275, 284). His goal is not be moved (cf. 276) and he does not move during the speech. To persuade the chorus, he visualizes himself for them: he imagines the chorus "looking upon his face, ugly to behold" (285-86), and he begs the chorus not to be influenced by his appearance. In keeping with the reversal noted above, by which the stage has become a stage with respect to the orchestra, he acknowledges the chorus as a spectator that might be horrified at what he sees. Oedipus' speech will be successful at least in causing the chorus to transfer the decision concerning banishment to "the leaders of this land," i.e., to Theseus (294-95). With the speech under discussion, following hard upon Antigone's supplication of the chorus in the name of herself and her father, Oedipus' seated posture reaffirms the suppliancy he has already proclaimed (44-45). He is the suppliant of the divinities in whose grove he finds himself (cf. 487, 634). His speech to the chorus is a

---

34. A conjecture of Elmsley in 250 accepted by Dawe and by L-J-W would remove an instance of the second person singular which the spatial conception of the scene would seem to require or at least allow.
35. Illustrated with an ancient and a modern example in Burkert 1979 figs. 3-4.
36. Pickard-Cambridge 1946:51 on 856-67; cf. Gould 1985:269.

Theatrical Space in Oedipus at Colonus 53

spoken version of Antigone's lyric petition. If it was not already clear, both their words and also the proxemic relations of Antigone and of her father to the chorus signify that they are suppliants.

The visual impact of these relations derives not only from the fact that theatrical signs are signs of signs (cf. on the embracing of knees in the paragraph before last) but also from the fact that suppliancy is an already established dramatic form attested in several earlier tragedies.[37] The questions thus arise of the relation of *Oedipus at Colonus* to this form and of the implications of this relation for the use of theatrical space in this tragedy. The form typically involves a triangular relation of suppliant, enemy, and rescuer. The suppliant is in flight from an enemy. He takes refuge at an altar as the suppliant of the god(s) to whom the altar is dedicated. In the land where he has taken asylum, he finds a rescuer whose aid he beseeches. An agon between the rescuer and the enemy ensues. The conclusion depends upon the circumstances of the flight. The suppliant is either received as a permanent member of the community in which he found asylum or he is assured safe return to his original community. Since, as said, *Oedipus at Colonus* clearly displays its affinity to this dramatic form, its deviance is all the more significant. The beseeching of the rescuer is already played out in the scenes just discussed, so that Oedipus does not have to humble himself before his true rescuer, Theseus, who in any case considers himself bound in advance by xenia to protect Oedipus. (Certain topoi of suppliant drama are nevertheless integrated into Theseus' reception of Oedipus.[38]) The main reason, however, for deviance from the form is that Oedipus offers as much as he asks: he comes indeed as the savior of Athens.[39] He can appeal to Theseus' self-interest (cf. 635). The spatial conception of Oedipus' relation to Theseus cannot therefore be that of suppliant to rescuer; nor, in general, is *Oedipus at Colonus* conceived in its proxemic dimensions as a suppliant drama. The act of sitting down is more fundamentally the occupation of the place in which the mana of his grave in the Eumenides' precinct will protect Attica. Since the spectators know what the sitting down means, they are then in a position to witness the frustration (which, as will be argued, becomes also a metatheatrical one) of Oedipus' need

---

37. Kopperschmidt 1971; Burian 1974. See also Taplin 1977:192-93. There are other studies of suppliant drama that I have not read: Burnett 1971; Gould 1973. Further bibliography in Taplin 1977:192 n. 3 and 451 n. 1. Suppliancy also had its stage conventions, which are discussed by Kaimio 1988: Ch. 5, who, however, omits both this scene in OC and the later one in which Polyneices is the suppliant of Oedipus.

38. Kopperschmidt 1971:331 on lines 631-41.

39. This rather radical variation of the suppliant form is the theme of Burian 1974.

to demonstrate his power. Both visually and in mimetic discourse, he is old, weak, blind, squalid, and destitute. How can this person have, i.e., show that he has, the power that he says he has?

To return to the opening of the first episode, once Oedipus has persuaded the chorus to remand the decision to Theseus (292-95), he immediately asks where Theseus is (296), and the relation of the mimetic to the diegetic space is thus brought into question again. Will Theseus come "near" (300)? The chorus conjures up a picture of movement between Colonus and Athens: the *skopos* who had summoned the chorus had continued to Athens; the name of Oedipus, who was not identified until after the departure of the *skopos*, will be carried by rumor (297-307). But before Theseus can traverse this busy space, to enter from the spectators' right, someone else appears in the left parodos, coming from abroad. Antigone says, "I see a woman approaching us" (311-12). Slowly, a figure on a horse, accompanied by an attendant (334), enters the stage.[40] In precisely mimetic discourse, Antigone describes horse and rider: it is a "colt of Etna" and the rider wears a "Thessalian hat" (312-14). At a certain point, the figure's bright eyes show Antigone that it is her sister (319-21). It is clear (*dêlon*) that this (*hode*) is Ismene (320-21). The entrance is thus enacted by Ismene and mimetically narrated by her sister. But the Ismene whom she can see Oedipus can recognize only by her voice (322-23; cf. 138: "I see by voice"). The contrast between the negative and positive spaces continues in the opening exchange between Ismene and her father. She calls attention to the fact that she is looking at him and Antigone (326) and also to her father's appearance—"ugly to behold" (327).[41] (As with subsequent entrances, it is not the one or ones on stage who give the welcome but the one entering, just as, in greeting scenes on countless vase paintings, the one arriving raises his or her hand in greeting and not the one receiving or awaiting.[42]) Oedipus has to ask if she has "appeared" (328) but his only way of confirming her appearance is by touch, and he bids her touch him (329). She embraces both him and Antigone at once, and a tableau is created that will be repeated at the reunion of the three after the abduction of the daughters by Kreon and also at the end of the play, when Oedipus takes leave of his daughters just before his death. What is a

---

40. On the length of the entrance, see Gould ibid.; Taplin 1977:297. Different commentators have different opinions on whether Ismene actually rides onto the stage. On horses and other animals on stage, see Dingel 1971:354.
41. Accepting, with L-J-W 1990a, Bücheler's conjecture in 327. Cf. 578.
42. Neumann 1965:43.

tableau for the audience is for Oedipus, however, a sub-visual reenactment of the arrival of Ismene, whose primary arrival belonged to the positive dramatic space from which he is excluded.

The ensuing exchanges between Oedipus and Ismene open up both a wild diegetic space, as he refers to his wanderings, during which he was supported by Antigone and occasionally visited by Ismene (337-60),[43] and also a wide political diegetic space, in which the main locations are Thebes, where Eteocles now rules, and Argos, where Polyneices, in exile, has formed a marriage connection and raised an army with which he will attack his native city (361-84). Oedipus learns that, because of an oracle, the Thebans intend to bury him outside their city and that Kreon is coming to get him (385-400). Another entrance is in the offing. Oedipus learns in particular of the power of his burial place to help or harm the Thebans (408-411), as a recent oracle has said, an oracle that thus makes specific what Oedipus had learned at Delphi long ago (cf. 92). He can thus state more emphatically than before his usefulness to "this city" (459), Athens: he will be a "savior" (460). Though the chorus is not, or at least pretends not to be, incredulous and proceeds to tell Oedipus how to atone to the Eumenides for his violation of their grove, Oedipus' predicament is worse than ever: the contradiction between his appearance and the efficacy of his grave is all the more pronounced. The former is demonstrable and perceptible; the latter is not. Thus the former can be represented in theatrical space in its various modalities; the latter cannot.

The chorus' detailed instructions for the rite of atonement further the diegetic creation of the inner grove. They conclude by telling Ismene, who will perform the rite, that she must go to a spot on the "further side" of the grove, where there is a custodian who will help her (505-506). When she exits, the chorus and Oedipus sing a kommos, at the end of which Theseus enters from the right.[44] The chorus announces his arrival with his name and with the usual particles and demonstrative (549), and no further identification is necessary. Whereas Theseus might still have opened with the self-introduction that begins only at 562, he in effect introduces Oedipus, as if Oedipus were the new character on stage (551-56). Theseus states in detail how he recognizes Oedipus. He had in the

---

43. Segal 1981:368: "The road is the single most dominant spatial metaphor of the play." The idea is captured in Pavese's "La Strada" (Pavese 1947), a dialogue between the old Oedipus and a beggar which takes place on the open road and in which, as in *Oedipus at Colonus*, the road is a metaphor.

44. The lyric dialogue preceding an entrance has the same structural function as, and thus can be taken as a substitution for, a choral song. See Taplin 1977:247.

past heard of Oedipus' self-blinding and, now that he sees him,[45] he is all the more certain of Oedipus' identity (551–54). For, Theseus goes on to explain, "your outfit (*skeuē*) and your wretched face show (*dēlouton*) me that you are who you are" (555–56). The verb refers to the evidence that confirms the identity of a character (cf. 146, 320). In this case, however, the character has no chance to participate in identifying himself: the restriction on the enunciative discourse of Oedipus is in full force. Oedipus is there as a character for Theseus to behold, i.e., Oedipus is in the same condition to which he was reduced in the parodos, and the word for "outfit," which is the regular word for the dress of an actor, is ambiguous: it refers, like the references to the face of Oedipus, to the character Oedipus and at the same time to this character as a character. Thus, with the arrival of each new character—the stranger, the chorus, Ismene, and now Theseus—through the blindness of Oedipus and the consequent discrepancy between his and the others' dramatic spaces, he is not only isolated and physically passive, but he becomes a character of a different order from the others, one who is deployed (sometimes at his own instigation) within the space that the others have already described for themselves and the spectators. Since Oedipus cannot participate in the action that goes on in that space except at the others' direction, his is in the nature of a secondary action (with the telling exception of 118–39 with its brief reversal of the positive and negative spaces).

Oedipus is well aware of the discrepancy between his appearance, i.e., what the others can see, and the benefit that his grave in Colonus will bring the Athenians, i.e., what he can foresee. He says to Theseus: "I come to give you my wretched body, a gift not excellent to the sight, but the gains from it are better than a beautiful physique" (576–78). The predicament of Oedipus' promise, which had arisen in his interchange with the chorus, now becomes more acute. What Theseus and the others have seen and referred to within the dramatic space is not a reliable sign of the future benefit. What Oedipus has to offer is indemonstrable (and thus not available to be dramatized). Theseus begins to question Oedipus. He asks, for example, when the benefit Oedipus will be shown (*dēlōsetai* 581). When will Theseus have a visual confirmation of the benefit? Only, Oedipus replies, when he dies and Theseus buries him (582), a statement that, in effect, repeats the indemonstrability (and thus the non-theatricality) of the benefit. "The body of the actor represents ...

---

45. Accepting, with L-J-W 1990a (and see 1990b ad loc.), Nauck's conjecture in 554.

the condition of the possibility of theater,"[46] but this body will never be able to demonstrate the benefit of Oedipus, which is post mortem. The contours of the predicament are now sharp. As blind, Oedipus cannot participate in the dramatic space of the other characters except under the limitations described above. They for their part are excluded from the space, which could be called future-diegetic, but which is already associated with the grove which they cannot even look at (cf. 130), in which Oedipus' benefit will become known. The play thus presents the spectators with the predicament of a non-dramatizable, non-theatrical action.

The chorus has been present during the exchange between Oedipus and Theseus. When the latter exits (667), the chorus begins a song, the famous praise of Colonus and Athens. The song is addressed to Oedipus, the "stranger" (*xene*: vocative 668), and implicitly refers to his choice of Colonus over Theseus' palace as his abode in Attica (638-46). The song is thus also a response to, and increases the semiotic force of, Oedipus' unchanged seated (or crouching) posture. The chorus begins by, in effect, reversing the hierarchical relation of Athens to Colonus that was epitomized in the figure of Theseus. They tell Oedipus: "you have come to earth's best abodes, white Colonus, belonging to this land [i.e., Attica] of goodly horses" (668-70).[47] The chorus' demonstrative, "this," though it is general and does not require that Oedipus be able to see its referent, is nevertheless probably accompanied by a gesture. *Cheironomia* "gesticulation" and *deixis* "pointing" are in ancient theory as much a part of the chorus' action as dancing.[48] Gestural and proxemic signs would have conveyed messages to the spectators that are invisible to Oedipus, and, as will be observed below, even the mimetic discourse of the chorus cannot, in some respects, be apprehended as mimetic by Oedipus. At the opening of their song, however, the chorus accommodates Oedipus' blindness, beginning their description of Colonus with the nightingale's song (672; cf. Antigone at 18). The lush vegetation described by the chorus reinforces the mimetic discourse heard at the beginning of

---

46. Fischer-Lichte 1983:98.
47. Taking the first genitive phrase, with Jebb, as "territorial genitive" referring to Attica as a whole, of which the "abodes" (Colonus) are a part.
48. *Cheironomia*: Athen. 14.631C; Plut. *Mor.* 747B; Lawlor 1964:25; Pickard-Cambridge 1968:246-57. *Deixis*: Plut. *Mor.* 747E; Lawlor 1964:32-33; Pickard-Cambridge 1968:249.

the play. The grapevine reappears (675ff.), and to the laurel and olive are added ivy (674), narcissus (683), and crocus (685).[49]

But as the chorus proceeds with their description of Colonus, they begin to introduce elements that, mimetic or diegetic in only a limited sense for Oedipus, have specific referential value for the spectators. Oedipus may never have heard of the Cephisus (687) and its irrigation of Colonus, but the name and the related phenomenon are well known to the spectators. The choruses of the Muses may be an allusion to their altar in the Academy, near Colonus (691-92; cf. Paus. 1.30.2; Eur. *Med.* 824-25). If so, the referent is lost on Oedipus, who can grasp only the general information that Colonus and the region are blessed by the Muses' dances. Similarly, the description of the self-generation of the olive would have reminded the spectators of the regrowth of the olive on the Acropolis (698; Hdt. 8.55) and perhaps also of the secondary phenomenon in the Academy (Paus. *ibid.*; cf. schol. *OC* 705). The description of the olive as "unvanquished" may be another anachronistic allusion: to Archidamus' sparing the sacred olives when he invaded Attica at the beginning of the Peloponnesian War (schol. *OC* 698, citing Philochorus and Androtion). Another allusion that would have been lost on Oedipus is carried by the adjective *euthalasson* (711), if it refers to the salt-water well on the Acropolis (Paus. 1.26.5; cf. Ch. 3§1 below). In sum, these details of the chorus' description must be apprehended in one way by the spectators and in another way by Oedipus, even though the song was addressed to Oedipus.

The question thus arises of the valence of the demonstratives used by the chorus in the context of these allusions (700, 707, 715). Like the one that opened the chorus' song (668), these demonstratives convey something to Oedipus: that the chorus is referring to the region in which he finds himself. Its gestural (and proxemic?) accompaniment is, however, perceptible only to Antigone (who is on stage, presumably next to her father, but whose presence is unacknowledged from 509 to 720) and to the spectators. These demonstratives must reinforce the "private" communication between the chorus and the spectators in the stasimon and thus the dramatic-semiotic (not physical) separation between stage and orchestra that was defined in the parodos. Since the chorus, somewhat in the manner of the comic chorus in the parabasis, can communicate directly with the spectators, outside its dramatic role (and here partly by means of anachronism), its ambiguous status becomes more clearly

---

49. See Kamerbeek's note on 681-85 for the symbolism of the narcissus and crocus: here is a perfect example of how the linguistic code can belong to multiple systems of meaning. Cf. Fischer-Lichte 1983:34.

defined: while it is a participant in the same dramatic action as Oedipus and the other characters, it is also the observer of this action and, as such, closer to the spectators than to the actors. The semiotic analysis of this ambiguity would be greatly aided if there could be any certainty about the direction in which the chorus is facing as it delivers its lines. The truism that the chorus, upon entering the orchestra, turned and faced the audience[50] cannot be true of the parodos of this tragedy nor can the chorus be facing the audience at the beginning of the stasimon under discussion. But, since the "private" meanings of the linguistic code commence in the first antistrophe, one can speculate that, from this point, the chorus' orientation changes and that its gestural (and proxemic?) signs are coordinated with its new perspective. These signs would have conveyed something to the audience that they did not convey to Antigone. In any case, the discrepancy within the linguistic code can be seen to belong to the function of the chorus as it has already appeared in the semiotic analysis of the parodos. On the principle (cf. the preceding chapter) that theatrical signs are signs of signs, it would still have to be asked how and why the chorus resemanticizes, for the spectators and to the exclusion, as it were, of Oedipus, linguistic signs, like the ones noticed above, having to do with Colonus and Athens. These questions are pursued in the second part of this book.

The first person to speak in the ensuing episode (720-1043) is Antigone, and her words show that she has understood herself to be one of the addressees of the chorus' song (a fact that may qualify what was said about demonstratives in the preceding paragraph). Indeed, she herself addresses the land that has just been praised, saying that now it must reveal this laudation to be real (720-21).[51]—Not for the first time, the challenge of visual presentation or concretization is posed.[52]—To her father, who immediately senses danger, she explains that Kreon and an escort are drawing near (722-23), and he, using the same verb as Antigone in her opening words, calls upon the chorus to make real their promise of his safety (724-25). They in turn refer to "this land," whose strength has not grown old, even if they are old (726-27).—The challenge is transferred back to the land, as in Antigone's opening words. But how can the land become an agent of protection?—Kreon first addresses the chorus,

---

50. Lawlor 1964:27; Pickard-Cambridge 1968:239-45 discusses the evidence, without arriving at the truism.
51. Cf. L-J-W 1990b ad loc.
52. Segal 1981:376 comments on the self-referential aspect of these lines and of the Muses in the preceding ode.

who are no longer facing the spectators, mimetically describing the fear that he sees in their eyes.[53] The chorus is for the moment the spectator and the audience of Kreon, and the situation of the preceding stasimon, in which the chorus had a distinct relation with the "real" spectators, has been canceled. Kreon's mimetic words interpret for the spectators whatever gestures and/or actions have expressed the chorus' reaction to his arrival. The word that Kreon uses to refer to his arrival, *epeisodos*, reinforces the new relation between orchestra and stage. The word, an unusual one,[54] is the base of the neuter diminutive *epeisodion*, which in the *Poetics* became the term for the part of tragedy falling between two choral songs (1452b20).[55] The latter word already had this sense in the fifth century, as a fragment of the comic poet Metagenes (14.1 Kock [vol. 1, p. 708]) shows.[56] Whether or not Kreon's use of *epeisodos* would have suggested the theatrical term, the compound noun, referring to his arrival in Colonus, suggests his arrival as a new or additional (*ep-*) character on stage,[57] and thus presents Kreon as a character to the chorus-spectators. The situation is like the one at the beginning of the parodos, where Oedipus was able to put the chorus in the position of spectators of a performance through his self-dramatized arrival from the depths of the grove. Now as then, however, the chorus will be able to reassert itself and even, to some extent, to cross the given theatrical boundary between stage and orchestra. Consider also, at the outset of his address to Oedipus, Kreon's description, beginning with the participle "seeing" (745), of the appearance of Oedipus and Antigone and compare Theseus' "introduction" of Oedipus at 551-56: Kreon, for his own purposes, describes

---

53. For such readings by one character of the eyes of another, cf. the chorus of Oedipus (149ff.), Antigone of Ismene (319-20), Theseus of Oedipus (551-54), and Antigone of Polyneices (1250-51). Kreon's speech, like Theseus' at 551-68, belongs to a type of entrance-speech in which the character addresses the chorus and provides various kinds of information about himself: Poe 1992:151.

54. Soph. frag. 273 Pearson = 273 Radt, from *Inachus*, where it refers to the advent of Plouton/Ploutos as an attendant of Zeus in Argos, may be the only other fifth-century example.

55. Aichele 1971:48 believes that *epeisodos* is already a technical theatrical term. The use in Soph. *Inachus* would then be metaphorical. Contra: Taplin 1977:133 n. 2.

56. I follow Kock's interpretation. The definition in LSJ is incorrect. Cratinus frag. 195K, where *epeisodion* occurs, is no help. For the formation of the word, see Meillet-Vendryes §644. Note, in the list of examples there, two other theatrical terms: ἡμιχόριον and προσκήνιον, and cf. other such diminutives in the index of Pickard-Cambridge 1946. Heath 1989:157-58 tends to doubt that the word already had its Aristotelian meaning in Metagenes.

57. Cf. Lucas 1968 on *Poetics* 12.52b20.

Oedipus and thus redescribes him for the spectators. Not only does Kreon "self-consciously" enter the stage as a new character but he takes over the stage, at least for the time being, as its master, and this mastery has to do with the fact that he can see and describe Oedipus, who cannot see him.

After Kreon has addressed the chorus, referring to Oedipus in the third person as "this man" (735, 739) and has then turned to Oedipus himself (740), he pleads with him at length to return to Thebes. Oedipus replies at even greater length (761-99: 38 lines to Kreon's 33), scornfully rejecting Kreon's appeal. Except for gestures by the speakers, the stage is still during these long speeches, as Thebes presents itself in the person of Kreon and the political-geographical poles of the play are diegetically restated; as the opposition between "here" (798) and "there" (787) is reinforced; as, likewise, within this framework, Oedipus repudiates philia (cf. 771, 775; Ch. 3§6), i.e., his former "nearness and dearness" to Thebes, in the name of his new relationship with Athens.[58] At the end of Oedipus' speech, he and Kreon break into stichomythy, as tension builds (800-19),[59] and then into antilabe (change of speaker within the line) at 820, and then, just as Kreon seizes Antigone (832), into an excited lyric strophe, full of antilabe, in which Oedipus, Kreon, and the chorus participate.[60] (The matching antistrophe [876-86] will begin just when Kreon seizes Oedipus.) The composition and versification of the episode are driven by the mounting conflict that will eventuate in drastic proxemic changes and in physical contact between some of the characters. Here is as clear an example as one could want of the spatial conception, i.e., of the deployment of the actors' bodies in the stage space, as determining the language of the text (cf. the hermeneutic circle proposed in the preceding chapter). In passing, one can observe that formal analysis of versification, which has already shown the relation of stichomythy, for example, to classifiable kinds of action,[61] would complement and support a general semiotics of Greek theater.

---

58. Cf. Jones 1962:63 for philia as "state of nearness and dearness."
59. See Mastronarde 1979:73 on 813-15 and contrast the text of L-J-W 1990a. In 1990b, they do not consider the Byzantine conjecture that Mastronarde accepts.
60. The participation of three speakers in the antilabe is unusual: Seidensticker 1971:204.
61. Seidensticker 1971:205. Cerbo 1989 establishes a metrical and formal typology of scenes in Euripides in which long-separated members of the same family are reunited. These scenes include an embrace, i.e., a particular spatial conception underlies the language of the text.

The physical conflict that begins to build at the end of Oedipus' long speech is marked almost diagrammatically in the speeches and song of actors and chorus.[62] Kreon's threats become deeds (cf. 817), and the chorus responds *pro virili* (or *senili*) *parte* to Antigone's challenge (720-21). Kreon has already seized Ismene, he says, and "I'll soon carry off this one [Antigone]" (819). Kreon to his henchmen: "Take her away by force if she will not go of her own free will" (826-27), though he still has his hands on her. Kreon: "I am carrying off what is rightfully mine" (832). Chorus: "Let go of her" (835).[63] They move toward Kreon. Kreon: "Keep away from me" (836). Chorus: "Let the child out of your grip and be quick about it" (838-39). "Let go of her" (840). Kreon to the chorus: "Get out of here" (840). The chorus turns away from him and calls upon the Colonans for aid (841-43). Antigone: "I am being dragged away" (844). Oedipus: "Where are you?" (845). Antigone: "I am being led off against my will" (845). Oedipus: "Reach me your hand" (846, cf. 173, 200-201, 501-502). Antigone: "I cannot" (846). Kreon to his henchmen, having handed Antigone over to them: "Take her away" (847). They do so. The chorus, advancing on Kreon again, brandishing their staffs and/or with the aggressive "flat hand"[64]: "Stop here" (856). Kreon: "Don't touch me" (856). Chorus: "I'll not let you go" (857). Kreon: "Then it won't be only these two girls that I'll lay hands on. I'll take this one [Oedipus]" (859-60). He breaks away from the chorus, which does not intervene physically again. (They have been cowed by Kreon, and the land of Colonus, in the form of these old men, has failed to protect Oedipus and his daughter.) Oedipus: "Do you dare to touch me?" (863). Kreon: "I'll carry you off even if I'm alone" (874-75; his henchmen have already left with Antigone in their grasp). Oedipus screams (876). During the ensuing antistrophe, Kreon slowly drags Oedipus away, and the chorus is reduced to merely verbal protest. Kreon has somehow dislodged Oedipus from his seated position, from the seat in the land that he had claimed as his and that his posture had symbolized. At the end of the antistrophe, as at the end of the strophe, the chorus calls for aid (884-86; cf. 841-43).

From one perspective, the sentences just quoted appear to be didascalic. They would be the tragedian's guides to a director and/or to

---

62. This scene is "perhaps the most elaborate and varied scene of violence in Greek tragedy": Kaimio 1988:76. See Kaimio's notes for various opinions on how the scene was or should be staged.
63. It is possible that these words are spoken by the chorus leader, who leaves the ranks of the chorus as he tries to stop Kreon; also at 857. Cf. Kaimio 1970:207, 230 n. 2.
64. Lawlor 1964:35-36.

actors. But if Honzl is right, sentences such as these do not redouble the characters' actions. They are not mimetic in the same sense as descriptions of the stage setting, which refer to what the spectators can see or, if the descriptions are mimetic-constative, should see. The characters' references to their actions presuppose that the actions seen by the spectators are *not* the same as the ones specified but abstract and stylized and therefore in need of that specification.[65] The actors' words complete their actions. If so, then these words that seem primary qua didascalia are actually secondary, serving to specify a more fundamental proxemic and gestural conception that is worked out on stage in a non-realistic acting style.[66] One has thus moved around the hermeneutic circle proposed in the preceding chapter from the dramatic text as script to the physical spatial conception informing the script.

From another perspective, the characters' references to their actions are the verbal reflex of a continual problematizing of the spatial dimension of the action that has already come out in various ways. When Antigone calls for the translation of words (the chorus' praise of Colonus and Athens) into deeds, she is restating, in new terms, a demand for dramatic representation already heard in various ways. This demand has taken the form of a dilemma. On the one hand, Oedipus must represent, but has no way to represent, except in words, the future benefit of his grave at Colonus: the benefit is by its nature unrepresentable in advance. No deed he can perform will express this benefit. Indeed, his wretched appearance, his age and weakness seem to belie the promise that he makes. On the other hand, since Oedipus is blind, no one can perform a deed that he can see; no one can represent himself to Oedipus except in words or by physical contact. In the episode under discussion, the breaking of the physical contact between Oedipus and Antigone and the attempted abduction of Oedipus by Kreon forcefully restate the isolation of Oedipus, his imperviousness to most of the theatrical codes. His question to Antigone, "Where are you?" (845), epitomizes his plight (cf. the remarks at the beginning of this chapter on the question that opens the tragedy). The spatial conception of the tragedy, then, is built on the blindness of Oedipus and his posthumous benefit to Athens. While in the nar-

---

65. Cf. Rossi 1989:76–77. Burton 1980:267: "we may acquiesce in a series of threatening movements accompanied by gestures."
66. Mastronarde 1979:111, citing *OC* 819–47 inter alia, refers to "the reluctance of the tragedians to diminish the decorum of performance in the interests of realistically rapid, highly mimetic movements" and in n. 52 on the same page he refers to "the unnaturalistic slowness of movement which the texts seem to require."

rative dimension of the play, as the action unfolds, this blindness is tantamount to weakness and physical dependency on others (at least until the hour of his death and miraculous disappearance into the earth), Oedipus' negative dramatic space, with all its limitations, is primary, determining the use of the positive space occupied by everyone else.

At the end of the antistrophe (884-86), the chorus call not upon the Colonans but upon "all the people" and "the leader of this land." The latter is Theseus, to whom Kreon has just referred contemptuously (862).[67] Theseus enters with attendants (887), stopping the exit of Kreon.[68] Kreon desists from his attempt to abduct Oedipus (so much can be inferred from what Oedipus says at 891-92 and 894-95). Theseus' opening words contribute another detail to the diegetic description of Colonus: the altar of Poseidon, which is nearby and perhaps, as the demonstrative indicates, can even be seen from the dramatic space of the stage (888-89; 898: *tousde*). He, the king of Athens, has been sacrificing at the altar with "all the people" (898; cf. the chorus' appeal at 884). Wherever he is, there is Athens; and he will now demonstrate the power of the city, as well as his fidelity to the relationship of xenia into which he has entered with Oedipus (902-903; cf. Ch. 3§9). Indeed, by his mere entrance on stage, he has stopped Kreon, which the chorus of Colonans had been unable to do. He has arrived in haste (890, where the reference to his own action is of the same order as in the examples discussed above apropos of the abductions), and addresses the chorus (n.b. the plural at 889). Oedipus answers, and Theseus then turns to him (893). Theseus then immediately mobilizes the pursuit of the abductors of Oedipus' daughters. He calls for one of his attendants to return to the altar and dispatch the people to a point where they can intercept the abductors (897-903). One of them steps forward and Theseus addresses him: "Go quickly" (904). Then he turns to the chorus, referring somewhat contemptuously to Kreon as "this one," using a demonstrative that, with only one other exception, is never used substantively in this play in any form to refer to a character on stage (904).[69] Finally, Theseus turns to Kreon, who is the last person

---

67. Cf. L-J-W 1990b ad loc.

68. On the social, political, and theatrical-historical resonance of the entry in response to *boê*, see Taplin 1977:219-20. On the Theseus - Kreon contrast, see Blundell 1993:292-96; 303-305.

69. The other exception, also from the mouth of Theseus, is at 1148, where the reference is to the daughters of Oedipus and is thus perhaps somewhat male chauvinist. For the contemptuous nuance of the demonstrative *houtos*, see Ellendt 1872:585/2 (c); LSJ s.v. C.I.3. At 904, the demonstrative may also have a legal nuance: see LSJ s.v. C.I.4 and cf. Ch. 3§10. Line 904 caught the attention of Ellendt 1872:582/2, though I think his

whom Theseus addresses (907). The sequence, then, of Theseus' proxemic relations is: chorus, for an instant (889); Oedipus; attendants as a group; a single attendant; chorus; Kreon. This sequence dramatizes and visualizes a rough scale of respect, with Kreon at the bottom.

But it will take Theseus some time to make clear what he expects of Kreon: that he see to it that the daughters of Oedipus are returned (932-36), and it will take even longer for anything to happen on stage, since now Kreon commences an indictment of Oedipus (939-59), to which Oedipus will reply at great length (960-1013). It is a trial scene (cf. Ch. 3§10). Finally, Theseus says: "Enough of words" (1016), and tells Kreon that he must lead him to where Oedipus' daughters are (1019-21, 1038), while Oedipus, Theseus says, is to remain where he is (1038-39). Thus at the end of the scene, as in Antigone's words at the beginning, the opposition between words and deeds is restated, though now in a way that begins to suggest that this tragedy is expressing a frustration belonging to its very medium, i.e., a generic frustration, at the limitation on its ability to fulfill its own spatial conception, the stage potentiality on which it is built. Somewhere off stage, in the diegetic space that has been and will continue to be evoked, a band of Thebans is carrying Oedipus' daughters toward the border of Attica, while here at Colonus, on stage, the characters deliver long dicastic speeches. The long retardation of the dramatic action is a frustration that belongs to the medium itself, its inability to represent such action, its allegiance to a unity of place.[70] Antigone's challenge (720-21) has not yet been met. If this inability is conceived in terms of the dilemma specific to this tragedy, which has already been articulated in various ways, it is the blindness of Oedipus that presents the challenge of visualization, i.e., of enactment in space, which is the fundamental requirement of drama (cf. Aristotle *Poet.* 6.49b24-27). To his inability to see corresponds the limitation on drama's or, in particular, Greek tragedy's, capacity for action (a limitation all the more acute because of its acting conventions: cf. the remarks above, following from Honzl's observations, on abstract, stylized acting).

Though Theseus says "Enough of words" (1016), in effect reiterating Antigone's challenge, the deeds to which he now turns at the end of

---

interpretation is incorrect. I do not count 1252 as an exception to the rule I am positing, since the speaker is blind. For *houtos* as vocative, which is very rare in tragedy, see Taplin 1977:220. The tendency of characters in tragedy is to use *hode* when they refer to the chorus, of characters in comedy to use *houtos*. See Kaimio 1970:202.

70. See Fantuzzi 1991 on the paradox that the standard of unity of place developed at the same time as scene painting, which might have seemed to provide greater flexibility.

the episode are not "made bright" (cf. 720-21) on stage but in a diegetic space opened up in the second stasimon (1044-95). The problem is transposed into the chorus' wish, expressed in its opening words, that it might be where the action is (1044) and its later wish that it might be able to observe the action, "lifting my eye above the struggle" like a bird (1081-84). The dilemma created by the blindness of Oedipus is thus transposed, and even to some degree self-consciously acknowledged by the chorus, into the chorus' own relation to the dramatic action. In this tragedy, conventional "escapist" motifs of choral odes find a new context, and thus a new sense, in a theatrical autoreflexivity in which the fundamental dramatic requirement of visualized action has become a theme.[71] The spectators hear the chorus' words, which take the form of wishes, surmises, questions, and prayers, and see its dancing and gestures, which have to take the place of the action that the chorus, and the spectators, would like to see. The spatial diegesis thus conveyed in effect replaces the demand for visualization by further enlarging the ever-growing environs of the immediate dramatic space. This choral diegesis looks in a particular direction, however, for a particular purpose. The chorus imagines the routes that the abductors of Antigone and Ismene might take. One is the Sacred Way, proceeding along which they will have reached either the "Pythian shore" (1047), i.e., the shore of the bay of Eleusis north of Daphne,[72] or, farther, "the torch-lit shores" (1048) of Eleusis. Along another route, it may be that they are fleeing "from Oeatid pastures and will move near to the western territory of the snowy rock" (1059ff.), i.e., according to the scholiast, Mt. Aigaleos, on the edge of the deme Oa, so that moving north into the Thriasian Plain, they would be west or northwest of this deme.[73] The chorus thus conjures up a picture of the northern frontier of Attica and, at the same time, conveys the conviction that Theseus controls this frontier. This ode indeed "dwells on the might of Theseus and his power to protect his friends."[74] Thus the question as to how the land can become an agent of protection now finds an answer: Theseus, acting in concert with the Colonans (cf. Ch. 3§1), even if the spectators cannot behold Antigone beholding the response to her challenge.

71. For references to other "escapist" passages in Greek tragedy and to secondary literature, see Burton 1980: 281 n. 32.
72. For this interpretation of the phrase see Jebb and Kamerbeek.
73. I am translating the text of L-J-W 1990a, who keep the reading of the mss. On the unusual linking of the end of the strophe to the beginning of the antistrophe (with emphasis on place), see Kranz 1933:178.
74. L-J-W 1990b:247.

What happens on stage during the stasimon, while the spectators' eyes are on the chorus? Oedipus is left alone. Here the converse of Honzl's law applies: without verbal reference to X's action by A or by another actor or by the chorus, no action or deed is realized visually on stage (though A may use gestures, I suppose).[75] Thus Oedipus does nothing. He is, in effect, fixed by Theseus' words in the place in which he debated Kreon: "Stay right here and be quiet (i.e., still, unmoving)" (1038-39).[76] In any case, he cannot move or even sit down without the aid of Antigone. His isolation is completed by the chorus' total lack of concern. The chorus begins with a reference to itself. The demonstratives that it uses ("this land": 1087, 1095), with whatever accompanying gestures, are addressed to the spectators. Its references to points on the northern frontier of Attica are lost on Oedipus. Its use of "sons of Theseus" for the Athenian contingent is an anachronism (1066).[77] But Oedipus does not even hear them, because, from the spectators' point of view, i.e., by the conventions of this theater, he is in a kind of dramatic suspension. He is not there.[78] The zero-degree of referentiality to which he was limited by his blindness has now been made absolute. While he is there physically on stage, he is a semiotic blank. He presents, in Fischer-Lichte's phrase, a pure "apriori of the body," in which, instead of affording the condition of theater, the actor's body denies it (cf. p. 29 above). In this way, as in the case of the "escapist" motifs, this tragedy accommodates a particular convention to its metatheatricality, using the semiotic blank to reinscribe the problem of dramatic visualization.

But what the body of Oedipus cannot do during the stasimon, the bodies of the other actors cannot do vis-à-vis the blind Oedipus when the action resumes. The problem of the blind old man's imperviousness to the dramatic space is made explicit again in the opening lines of the next episode, when the chorus leader refers to his sight of Oedipus' daughters approaching ("I see": 1097). Oedipus asks: "Where, where?" (1099). And Antigone, as she draws near, instead of saying "Here we are" or the like, says, "Would that some god would grant you to see this noble man who has brought us here to you" (1100-1101). (The unusual, visually arrest-

---

75. For Honzl's law and for the sigla "A" and "X," see Ch. 1 above.
76. For this meaning of ἔκηλος, see LSJ s.v.: "of mere inaction, *quiet*."
77. Campbell 1879 ad loc.
78. "During the pause created by the choral ode any actor who remains on stage stands, so to speak, in suspended animation": Poe 1992:149 n. 85. Cf. Ritchie 1964:116 n. 6 on places in Sophocles and Euripides in which no notice is taken of the presence of the actor.

ing triple entry [of Antigone, Ismene, and Theseus] establishes a semiotic tension, to be discussed below, between what the spectators see and what they hear.[79]) Thus, at the narrative and thematic level, she confirms "the might of Theseus and his power to protect his friends," the concern of the preceding stasimon, and, at the same time, at the level of theatrical autoreflexivity, makes explicit the problem posed by the relation of chorus to actor during that stasimon. For that matter, the chorus leader, in the very opening lines of this episode, retrojects onto the stasimon a dramatic relation between the chorus and Oedipus of which there was no evidence whatsoever: the chorus leader now tells Oedipus that he will not say that the chorus was a false prophet, referring explicitly to the song it has just sung (1098, cf. 1080), i.e., the chorus leader in effect pretends that the chorus was addressing Oedipus, that it was for him that it was conjuring up scenes of his daughters' rescue. But if it was addressing Oedipus all along, why does the chorus leader begin "Oh wandering friend" (1096), in which phrase the interjection "Oh" in line-initial position in the first line of the speech shows that he has to get Oedipus' attention (cf. 724, where Oedipus has to get the chorus' attention),[80] as is natural, since he cannot have been facing Oedipus as he looked toward Antigone and Ismene advancing from the wings nor was the chorus likely to have been looking at Oedipus during the stasimon? This slight contradiction between the chorus leader's form of address to Oedipus and his statement, implying a dramatic relationship during the stasimon, already establishes the metatheatrical dimension of Antigone's opening words (1099-1100).

The chorus leader's three-line speech also calls attention to itself for another reason. This is the only place in Sophocles in which the chorus leader, in a spoken meter, announces an entrance.[81] This peculiarity should be placed in the framework of tragedy's general reluctance to announce entrances after a strophic chorus.[82] Since the audience expected an entrance at such a juncture, announcement was unnecessary.

---

79. See Taplin 1977:241 on triple entries.
80. The uses of ὦ in line-initial position in the first line of speeches (i.e., outside of lyric passage) fall into fairly clear categories: prayers and entreaties (e.g., 84, 237, 465), commands (1169, 1457), emotionally charged greetings (324, 327, 330, 1102, 1108, 1109), reinforcement of epithets (863, 960) and of solemn forms of address (607, 940), and attention-getting, as in 1096, the case under discussion (cf. 891). The attention-getting ὦ also appears in the midst of speeches when the speaker turns to a new addressee (1542).
81. As observed, though not exactly in these terms, by Campbell 1879 on 1096. The closest parallel in Sophocles may be *Ant.* 626-30 (lyric).
82. Statistics and discussion in Hamilton 1978.

This general rule will be violated only for a special reason. In the case of *Oedipus at Colonus*, the reason is obvious: since Oedipus is blind, all entrances have to be announced for his sake.[83] Once again, then, the blindness of Oedipus tests the genre itself. In the same way that (for other reasons), the demarcation between stage and orchestra was crossed in the second episode, so here the chorus leader's iambic trimeters in themselves signify an unusual relationship between him and the character on the stage. In this metrical setting, the "I" of the chorus leader, in its difference from the collective "I" of the chorus that has just completed its song, *which is also a difference from the normal "I" of a chorus leader in Greek tragedy*, momentarily makes of him a dramatic character, and in such a way as to create a "you" of Oedipus and to bring him back to life as a character, to animate the body of the actor that was standing there behind the chorus during its song.

The straining of generic rules continues in the third episode from the moment that Antigone, Ismene, and Theseus (with a retinue: 1103) appear on stage. For now the spectators have four actors before them, of whom, by the "three actor law," only three can speak. From Antigone's opening speech, answering the urgent questions that her father had put to the chorus leader (1099), the spectators know the identities of the three who have just entered; further, they know that Theseus will have to speak. Ismene is then already the supernumerary. She will be a *persona muta*, a non-speaking actor. She will thus have in this episode the function that her father had during the preceding stasimon, except that she will act. And since she will act, she, that is, the movement of her body in the stage space, will create the need for its verbal counterpart, as Honzl's law requires. As Pickard-Cambridge observed (though not from the point of view of Honzl's law!), "speech is expected" from Ismene.[84] Since she cannot speak, verbal reference to her and to her actions will have to come from Oedipus and from Antigone. Indeed, the tension created by the acting *persona muta* is translated into the syntactic inconcinnity of Oedipus' use of a singular vocative, addressed to Antigone, with a plural or dual verb (1102, 1104, 1112, 1204).[85] The singular observes the three actor

---

83. Hamilton 1978:70 n. 25.
84. Pickard-Cambridge 1968:143.
85. Kamerbeek 1984:156-57: "We have to bear in mind that throughout both this and the next epeisodion Ismene is κωφὸν πρόσωπον ... : the three actors are needed for Oedipus, Antigone and Theseus or Polynices respectively. Hence perhaps the rather inconsistent use of singular and plural (or dual) in Oedipus' addressing his daughter(s)." The scholiast on Aristoph. *Pl.* 66, cited by Ellendt 1872:797/2 and LSJ s.v. ὤ II.1, is not formulating a rule about singular vocative with plural verb but observing that ὤ τάν may

law, while the dual or the plural acknowledges the presence of the supernumerary. Here, then, is another rather clear example of how the spatial conception, i.e., of the deployment of the actors' bodies in the stage space, determines the language of the text.[86] The consistency of this spatial conception is shown in the fact that, even at the end of the episode, when Ismene has nothing to do, her presence and even her cooperation continue, rather unexpectedly if one does not visualize the scene, to be acknowledged: note line 1204, already cited, which is Oedipus' response to an exhortation by Antigone in which she has maintained the viewpoint of both her and her sister (note the dual [1184] and the plurals [1201-1202]).[87]

The presence of Ismene is necessary for the reenactment of the tableau already seen in the first episode, the triple embrace of father and daughters. This reenactment is not some dramatic over-determination of the helplessness of Oedipus nor is it simply a repetition of the need for a sub-visual confirmation for Oedipus of the arrival of his daughters. It is the visualization for the spectators of the philia, of the relation of "nearness and dearness" between Oedipus and his daughters that is the emotional and pragmatic basis of Oedipus' existence.[88] Not only is Oedipus a stateless person as he arrives in Attica, he is also completely desolate of human relations except for his daughters. Thus he can now say to them: "make him who was before (i.e., in your absence) desolate cease

---

be followed by a plural verb. Elsewhere in *OC*, when Ismene is free to speak, Oedipus uses the dual of the vocative and the dual of the verb (493). And when in the fourth episode only Oedipus, Antigone, and Ismene are on stage (1446-99), even though Ismene remains mute, Oedipus "realistically" uses the plural vocative and the second plural of the verb (1457-61; cf. 1472, 1486). When Theseus returns to the stage in the fourth episode, even though the tension of four potential actors is restored, Oedipus' language remains "realistic": he consistently uses plural vocatives, dual pronouns, and second plural verbs (1542-47). Likewise, Polyneices uses plurals and duals in addressing his sisters (1405-12, 1435-46), except for a passage in which he is engaged in dialogue with Antigone (1414-31). Nevertheless, a trace of the inconcinnity reappears just before Polyneices' exit: cf. the plural at 1437 (both sisters) with the singular at 1439 and 1442 (Antigone), followed by a dual and plurals in his closing lines (1444-47).

86. For the affective value of the dual of the personal pronoun, see Solomon 1987:72-80.

87. The reflex of the three actor law can be seen in the forms of address, numbers of the verbs, etc. in the exchanges between Polyneices and Antigone in the fourth episode at 1432-46.

88. Sophocles thus again exploits for his own purposes a conventional scene (cf. Kaimio 1988:39-40).

from this grievous dismay" (1113-14).[89] The tableau of philia indeed serves to isolate Oedipus from the other actor on stage, Theseus, who stands by in silence as Oedipus is reunited with his daughters. For Oedipus cannot even touch the hand of Theseus. So he realizes when, in his gratitude, he turns to Theseus, somehow knowing where he is, and reaches out to him, saying "Give me your right hand, my lord, that I may touch it and that I may kiss your cheek" (1130-31).[90] The word for kiss is formed on the same base as philia: the gestures that Oedipus proposes belong to another kind of "nearness and dearness," which goes with the relation of xenia between him and Theseus (cf. Ch. 3§9). But Oedipus immediately realizes that, because he is defiled, he must not touch Theseus (1132-35). The withdrawal from contact with Theseus is also a reestablishment of the unique relation with the daughters. In the final significant development in this episode, Oedipus learns that his son, Polyneices, is a suppliant at the altar of Poseidon (the importance of which is thus again diegetically affirmed). Oedipus' loathing of his son and initial refusal to meet him are yet another expression of the primacy of the relation with the daughters. Indeed, it is only in virtue of his relation of philia with them (note 1194 and 1205) and the obligation to them thereby entailed that Oedipus can be persuaded to listen to Polyneices.

At the end of the episode, Theseus departs, assuring Oedipus of his safety. Oedipus is left with his two daughters beside him. He is more secure than at any time in the play until now. The chorus then begins a song full of gnomes on the sorrows of old age and on the futility of human life in general. In the epode, the chorus speaks not only for itself but for Oedipus, who is likened to a storm-lashed promontory. The contrast between this song and the situation at the end of the preceding episode is stark and unexpected. The chorus speaks of old age as *aphilon* (1237), and yet Oedipus has just been seen and is perhaps still seen in a tableau of philia.[91] Furthermore, despite the chorus' reference to Oedipus by means of a demonstrative, with an accompanying gesture (1239), this

---

89. Following the text of L-J-W 1990a. πλάνου "wandering" has to be metaphorical; I have translated it "dismay." The demonstrative ("this ... dismay") has to refer to an inner, mostly invisible state (i.e., invisible as apart from gestures) and is another example of the zero degree of referentiality of Oedipus' demonstratives.

90. Cf. Campbell 1879 on 1130ff.: "The action which no doubt accompanied these lines would make them clearer to the spectator than they are to the reader. Oedipus reaches forth his hand towards Theseus, then draws it back, and on becoming aware [how?] that Theseus is bending towards him, repels him gently with a movement of his hand." Cf. Kaimio 1988:27: Oedipus' gesture plays on the stage convention of the handshake.

91. Cf. Ch. 3§1 sub fin. for further remarks on this stasimon.

stasimon is more detached from the action of the play than any of the previous strophic performances. The parodos was an example, rare in Greek tragedy, of the dialogization of a strophic song[92]; the first stasimon was addressed to Oedipus, in effect congratulating him on his choice of Colonus as his new home; the second referred to events taking place offstage that would confirm the promises of Theseus and restore Oedipus' daughters to him. The third stasimon is of a different sort: it is one of those Sophoclean stasima that through general reflection introduces ambiguity, irony, and contrast into the midst of the action.[93] The chorus is completely detached from the stage; Oedipus becomes an example that illustrates a theme, as in the fourth stasimon of *Oedipus the King*.[94] He becomes, in short, a character in a play from whom the chorus, now in the role of spectator, can draw a lesson. In a tragedy in which the boundary between stage and orchestra has been permeable and changing, the stage is now definitively a stage.[95]

So much for the contrast between stasimon and preceding scene. What, however, of the relation of the chorus' words to its own action, i.e., to its dancing and gestures? If Honzl's law applies to the chorus as well as to the actors, one should expect an incongruence between words and action (which is practically guaranteed by the abstractness of this song) that the spectators are able to synthesize into an esthetic unity. Though we have no idea what the chorus' dance looked like, if it is assumed that its song, like any verbal element of any play, is the "linguistic transcription of stage potentiality" (cf. Ch. 1), i.e., of a spatial dramatic idea, then the song should provide some clue to the nature of the action that the spectators have to synthesize with the words of the text that we have. That clue lies in the very demonstrative that isolates Oedipus on the stage (1239) and, in the same line, in the chorus' likening of Oedipus, an old man, to itself (fifteen old men). The semiotic matrix of the strophic performance is the sympathy of old men for the old man Oedipus (cf. 255, 461, 1014-15). Their dancing and gestures express (to repeat, we do not know how) this sympathy, and these are the actions that the spectators can synthesize with the chorus' abstract thoughts.

92. Cf. Rode 1971:100.
93. Cf. Rode 1971:114. On the use of the first person singular at the beginning of this stasimon, see Kaimio 1970:96-97.
94. Cf. Kranz 1933:194-95.
95. For which reason I do not agree with Rode 1971:110 that this stasimon is in any way integrated into the dramatic action.

At the beginning of the fourth episode, Antigone announces, in formulaic terms, the arrival of a new character, the stranger of whom Theseus had spoken. He enters from the spectators' right, the Colonus and Athens side of the theater, in contrast to Kreon.[96] This character is weeping and unaccompanied (1249-51), already, no doubt, expressing his suppliancy (cf. Theseus' description at 1156-60) in his manner of approaching Oedipus. "Who is this?" Oedipus asks (1252), and the demonstrative *houtos*, the most distant form of reference to a character on stage, reflects an already established hostility,[97] in contrast with the normal *hode* that Antigone has just used (1249). Polyneices begins by addressing not his father but his sisters, and, using exactly the same participle as Kreon had used earlier, he refers to himself as "seeing" the ills of his father, to whom he refers with a demonstrative, pointing at him at the same time (1255). As at the entrance of Kreon, Oedipus is a third person, and what he is grammatically he is also dramatically: he cannot be a subject; he is the object of another character's action. Polyneices proceeds to give a detailed description of Oedipus' wretched appearance (1255-63). The effect of this description or redescription is that, once again, Oedipus is isolated in his negative dramatic space and becomes a character for the other characters.

But Polyneices is not a character in the same sense as the others in this tragedy. Whereas, thanks to the innovation in the Oedipus myth by which Oedipus dies in Colonus (cf. Ch. 3§2), Kreon has never before tried to take Oedipus back to Thebes and Theseus has never welcomed him to Athens, the curse on Polyneices is as old as Theban epic. Oedipus curses his sons in two fragments of the *Thebaid* (frags. 2-3 Bernabé). The curse is thematic in Aeschylus' *Seven Against Thebes* and in Euripides' *Phoenician Women*. *Oedipus at Colonus*, then, dramatizes a well-known motif, and, when Polyneices appears on stage, he is already the accursed son, in a way that Theseus cannot already be the Attic *xenos* of Oedipus and Kreon cannot already be an emissary from Thebes to bring Oedipus home. Polyneices' status is reflected at several points in the scene. Explaining why he has come as a suppliant, he refers to the army that he has raised in Argos as "the expedition with seven bodies of spearmen" (1305). His use of the definite article, which implies that the expedition is the one already known, the famous one, is, as Campbell

---

96. Taplin 1983b:158-63.
97. On this demonstrative, see above on line 904 and n. 69.

observed, anachronistic.[98] Polyneices speaks of the Erinyes of his father (1434) "without any reference to the Erinyes at whose sacred place he is standing,"[99] though in cursing Polyneices, Oedipus had called upon the local Erinyes (1391) and his son had heard him. The Erinyes of which Polyneices knows are indeed the ones that in the poetic tradition always attach to Oedipus, beginning with *Odyssey* 11.280 (cf. Ch. 3§11). When Polyneices sets out on his return to Argos, he calls upon his sisters to perform the proper funeral rites for him, if his father's curse should be fulfilled and if they should return to Thebes (1405-10). Sophocles thus alludes to his own *Antigone*, and Polyneices speaks directly out of a poetic tradition of which Sophocles himself is already a part. Polyneices promises his sisters a fame that they already have.[100]

In the spatial conception of this scene (the first half of the fourth episode), this character, who is to some extent also a metacharacter, presents himself as a suppliant (1327), as Antigone had presented herself to the chorus at the end of the parodos. The proxemic relations of the characters on stage are, for some moments of the supplication, all that the spectators have, as Oedipus remains silent (note the pause at 1271). His turning away signals the rejection of his son's plea (1272). The power that Oedipus has as rescuer in the triad of supplication (cf. above on suppliant drama) is then turned against Polyneices and takes the form of the curse. Though Oedipus acknowledges the traditional position of the curse in the myth when he says that he had also formerly cursed his sons (1375), the curse as here dramatized is an innovation in the narrative sequence, coming when Polyneices' Argive army is already in the field, and it is also, so far as we know, an innovation in Athenian tragedy. This new curse thus finally answers the question: How can the blind old Oedipus have, i.e., show that he has, the power that he says he has? The illocutionary speech-act (n.b. 1384-85, 1389, 1391), with the gestures that accompany it, at last makes an agent of Oedipus, who has until now been an object in the struggles of the other characters. The problem of the representation of the power of Oedipus is finally solved. But the curse could not have had its dramatic efficacy if Polyneices was not the kind of character that I have described. The curse has its dramatic efficacy because Polyneices is already accursed, given as accursed in the poetic

---

98. Campbell 1879 ad loc.
99. Campbell 1879 ad loc.
100. Polyneices' description of his army (1286-1301) is to some extent a heroic geography of the Peloponnesus, which is in contrast to the indeterminate space through which Oedipus wandered for many years (1335-36, 1363-64; cf. Ch. 3§5 on wandering).

tradition reaching back to archaic epic. The problem of representation is thus finally solved (and over-determinations of this solution are in the offing) in the metatheatrical dimension of the tragedy, in which Polyneices is, from the moment of his entrance, a metacharacter.

During the scene, Antigone and Ismene have left their father and gone over to Polyneices, whom they try to restrain as he announces his decision to return to his army and meet his fate. "Release me," he says, "and farewell" (1437).[101] He exits on the spectators' left, heading away from Athens.[102] In response to the curse it has just heard, the chorus breaks into excited dochmiacs (1447).[103] Before it can finish its distraught reflections, thunder is heard (1456). The stage space is invaded by repeated claps of thunder coming from off stage (produced by the "thunder-machine" [*bronteion*]),[104] and the chorus "sees" repeated lightning flashes (1466, 1477, cf. 1514-15). Its fear and agitation are expressed in a sequence of strophes separated by five-line passages of calmer iambic trimeters spoken by Oedipus and Antigone—calmer, but Oedipus knows that the hour of his death is at hand and he repeatedly summons Theseus (1457-57, 1461, 1475-76, 1486). (One of the places where they think he may be is the altar of Poseidon, that nearby point in Colonus: cf. 888-89, 1158.) The arrival of Theseus brings calmness. Indeed, he seems not even to have heard the thunder (1501-1505). And yet the thunder has changed the whole spatial orientation of the play from the stage to the diegetic space off stage (cf. 1514-15 and especially 1540). The scene mirrors the earlier one in which Theseus had rescued Oedipus from Kreon; Theseus' own words call attention to the similarity (1500, 1507).[105] After a brief series of exchanges between Oedipus and Theseus, the rest of the scene (the second half of the fourth episode) is taken up with a speech of Oedipus in which he gives Theseus instructions concerning his burial place and then instructs his daughters to follow him as he is now their guide (1518-55). This speech focuses the attention of Theseus, and of

---

101. I believe that the verb ἐπέχω at 1432 (Polyneices to Antigone: "Do not detain me") does not indicate physical restraint. On the interchange between Polyneices and Antigone, see Zeitlin 1990:162: it "takes us back all the way to Aiskhylos' *Seven against Thebes*."

102. Cf. n. 1 above.

103. On the scholarly Titanomachy over the reference of the chorus' words at 1447ff., see Kamerbeek ad loc. I agree with the analysis of Burton 1980:268-69.

104. Burton 1980:269: "It is to be noted that the peals of thunder occur at unsymmetrical and therefore unexpected intervals during the chorus' lyrics, the first at the end of the first strophe (1456), the second during the antistrophe (1466f.), the third at the beginning of the second strophe (1477f.)."

105. As observed by Taplin 1971:31-32.

the spectators, on the spot (*khôros* 1520, 1540; cf. Ch. 3§3) where Oedipus will die, a spot that will be revealed to Theseus alone. Not even his daughters will be allowed to see it. Thus a spot that is off stage and proleptic-diegetic is overdetermined as off-limits within that proleptic-diegetic space. What is off stage is in this case doubly invisible.

Having finished his instructions to Theseus, Oedipus says, "Let us set forth" (1541), and he bids his daughters follow. As he had promised to do shortly before (1520–21), he leads the way. As they were once his guides, he says, he is now theirs (1543): in this respect, they have changed roles. The fundamental passivity that was expressed in his physical dependence on his daughters is now exchanged for independent action, as his movement on stage shows. In keeping with Honzl's law, his action must have a verbal counterpart. Oedipus does not, however, refer directly to his action but speaks instead, with an agent noun, of the function that he is now fulfilling: "I am manifested as a strange guide" (also 1543). The verb (*phainô*) can express the appearance of a character on stage (77, 328), the self-presentation of one character to another. Here Oedipus' new and strange capacity to move like a sighted person is expressed in terms of a self-presentation or revelation of a new function to his daughters, whose attempts to help him physically he now thwarts with a restraining gesture (1544). It is also a revelation to the spectators, as Oedipus, who was already visible, becomes visible as something new. The stage is also seen anew. As Oedipus leads the other characters away, he uses six demonstratives in two lines (1546–47), in a way in which he was heretofore unable to use demonstratives.[106] As the stage is now visible to him and is thus a dramatic space for him as for the other characters, it is also transformed and newly visible for the spectators. Seen by Oedipus for the first time, it is also seen by the spectators as new. Oedipus leads all the other characters off stage, and the stage is thus then also seen empty for the first time since the very beginning of the tragedy. The stage convention of the exiting character's farewell creates an inconcinnity in Oedipus' farewell to Theseus, who follows him, along with Ismene and Antigone, through the opening in the center of the stage building into the inner grove. The inconcinnity has the effect of calling attention to, and reinforcing, the visual fact that there is no one there on stage any longer. Once again, as through the curse, the power of the old man finally finds proof, this time through his self-presentation as a guide. As he leads the other two actors and the *persona muta* off stage, the tableau perhaps resembles the procession at the Proagon in which the tragedian led his

---

106. Jebb on 1547: "The number of forms of ὅδε in this v. and 1546 is curious."

troupe up onto a platform in the Odeon (Plat. *Symp.* 194; cf. *Vit. Eur.* 2 sub fin. Schwartz), except that here Oedipus leads the other characters off a platform and out of the public's sight. In any case, the procession led by Oedipus, comprised of Antigone, Ismene, Theseus, and Theseus' retinue, not only marks a narrative ending of the play, since the action is effectively complete, but also a formal ending, since it leaves the stage empty, like the processions in the exodoi of Aeschylus' *Eumenides* and Sophocles' *Ajax*.

This is not, however, an exodos, as the chorus shows by beginning a strophic song. This song takes the form of a prayer to Aïdoneus (Hades), Persephone, the Infernal Goddesses, and Kerberos for Oedipus' safe passage to the underworld. As Kamerbeek observed, the prayer conceives of the descent as a katabasis.[107] May Oedipus reach the plain of the dead and the Stygian house (1560-67). May Kerberos leave a clear path for him (1568-78).[108] The prayer contains, in short, a generalized, proleptic narrative sketch of Oedipus' descent, in the same emotional vein of sympathy and concern as in the previous stasimon. The chorus sings and performs in front of the newly emptied stage space. Their song thus reinforces the new orientation of the action to off-stage space, and, in their first line, they refer to Persephone with the unusual epithet "unseen" (1556). The region in which they place Oedipus is, indeed, unseen by definition and thus radically unvisualizable, except on the authority of "the account of these things that has always held" (1573)—what we would call the mythical geography of the underworld. Oedipus' descent is not like an action on the northern frontier of Attica, which characters or chorus in a tragedy can only long to see because of various constraints of the genre, beginning with unity of place. Against the background of an empty stage, the chorus sing of a radically undramatizable action. This stage is not only, to repeat, newly emptied, it is also newly created by Oedipus' surprising action, and for this reason it is left, even in its empty state, full of potential for representation, by contrast with the unseen, unseeable, dramatically unrepresentable underworld whither, the chorus imagines, Oedipus is already journeying. The chorus' invocation of the Infernal Goddesses (1568), i.e., the Eumenides, does nothing to change the emptiness of the stage, since they, too, are invisible, and, in relation to the action of this tragedy, they are, as cult figures, deeper in the grove,

---

107. Kamerbeek on 1658-73.
108. See L-J-W 1990b on 1575. The text remains a problem, and therefore the action of Kerberos for which the chorus prays remains in doubt.

78   Chapter 2

in the diegetic space already established by the chorus in their instructions to Ismene (465-92).[109]

Before the stasimon, the spectators saw Oedipus lead a procession off stage. Now a messenger (someone who must have been in Theseus' retinue [1589]) appears, entering from the opening in the center of the stage, through which Oedipus and the others had exited toward the inner grove, and relates what has happened. He begins

> Fellow-citizens, the briefest
> account I could give is that Oedipus is dead;
> but, as for what happened, neither can the speech in brief
> be told nor can all the deeds that took place there.[110]
>
>   1579-82

The messenger thus reestablishes the opposition between words and deeds that, at least from the beginning of the second stasimon, began to entail the play's acknowledgment of the challenge of visual presentation or concretization. In a messenger's speech, however, it is a foregone conclusion that the action took place off stage. Such a speech in itself signifies the genre's limits as regards the representation of action, its inability completely to fulfill the requirements of a definition according to which "Tragedy is an imitation of an action ... on the part of men acting (*drôntôn*), not through narration" (Aristotle, *Poet.* 6.49b24-27). And here the messenger's opening words, distinguishing between words and deeds, inevitably call attention to the fact that words are now replacing the enactment of deeds. The stage that had been left empty is denied the enactment for which it was full of potential.

The messenger begins his narration with the action that the chorus saw at the end of the preceding episode—how Oedipus departed without a guide, he himself leading the others, which "you, too, know, I think, because you were here" (1587-89). The presence of the chorus at that action is thus implicitly distinguished from its absence from what happened thereafter. This opposition between presence and absence, here structuring his narration, will reappear as part of the content of the narration, within its diegetic space. At first, however, the messenger can sim-

---

109. They cannot be addressed by their cult titles (129-32), though they are necessarily referred to by general names (39-43; cf. Oedipus' prayer: 84ff.). The chorus' appellation in this prayer ("Infernal Goddesses") is clearly in the category of general names.

110. I construe the sentence in what I think is the most self-evident fashion. Cf. the distinction between words and deeds in Thuc. 1.22.2 and the use there, as here in *OC* 1581, of the aorist passive participle of πράττω in the neuter plural to refer to events in the broadest sense, as including words and deeds.

ply report what he saw. After Oedipus left the presence of the chorus, he went to a spot that can be defined, for the elders of Colonus, very precisely, by a variety of details (1590-97a; cf. Ch. 3§3). He then sat down, an action that the spectators can easily visualize, since they have seen this action twice on stage already (11ff., 195-202; and again at the beginning of the third episode?). He removed the rags (to which attention was often called in the course of the play) and ordered his daughters to bathe and dress him appropriately (1579b-1603), i.e., for burial. The next event is introduced as occurring after "he had got all the pleasure belonging to a doer (*drôntos*)" (1604).[111] The word for "doer" is closely associated with theater (especially in Aristophanes' *Frogs*) and is perhaps a way of expressing the idea already visually expressed in Oedipus' leaving the stage. (This will not be the only occurrence of this word in the messenger's report.)

Then a clap of thunder was heard (not heard on stage; cf. my remarks on 1501-1505 above), which comes coincidentally just as Oedipus finishes what he was doing. The frightened daughters fall at his knees (he was sitting on something, then), and he puts his arms around them. It is the tableau of philia that the spectators have already seen (329ff., 1110ff.), and indeed Oedipus affirms his philia as a recompense for all that they have had to endure on his behalf (1604-23a). When they have exhausted their grief, there is a moment of silence, and then a voice is heard. (Like the thunderclap, it waits for an interval in the action.) The god called on Oedipus again and again from many places in the grove,[112] and chided him for his procrastination (1623b-28). The messenger quotes the god, the source of the voice, who addressed Oedipus with the demonstrative *houtos* (1627). Within the drama, no character could use this demonstrative of another, with the two exceptions already noted, Theseus' of Kreon (contemptuous; 904) and of Oedipus' daughters (patronizing? 1148; cf. n. 68). Though Oedipus may at the end of the last episode have become an actor in the full theatrical sense, an extra-theatrical perspective is now in force, since the disembodied voice cannot be located in the diegetic space (it came from many places) and as the voice of a god it comes from outside that space. The characters, the action, and the space of the messenger's narrative are all continuous with what has transpired on stage; the voice is not. Upon hearing the voice, Oedipus procrastinates further, calling for Theseus, who is to pledge protection of the daugh-

---

111. In this translation, I follow the discussion of L-J-W 1990b:262 on 1604. Their tentative emendation squares with this tragedy's tendency to problematize enactment.
112. L-J-W 1990b:262 support Jebb's interpretation of the adverb πολλαχῇ.

ters. At Oedipus' bidding, Theseus and the daughters clasped hands to cement the pledge, and Theseus swore to do (*drasein*) what he had promised (1629-37, cf. 1773). When Oedipus had done (verb *dran*) these things, he "felt for his daughters with blind hands" (1638-39),[113] a reminder that he is still, and always was, blind; thus his independent movement, his "acting," was not the result of regained sight but had some other source. He dismissed them and the others. Only Theseus was to be present at what was to happen (*ta drômena* 1644).[114] The daughters, the messenger, and the others withdrew. After a short time, they turned and looked back. Oedipus was nowhere to be seen. Theseus was shielding his eyes with his hand, and then they saw him "supplicating both earth and Olympus at the same time,"[115] i.e., making the appropriate gestures of supplication.

While the messenger was present at the scene of Oedipus' death and the chorus was absent, the messenger himself was absent from the final moments (and also from the final place). While the messenger can describe the penultimate actions of Oedipus, which he does in terms of theatrical actions (verb *dran*), they lead up to a final scene, referred to in the same terms (*ta drômena* 1644), which he cannot describe. The messenger's relation to the death is thus the same as the chorus' to the messenger. The messenger has to rely on someone else as witness, namely Theseus, the only one present (though, when seen again by the chorus' witness, the messenger, even Theseus was shielding his eyes). As planned by Oedipus (cf. his own proleptic-diegetic account of his death: 1522-32), the place of his death remains concealed from everyone but Theseus and is thus beyond diegesis. (Theseus has been sworn to secrecy; only his successor will know the location of the grave.) The action of the play culminates in "actions" (*drômena*) of a different order from any other represented in any way in the tragedy. The final "actions" and the voice, the force that sends Oedipus into the extra-diegetic space, are a trope for the play's own mode of representation, which, as the play itself has shown, entails a gap between word and deed, between promise and demonstration. Oedipus has now gone over into the unrepresentable. Lacan's aphorism "I am not where I think, and I think where I am not" can be recast for *Oedipus at Colonus* as: "I am not where I act, and I act where I am not." The play dramatizes its own problematic, which is that of the *locus standi* or *agendi* of the dramatic agent. How can the dramatic agent represent

---

113. Jebb's translation.
114. See Nagy 1990b:31-32.
115. See L-J-W 1990b:263 on the readings in 1653 and 1655.

the action that his or her or some other character's words demand? This larger problematic is implicit in Honzl's law, which has formulated the gap between words and action at the pragmatic level of acting style. It is also implicit in the various pragmatic discontinuities in the speech of tragic actors and in particular in what has been called the "interstitial" character of entrance-announcements.[116]

At the end of the messenger's speech, the chorus asks where Oedipus' daughters and their escort are, and the messenger says that they are nearby, "for the very clear sounds of mourning show that they are coming hither" (1667-69), and these sounds are heard from off stage, as Ismene and Antigone enter through the opening in the center of the stage, as the messenger had done. The stage is left to them, as the messenger exits, through the parodos to the spectators' right, in the direction of Athens.[117] He came from the inner grove but he does not return there. It was possible to enter the forbidden grove only under the special circumstances of Oedipus' death; the impossibility of a return in that direction, manifested in the messenger's exit, will become a theme of the rest of the exodos, and, in this way, the focus of attention will continue to be on the diegetic (and extra-diegetic!) space. Though Antigone and Ismene enter accompanied by attendants, they are seen for the first time without their father, to whom they were always in close proximity when they were on stage.[118] Their desolation will be another theme of the exodos. Antigone addresses the chorus, beginning with the interjection *aiai* (1670), a sound of mourning. She commences a kommos of two antistrophic pairs (1670-96 = 1697-1723, 1724-36 = 1737-50) in which she, Ismene, and the chorus will participate. Both in sound and visually (with, no doubt, conventional gestures of grief), this kommos is a lamentation typical of the exodos,[119] and yet it manages to verbalize

---

116. For discontinuities, see Mastronarde 1979. On the inorganic, unrealistic, "interstitial" character of entrance-announcements, see Poe 1992:130-31, who poses the question: "Why did the spectators need to have pointed out what they could plainly see?"

117. By convention without a farewell. Cf. Taplin 1977:88: "Most of the major named characters of Greek tragedy are given an existence off-stage.... So when they go off they generally motivate their exit and say where they are going.... On the other hand, the majority of unnamed lower-status characters, which includes most messengers, have little or no existence beyond their role on stage. Their exit is, therefore, the end of their existence. So they are given no proper departure: when their part is played, they simply go away." Thus the departure of a messenger is a conventional exception to Honzl's law.

118. Just as the messenger who reported the death arrived without the corpse, contrary to the usual practice of Greek tragedy: see Taplin 1977:172.

119. Kremer 1971:118-19, 140. Kremer renounces an analysis of the exodos of *OC* (131 n. 26).

precisely the dilemma of the messenger's speech. Antigone says, in her very first sentence, "at the end we shall carry away things of which we cannot give an account, though we have seen and suffered them" (1675-76).[120] Her words attest to the unnarratability of the event that, in the context of the messenger's speech, signified also the extra-theatricality of the event. Like the messenger, and in similar language, Antigone describes as best she can the death that she did not see (cf. Antigone's description [1679-83] with the messenger's [1658-62]). She then turns to her sister and to their desolation. How will they survive the life of wandering that seems to lie ahead (1685-89)? Ismene chimes in with like despair, and the strophe ends with the chorus' attempt at consolation (1690-96).

In the first antistrophe, Antigone continues the theme of her desolation, now in terms of philia that hark back to the messenger's account of Oedipus' final words to his daughters, when Oedipus said philia was the recompense for all that they had had to suffer on his behalf (1614-19). The chorus intervenes at exactly the same point as in the strophe and again brings Antigone back to the perspective of her father, who, she concedes, died "as he wished" (1704). She reverts, however, to her desolation, and again Ismene chimes in and again the chorus consoles them (1712-23). At the beginning of the second strophe, Antigone exclaims, "Let us rush back," and Ismene interrupts her to ask for what purpose (1724). The strophe consists of an emotionally charged series of exchanges (in the form of antilabe) between the sisters. Antigone wants to see where her father died. Ismene objects that it is not right to do so and that he died without burial and apart from everyone (i.e., it is practically impossible to return to the scene of their father's death).[121] The place that has been represented in various ways as unrepresentable now appears concretely, in the context of Antigone's grief, as inaccessible. Like both units of the first strophic pair, the second strophe reverts to the theme of desolation, which is then continued in the antistrophe in a series of exchanges between Antigone and the chorus. The kommos thus ends with the plight of the daughters, preparing for the appearance of Theseus, who will assure them of safe conduct back to Thebes. Theseus will also assert himself as the sole sanctioned witness of the death of Oedipus.

Theseus enters. His first words are: "Children, cease your lamentation" (1751). His anapests by themselves signify that the play is coming

---

120. I have followed the interpretation of 1675 of L-J-W 1990b.
121. See Jebb and Kamerbeek on 1731ff.

to an end, and his injunction, putting an end to the lamentation that has just ended with the conclusion of the kommos, only articulates at the formal level of the tragedy what has just happened at the level of action. (One can compare the stopping of the rocking chair in Beckett's *Rockaby*, an example used in the preceding chapter. The action of stopping both ends the play and is the end of the drama that was presented in that play.) Theseus thus functions both within the action and outside it. Antigone beseeches him to let her and Ismene (contrary to Ismene's recently expressed opposition) see the tomb of their father (1754-57). Theseus refuses, reiterating the conditions that Oedipus had imposed (1760-67). According to these conditions, Theseus is the sole witness. As he now returns to the stage as the sole custodian of the tomb (which is now a tomb, a definite place, contrary to 1732 [Ismene]), he is thus the sole confirmation within the dramatic space of the death (with all its promises) that took place in an extra-diegetic space under extra-theatrical conditions. He is the tragedy's way of representing the death of Oedipus, otherwise radically unrepresentable: he is a character who returns to the stage (cf. the discussion of *epeisodos* above) from the dimension of the unrepresentable, whose speech is testimony to that dimension, and who is a character always bearing the trace of the fact that he is a character. Antigone, thwarted, now asks that she and Ismene may be sent back to Thebes, where they hope to prevent the mutual slaughter of their brothers, and Theseus complies (1768-76). The chorus then repeats Theseus' injunction to cease mourning and says that these events have been ratified, i.e., by the gods (1777-79), and the tragedy is over. Like Theseus they decree the end of something that has already ended, signaling the end both of the action and of the tragedy. The dispatch of the sisters to Thebes and the reference to the imminent battle are continuous with the scene (the first half of the fourth episode) in which Polyneices is sent packing and goes off calling upon his sisters to give him a proper burial. Like that earlier scene, the closing lines of the tragedy present characters (here Antigone and Ismene) who are already characters in other tragedies and who are going to do things that they have already done in tragedy, in Antigone's case, to die. Theseus' promise ("I will do" [verb *drasein*] 1773) is confirmed by the tradition of Attic tragedy, indeed by Sophocles' own earlier work. When, in the concluding lines, the chorus says that these events have been ratified, they (who are a chorus in a tragedy) are talking about tragedy as much as about the gods.[122]

---

122. For suggestions, from another point of view, concerning *Oedipus at Colonus* as a tragedy about tragedy see Segal 1981:406-408.

PART II

3

Historical Place in *Oedipus at Colonus*

§1 The historical background of *Oedipus at Colonus*

Date of the tragedy

The tragedy was produced posthumously in 401 B.C.E. (arg. II). Sophocles had died in 406 sometime between Feb./Mar. (the Dionysia), when he and his chorus had appeared in mourning for Euripides at the Proagon to the tragic performances, and Jan./Feb. (the Lenaea) 405, when Aristophanes' *Frogs* locates him in the underworld.[1] Since *Oedipus at Colonus* completes a story-pattern,[2] it is integral to the conception of Oedipus and could in theory have been written at any time in Sophocles' productive life, even before *Oedipus the King*. Indeed the proposed dates of composition and/or recomposition differ widely.[3] And yet there are reasons for believing that Sophocles still had the tragedy *in manibus* in extreme old age, as Cicero said (*de sen.* 7.22). First, Sophocles is unlikely to have fabricated Oedipus' mythologically unexpected arrival at Colonus, and the first reference to the Theban king's new resting place can be connected with an event that occurred in 410 or

---

1. See Nemeth 1983.
2. Cf. the argument, based on comparative materials, in Edmunds 1985a:36–38; 41–42 and the demonstration of the ring-compositional relation of *OC* to *OT* by Seidensticker 1972.
3. See Jebb 1928:xliii; Schmid-Stählin 409 n. 1. The ancient evidence for the date (i.e., the period in the life of Sophocles) of composition is surveyed by Tanner 1966:153–58 by way of introduction to an argument that *OC* was revised after the battle of Arginusae (July 406) to harmonize the tragedy with the earlier *Antigone*.

407 (§2 below). Second, the verbal parallels between *Bacchae* 1078-90 and *Oedipus at Colonus* 1621-29 suggest that Sophocles was working on the tragedy as late as 406.[4] Third, the tragedy provides various models of acceptance and reconciliation pertinent to Athens in the aftermath of the revolution of the Four Hundred (§§4, 9-10, 12 below). (These models were no less relevant at the time of the tragedy's production, again a period of recriminations under a restored democracy.) *Oedipus at Colonus* thus dates from the last years of Sophocles' life. Since the *Philoctetes* was produced in 409 (arg.), it can be assumed that much if not all of the composition of *Oedipus at Colonus* took place after 409.

Athens between 409 and the year of Sophocles' death[5]

Lysias 20 (For Polystratos), dated to 409, provides a starting point for a discussion of Athenian politics under the restored democracy.[6] This speech has often been used as a source for the history of the oligarchic revolution; it also shows the mood and conditions in Athens after that revolution. The speech is prima facie evidence of the spirit of reprisal that prevailed from the moment of the collapse of the 400.[7] Polystratos was prosecuted right after the 5000 succeeded the 400 (22) and then again after the restoration, as an enemy of the democracy (Harp. s.v. Πολύστρατος). The charge against him the first time is unknown; the speaker says that it was unrelated to the office of *katalogeus* (compiler of the citizen list) that Polystratos held under the 400 (17). How, the speaker argues, could they have used that office against him when he left Athens

---

4. Dodds 1960:212.
5. In this sub-section, I shall call attention to *atimia* as a typical penalty because I intend later to discuss *atimia* as a theme in *OC* (§5).
6. Dover 1968:44: "The earliest datable speech in the corpusculum [the second part of Palatinus 88, comprising 30 speeches of Lysias] is XX.... No allusions in the speech positively indicate a date later than 409, and an accumulation of arguments *ex silentio* shows that it was certainly composed before the defeat of Athens."
7. Analysis and judgment of Athenian politics in the period after the collapse of the 5000 have varied greatly from one historian to another. I tend to adhere to the view of Hignett 1952:282: "The radical democracy had triumphed and its leaders could afford to be generous; if they had any real insight, they ought to have proclaimed an amnesty for all political offenses during the last two years. Instead they preferred to show to all the world that they had learnt nothing and forgotten nothing. They carried the intemperance of party strife no less far than their oligarchic opponents, and like them undermined the unity of Athens at a time when the energies of all the citizens should have been concentrated on the struggle against the external enemies of the state." Busolt 1904:1541ff. paints a dismal picture. For a milder assessment, see Kagan 1987:257.

after only eight days of service to the new government (14, 16)? He was assessed a large fine, however (14, 18). Compared with Antiphon and Archeptolemos, leaders of the revolution who remained in the city, he got off light (Lysias 12.67; Thuc. 8.68.2; [Plut.] X orat. 833E-F, 834A-B).[8] The only aspect of the earlier prosecution that emerges from Lysias 20 is that the attempt was made to associate Polystratos with Phrynichos (11), "i.e., with the now discredited right wing of the oligarchs."[9] At both trials, then, no matter what the details of the cases (which are simply lost), Polystratos was prosecuted as an enemy of the democracy. His son begs that he, his father, and their family be permitted to enjoy the rights of citizens (ἐπιτίμους 9). But Polystratos seems to have been a target of opportunity for malicious accusers—old, helpless, convinced that his innocence was a shield (6, 10, 22). He was another casualty of the judicial reign of terror conducted by Epigenes, Demophanes, and Cleisthenes after the restoration, which brought the death penalty without trial, confiscation of property, exile, and loss of civil rights (ἀτιμῶσαι Lysias 25.25-26).[10] This last penalty could take various forms. The soldiers who "remained in the city under the 400" (Andoc. 1.75) could not speak in the Assembly or be members of the Boule. Others suffered other restrictions (Andoc. 1.75-76: a list).

A better-known Athenian who suffered (according to him) at the hands of his fellow-citizens was Andocides. His *De reditu* was delivered to the Assembly of the restored democracy (26) at some time after April 410 (if the reference in 12 is to the battle of Cyzicus), while Athens was still short of grain (19-22). Unlike Polystratos, who at least was able to live in Athens, Andocides pleads for the right to return from exile. He presents himself as a victim of the Four Hundred, of Peisander in particular (13-16). As their enemy, he should be the friend of the democracy; and yet every sentence in the speech reveals that the democracy was no less opposed to him than Peisander had been. While he has legal grounds for his appeal, the decree of Menippus granting him immunity (23), he obviously does not think that his audience will be persuaded by a legal argument. He bases his case on the benefits he has conferred on Athens. These ought to carry weight when even slaves and foreigners who have done some service (by implication far smaller than Andocides') can re-

---

8. On Antiphon and his speech of self-defense, see Raaflaub 1992:26 and nn. 64-65.
9. Andrewes, in *HCT* 5.203.
10. See Ostwald 1986:421 n. 37 on the problem of the identity of these persons.

ceive gifts from the Athenians and become citizens. This is an argument that Aristophanes will make again in 405.

In that year, the passions of the Athenians had not yet burned themselves out. At the Lenaea (Jan.-Feb.), in the parabasis of *Frogs* Aristophanes called for re-enfranchisement of the citizens who had lost their rights (687-88) and forgiveness for those who had been "tripped up" by Phrynichos in 411 (689-91). No one in the city should be deprived of civil rights (adj. ἄτιμος 692). For even slaves had been made citizens as a reward for service in a single naval battle, at Arginusae (693-94). You Athenians should give up your anger and accept everyone who fights in the navy (i.e., every free man?) as a kinsman and as in possession of his rights (adj. ἐπίτιμος) and as a citizen (700-702). In the antistrophe of the song (706-15), Aristophanes mocks Cleigenes, a supporter of the demagogue Cleophon, who was the main instigator of the disenfranchisements.[11] In the anapests (716-36), Aristophanes apologizes for the *chrêstoi*. The situation was not remedied until the Decree of Patrocleides in autumn of 405, when, after Aegispotamoi and the beginning of the Spartan siege, the Athenians perforce sought harmony (Andoc. 1.73: ἐβουλεύσασθε περὶ ὁμονοίας, καὶ ἔδοξεν ὑμῖν τοὺς ἀτίμους ἐπιτίμους ποιῆσαι: the Decree is quoted at 77-79).[12]

While the mood of the roughly four-year period from the restoration to the last year of Sophocles' life has to be judged mainly from the passages just cited and from references to this period in the orators, the heated "trial" scene in Euripides' *Orestes* (Feb./Mar. 408 B.C.) can be taken as a dramatization of typical types, attitudes, and rhetoric (866-956).[13] The scholiast (on 772 and 903) sees in "the Argive not an Argive" (904) the figure of Cleophon. This person, unnamed in the play, proposes death by lapidation as the penalty for Orestes. Oddone Longo has pointed out that lapidation, long considered an inhuman penalty (cf. Aesch. *Eum.* 189), had come back into use in 409 B.C.E., when Thrasyllus had Alcibiades, the cousin of Alcibiades son of Cleinias, stoned to death

---

11. Aeschin. 2.76, 3.150; Aristot. *Ath. Pol.* 28.3, 34.1; Lys. 13.7-12, 19.48, 30.12; D.S. 13.53.2. Vanderpool 1952 supplies, from an ostrakon, the name, Kleippides, of Cleophon's father. On the death of Cleophon see Xen. *Hell.* 1.7.35

12. But not even then was the situation remedied, since the main divisions inevitably persisted. Cf. the Oxyrhynchus historian VI.2-3, on the year 397/6: the γνώριμοι καὶ χαρίεντες are opposed to the party of Thrasybulus, Aisimos and Anytos, and the ἐπιεικεῖς and the rich are opposed to the majority. On homonoia, see Raaflaub 1992:36 n. 99.

13. For bibliography on *Orestes*, see Raaflaub 1992:10 n. 28.

(Xen. *Hell.* 1.2.13).[14] This Alcibiades was one of those who was accused of the mutilation of the herms and had gone into exile (Andoc. 1.65).[15]

Colonus

The assembly at which the 400 came into power was held at Colonus, the place in which *Oedipus at Colonus* is set. Colonus was a cult center, the only one in Attica, of the Knights, where they sacrificed to Poseidon Hippios, and, as such, the place was closely identified with them. In a fragment of the Old Comic poet Pherecrates, someone says, "I was rushing to Colonus, not the one by the Agora but the Knights'" (εἰς Κολωνὸν ἱέμην, οὐ τὸν ἀγοραῖον, ἀλλὰ τὸν τῶν ἱππέων frag. 134K). Likewise, the Knights were closely identified with Poseidon. The chorus of Knights in Aristophanes' comedy of that name invokes its patron, Poseidon Lord of Horses (551). Thucydides seems to equate Colonus with the shrine of Poseidon (8.67.2), i.e., with the Knights' cult center. The two Colonuses of the Pherecrates fragment in fact represented the extremes of Athenian citizenship, since the one near the Agora was the place where laborers were hired and thus had the epithet μίσθιος (schol. Ar. *Av.* 998; cf. Soph. *OC* arg. II) or ἐργατικός (schol. Aeschin. 1.125). At Colonus of the Knights, the Hipparchs sacrificed an ox to Poseidon.[16] An inventory of the Poseidon cult-center, dated to ca. 406/5 B.C.E., includes ox-flayers (β]ουδόροι).[17] The choice of Colonus for the meeting of the assembly in 411 B.C.E. that established the Four Hundred (Thuc. 8.67) would not have been by accident.[18] After the assassination of Phrynichos, with the Four Hundred on the verge of collapse, Aristarchus and "young Knights" (τῶν ἱππέων νεανίσκοι Thuc. 8.92.6) supported Theramenes' attempt to free the oligarch Alexicles, who had been put under house-arrest in the Piraeus. In sum, the events of 411 B.C.E. would have given many Athenians reason

---

14. Longo 1975:282-83. On Xenophon's report of the incident, see Kagan 1987:272 n. 105.

15. Longo has also shown a series of parallels between Thucydides' description of stasis (3.82-83) and the action and themes of *Orestes*.

16. Siewert 1979:281-82 gives the evidence, which is mostly late, but which, combined with the inscription cited in the next note and with *OC* 887-89, makes it fairly certain that this sacrifice was already customary in Sophocles' time.

17. Line 9: see Woodward 1963 for the text.

18. Siewert 1979:287 and n. 41. Cf. Ostwald 1986:373-74: the choice of Colonus "will have discouraged the lower classes from attending."

to believe (if they did not already believe) in the truth of the Paphlagonian's charge against the Knights in Aristophanes' *Knights* (424 B.C.E.), that they were conspirators (257, 314, 452, 461-63) against the democracy. Even if we do not know why Colonus was chosen as the place for the extraordinary meeting of the assembly in 411 B.C.E. that established the Four Hundred (Thuc. 8.67),[19] we can be fairly confident about what that place represented.

Given the mood of recrimination in Athens between 409 and the year of Sophocles' death, it is difficult to see how a tragedy composed in this period, a tragedy that is set in Colonus, praises Colonus, praises Colonus with respect to Poseidon and horses, cannot be in some way apologetic. The second stasimon of the tragedy provides evidence for this hypothesis.

Poseidon, horses, and horsemen

Not only does Sophocles create a Colonus-Athens axis, in ways to be shown below (§3), so as to reverse the assumed associations of Colonus in the minds of the Athenian demos, he also presents the horsemen of Theseus' day, implicitly the ancestors of Sophocles' contemporary Knights, in a most favorable light. Using the same strategy as Aristophanes in the parabasis of *Knights*,[20] he brings the horsemen and the rowers into a kind of equality, and couples Poseidon's two main aspects, the equestrian and the maritime. The second antistrophe of the first stasimon exemplifies this strategy, which will be continued in the second episode.

> I have another very great praise for this mother city (ματροπόλει), the gift of a great god—a very great vaunt—a gift of good horses, of good colts, and of sea power (εὔιππον, εὔπωλον, εὐθάλασσον). For you, son of Cronos (i.e., Poseidon), enthroned her on this vaunt, having established first in these roads (i.e., Colonus) the taming bridle for horses (ἵπποισιν). And the well-bladed oar, fitted to men's hands, leaps wonderfully on the sea, companion of the hundred-footed Nereids.
>
> 707-19

The third of the εὐ- adjectives in this passage (translated "of sea power") perhaps also alludes to the salt spring in the Erechtheum, which Poseidon was believed to have created with a blow of his trident (Hdt. 8.55; Apollod.

---

19. Andrewes on Thuc. 8.67.2. Cf. Siewert 1979:287 and n. 41.
20. Cf. *OC* 707-19 with *Eq.* 551-67. Cf. Edmunds 1987:39-41.

3.14.1). The chorus already in a single phrase combines the sea god with the god of horsemanship. In the last lines of this strophe, the oar is a metonymy for the sea power of Athens, another vaunt that she owes to Poseidon.

In the second episode (720-1043), Kreon appears with attendants. He has come for Oedipus, who refuses to go back to Thebes. Oedipus curses Thebes and his sons. Kreon then says that he has seized one of the daughters (Ismene) and that he will now seize the other. His attendants take Antigone. The chorus calls upon the people of Colonus (ἔντοποι 841) and then upon the "whole people" (πᾶς λεώς) and "the rulers of the land (γᾶς)" (884). Theseus then enters:

> What is this shout? What is happening? What was the fear that made you stop me when I was sacrificing an ox at the altar to the sea god, the tutelary god of this Colonus?
>
> 887-89

By coincidence, then, Theseus was still in Colonus, performing a sacrifice to Poseidon. As far as we know, the Poseidon worshipped at Colonus was Poseidon Hippios. In the days of Theseus, Sophocles seems to say, it was Poseidon the sea god (cf. 1494, where again it is an altar of the sea god).[21] When Theseus learns what has happened, he gives a command:

> Will not someone of the attendants go as quickly as possible to these altars and compel the whole people, horsed and without horses, to speed from the sacrifice with slackened rein to the place where two roads of merchants meet?
>
> 897-901

Colonus was not the cult center, then, of the *kaloi kai agathoi* (cf. Aristoph. *Knights* 225, 227) but of the whole people. Theseus divides them into two categories, which we could call horsemen and non-horsemen, and urges them all to speed to the rescue "with slackened rein," though one group does not have any reins and its difficult to see how they could dash on foot the many kilometers to the place at which Ismene and Antigone would be carried over the border into Boeotia. The awkwardness of Theseus' command is of the same order as the worship of the sea god at Colonus. Sophocles wants to suggest an Athens in which the people were unified, and, even if some had horses and some did not, the distinction had no practical consequences.

---

21. The aspect of Poseidon is unspecified at 55 and 1158.

In the second stasimon, the chorus excitedly imagines the clash between the abductors of Oedipus' daughters and Theseus and his troops—the latter moving at high-speed on horseback and in chariots (1062). The horseless element is now forgotten. The contingent is divided into a new pair of groups, the men of Colonus and Theseus' men (1065-66). Even in this imagined scene, however, the maritime aspect of Poseidon is not forgotten. The horsemen are described as honoring "Athena Hippia and the earth-holding sea-god, the dear son of Rhea" (1070-73).[22] In the concluding strophe, the same division of the troops is preserved. The chorus prays to Zeus and Pallas Athena (who was worshipped at Athens, not at Colonus) to aid the "protectors of this land" (γᾶς τᾶσδε δαμούχοις 1087; cf. ἄνδρες τῆσδε δημοῦχοι χθονός 1348, where Oedipus addresses the chorus, i.e., men of Colonus, who might be the men of Colonus.[23] Then they call upon Apollo and Artemis to aid "this land and the citizens" (γᾷ τᾷδε καὶ πολίταις 1095), i.e., all the Athenians. The identity of these troops is all a matter of perspective. When Antigone reappears on stage, she attributes her release to "the hands of Theseus and those of his closest followers" (1102-1103).

Third stasimon

At the end of the third episode, Oedipus agrees to hear his son Polyneices on the condition that he be protected from seizure. Theseus assures him of protection, and the scene ends. Moved by the helplessness of the old man, the chorus, old men themselves, comment in the third stasimon (1211-48) on the folly of wishing to live to extreme old age (strophe). Not to be born is best; none of the three stages of life is good (antistrophe). Not I alone but also Oedipus is an example of the evils of old age (epode). Such in outline is the chorus' song. But is Oedipus also an example of the other stages of life described by the chorus? They characterize the middle stage as one of "envy, factions, strife, battles, and murders" (φθόνος, στάσεις, ἔρις, μάχαι / καὶ φόνοι 1234-35). All of these experiences are political. For years, however, Oedipus has wandered as a blind beggar. He is *apoptolis* (207), *apolis* (1357). The cho-

---

22. Paus. 1.30.4 refers to an altar of Poseidon Hippios and Athena Hippia at Colonus, and to a heroön of Peirithous and Theseus and of Adrastus and Oedipus.

23. In earlier editions of Schneidewin-Nauck, one found the comment: "den Attikern, zunächst aber den Bewohnern von Kolonos." Radermacher removed this comment in Schneidewin-Nauck 1909. Kamerbeek 1984:155: "the simple interpretation *incolae* can be defended."

rus' words do not fit Oedipus but they would well describe the situation in Athens in the period of the restored democracy. Oedipus the Theban thus represents the experience of many Athenians who had had to bear their fellow-citizens' wrath. The acceptance of Oedipus in Colonus and in Athens can thus be a model for the Athenians' acceptance of their own.[24] Elaborated in this fashion, my hypothesis requires not only an investigation of the relation of Colonus to Athens as represented in *Oedipus at Colonus* (§3) but also of the modes and conditions of Oedipus' reception (especially §§4–5, 9–10).

§2 Mythical background and apologetic tendency

As the tragedy begins, Oedipus arrives in Colonus. Oedipus is thus, for future time, both the future projected within the tragedy, and the real future that includes us, at Colonus. But when the tragedy had its first performance in 401 B.C.E. was Oedipus already there, so that his arrival was only the dramatization of an event that the audience knew had taken place in the distant past?

For the end of Oedipus' life, the myth had two main variants. Either, in the epic tradition, Oedipus died and was buried in Thebes (Hom. *Il.* 23.679 and schol. thereto = Hes. fr. 192 M-W; Soph. *Antig.* 53–54; Aesch. *Sept.* 914 and 1004) or, in local traditions, he left Thebes, wandered, died and was buried somewhere else. Besides Colonus, which is Oedipus' final resting place for the first time in Sophocles' tragedy, only Eteonos, a town in Boeotia is attested. For Colonus, the next-earliest source after Sophocles is a fragment of Androtion, the fourth-century Atthidographer. The fragment is difficult to use,[25] but seems to be independent of Sophocles. The relevant part runs as follows:

> Later, Jocasta, recognizing that she had married her son, hung herself. Oedipus, banished by Kreon, came to Attica and dwelt on (ᾤκησεν) the so-called Hill of the Horseman. And he was a suppliant in the shrine of the goddesses Demeter and Athena Poliouchos, and when he was forcibly carried off by Kreon he had Theseus as his defender. When Oedipus was dying of old age he called upon Theseus not to reveal his grave to any of the Thebans, for they wanted to maltreat him even as a corpse.
>
> *FGrH* 324F62

---

24. For the relation of *OC* 1231 to 205 see Di Benedetto 1979 and 1983:218–19.
25. Edmunds 1981:222 n. 6.

On the assumption that, if Androtion had wanted to summarize Sophocles' *Oedipus at Colonus*, he could have done so, the narrative just quoted can be taken not as a misrecollection or misunderstanding of the tragedy but as Androtion's summary of an Attic tradition concerning the end of Oedipus' life parallel to and varying from Sophocles'. In Androtion, not Ismene and Antigone but Oedipus is carried off by Kreon. Kreon's motive is not to bury Oedipus near Thebes but, apparently, to maltreat him. At Colonus, Oedipus is a suppliant not of the Eumenides but of Demeter and Athena Poliouchos.[26] The existence of this parallel tradition, however, shows that Sophocles' location of the death of Oedipus had a warrant in popular belief and that Sophocles is recoding an existing narrative for his own purposes.

The most striking difference, however, between Androtion and Sophocles is perhaps the absence in Androtion (as in the Eteonos tradition, to be discussed below) of any sense that Oedipus' burial place was to be a source of great benefit. Did Sophocles have any warrant for the notion of Oedipus as a savior (460, 577, 621–22, 629–30)?

There is some slight evidence that Oedipus was believed to have appeared to the Athenians at a certain point in the Decelean War and to have inspired them to defeat a hostile cavalry contingent.[27] The evidence for this belief is a scholium on an oration of Aristeides (*Hyper ton tettarôn* 172) that says that, after Oedipus came to Colonus and was buried there, he once appeared when the Thebans were attacking and inspired the Athenians to rally and defeat them. A historical event with which this scholium can be combined is attested in Diodorus Siculus 13.72.3–73.2, where it is said that, during the Decelean War (410 or 407 B.C.E.),[28] Agis led a raid against Athens in which Boeotian cavalry participated; the Athenian cavalry routed the Boeotian. This attack is also mentioned by Xenophon, who does not, however, refer to Boeotians or cavalry (*Hell.* 1.1.33).[29] The dating of the attack fits well with the proposed date of the composition of *Oedipus at Colonus*. Furthermore, the place of the attack would have been somewhere north of Athens proper in the vicinity of Colonus. The inspiring apparition is not unparalleled. There was the belief, for example, that Theseus rose out of the ground at the battle of Marathon (Paus. 1.15).

26. See further Edmunds 1981:224 n. 12.
27. My argument is essentially that to be found in Schmid-Stählin 1934:407–408.
28. On the problems see Edmunds 1981:232 n. 44. Kagan 1987:321 n. 113 holds that Diodorus Siculus 13.72.3–73.2 and Xenophon *Hell.* 1.1.33 refer to two different events.
29. Cf. Kagan 1987:262–63.

Whether or not the apparition of Oedipus was the source of the Attic tradition concerning his wandering to and burial at Colonus, it surely could have provided the belief (of which Androtion offers no hint) that that burial was of great benefit to Athens. To sum up the discussion to this point, Sophocles would have had warrants both for the burial of Oedipus at Colonus, as the Androtion variant showed, and for the benefit to Athens of that burial. *Oedipus at Colonus* in effect makes that benefit the point of the myth. For this reason, much care is given to the ritual aspects of Oedipus' reconciliation with the Eumenides and to the cultic aspects of his grave (cf. §11). Again, the type of grave is not unparalleled.

The distinguishing characteristic of Oedipus' grave is that its location is unknown to anyone except Theseus, who will pass this knowledge on to his successor. One parallel for this type of hero cult is Theban. In Plutarch's dialogue *de genio Socratis*, a character speaks of a certain Lysanoridas who "on his return to Thebes intends to search out the tomb of Dirce, which is unknown to any Theban who has not served as hipparch. For the retiring hipparch takes his successor and shows him the tomb in private and at night; and on performing certain rites there in which no fire is used, they rub out and destroy all trace of them and return their separate ways in the darkness" (*Mor.* 578B).[30] Another parallel is the graves of Sisyphus and Neleus in Corinth. Pausanias says: "The graves of Sisyphus and Neleus ... I do not think that anyone would look for after reading Eumelus. For he says that not even to Nestor did Sisyphus show the tomb of Neleus, because it must be kept unknown to everyone alike, and that Sisyphus is indeed buried on the Isthmus, but that few Corinthians, even those of his own day, knew where the grave was" (2.2.2).[31] Originally the reason for the concealment of the grave would have been the belief that the bones of the hero, if carried off, could confer power on an enemy. Thus the Spartans brought home the bones of Orestes from Tegea (Hdt. 1.67.3 ff. Cf. Plut. *Cimon* 8.3ff.: Cimon found the bones of Theseus on Skyros and brought them back to Athens.).[32]

Oedipus at Colonus could have given some such reason for concealment—Oedipus' fear that the Thebans would carry off his bones. Though it may be implicit, neither Oedipus nor any other character in the tragedy gives this reason. There may, however, be a reason external to the drama, and that would be contemporary uncertainty about or even

---

30. Trans. de Lacy and Einarson 1959:391-93.
31. Trans. Jones 1918:255.
32. Other examples of secret graves in Kearns 1989:51-52.

ignorance of the grave of Oedipus at Colonus. The Colonan stranger in the tragedy had to apologize for the obscurity of the cultic lore of his deme (62-63). (The comparison of *Oedipus at Colonus* with Androtion suggested an Attic tradition well enough established to exist in two variants, but a tradition concerning the death of Oedipus at Colonus and the knowledge of his grave there, let alone a cult, are two different things. The former does not entail the latter.) Besides a dubious reference in Euripides' *Phoenician Women* (1703-1707, a passage generally considered spurious),[33] there is no other fifth-century reference to Oedipus' grave at Colonus and there is none earlier. We have to wait until Pausanias in the second century C.E. to hear about Oedipus' grave at Colonus. But Pausanias' reference is not very satisfactory. He says: "There is also pointed out a place called the Hill of Horses, the first point in Attica, they say, that Oedipus reached ... and an altar to Poseidon, Horse God, and to Athena, Horse Goddess, and a chapel to the heroes Peirithous and Theseus and Oedipus and Adrastus" (1.30.4).[34] This quadruple hero cult does not sound much like the situation in *Oedipus at Colonus*. The burial of Oedipus on the Areopagus in a precinct of the Semnai (Paus. 1.28.6-7; cf. Val. Max. 5.3.3) does not shed any light on the problem, because the chronological relation of this burial to *Oedipus at Colonus* is indeterminable.[35]

The hiddenness of Oedipus' grave at Colonus might, then, have served two purposes: to accommodate and exploit contemporary uncertainty about the matter[36] and, at the same time, to take account of the recent apparition at the cavalry skirmish: Oedipus was a potent hero, a source of strength to Athens. Though Sophocles' audience was presumably unaware of any successor of Theseus in their generation who had knowledge of the grave's location, Sophocles' tragedy provides concrete indications of the immediate vicinity (1590-1655). The tragedy indeed guarantees Oedipus' presence at Colonus and the potency of his help. Scenes that from the literary-critical point of view have seemed

---

33. The passage has been defended, however, by Valk 1985:44-46 and by Craik 1988:267.
34. Trans. Jones 1918:167.
35. Kirsten 1973 argues that the burial at Colonus antedates the one on the Areopagus and that the cultic association of Poseidon the Horse God and Athena Hippia (cf. OC 1070-71) at Colonus antedates that on the Acropolis (represented on the west pediment of the Parthenon, where each has a team of horses). Kearns 1989:50-52, 208-209 tends to the same view concerning the chronological relation of the burials.
36. Good remarks by Jebb on 1522ff.

unintegrated,[37] can be understood as demonstrations of this potency. Oedipus' repudiation of Kreon and his curse on his son Polyneices can be taken as proleptic characterization, as a display of the power that Oedipus will have to destroy Thebans in the future (cf. 621-22).[38]

Sophocles has, then, given the tradition of Oedipus' death at Colonus a particular application. Not only did Oedipus die there but he is a potent hero, still appearing from his hidden grave. Because Oedipus is there at Colonus, Colonus is a vital asset to Athens. It is, the stranger says, "the bulwark of Athens" (58). In this way, the Attic tradition concerning Oedipus is recoded to suit the apologetic tendency of the tragedy.

Another local tradition, the one concerning Eteonos, can be compared with the Attic tradition preserved in the two variants, Sophocles' and Androtion's. This comparison can be used heuristically as a way of establishing some of the principal narrative features of the myth. These, in turn, will provide a check on the idea that the hero cult, as the particular, etiological thrust of Sophocles' recodification of the myth, is the main vehicle of the apology for Colonus. The Eteonos version of the death of Oedipus comes from the Alexandrian Lysimachus:

> When Oedipus died, his friends thought to bury him in Thebes. But the Thebans, holding that he was an impious person on account of the misfortunes which had befallen him in earlier times, prevented them from so doing. They carried him therefore to a certain place in Boeotia called Keos and buried him there. But the inhabitants of this village, being visited with sundry misfortunes, attributed them to the burying of Oedipus and bade his friends remove him from their land. The friends, perplexed by these occurrences, took him up and brought him to Eteonos. Wishing to bury him secretly, they interred him by night in the sanctuary of Demeter—for they did not know the locality. When the facts transpired, the inhabitants of Eteonos asked the god what they should do. The god bade them not to move the suppliant of the goddess. So Oedipus is buried there and the sanctuary is called Oedipodeion.[39]
>
> *FGrH* 382F2

Oedipus could not be buried at Thebes, nor at Keos, nor, at first at Eteonos.

---

37. Lesky 1966:296: "[I]t cannot be contended that the connection of the various parts achieves the same closeness that we find in the plays of his maturity; nor does it have the same continuity and ease in the unfolding of the action."
38. Edmunds 1981:229; Henrichs 1983:94-95 (with bibliography in n. 32).
39. The translation, with very minor changes, is that of Cook 1925:1152.

As a defiled person, he was a risk to any place in which he might come to rest. (Cf. the reaction of the Colonan elders to the discovery of Oedipus' identity at OC 226ff.) Thus Androtion, who says that Kreon tried to carry Oedipus away from Colonus, does not seem to have imagined that Kreon saw any positive value in Oedipus. Androtion's account ends with the idea that Thebans would maltreat even the corpse of Oedipus if they could find it. Against this negative concept of the burial place of Oedipus, one must set the positive one in *Oedipus at Colonus*. Furthermore, as against the preordained burial of Oedipus in a sacred precinct (*Oedipus at Colonus* 84-110: Oedipus quotes the oracle), in Lysimachus the burial of Oedipus in a precinct of Demeter takes place by mistake, and is sanctioned by Apollo only after the fact. The Oedipodeion is presumably known to and accessible to everyone.

In other respects, however, the two local versions, the Attic and the Boeotian, are similar. In both, Oedipus is a suppliant. In both, he has his own shrine within a larger precinct. In both, Demeter is important. She is one of the two deities of which Androtion says Oedipus was a suppliant; there was a shrine of Demeter Euchloös near the place where Oedipus was buried in *Oedipus at Colonus* (1600). Given these broad similarities, the particular differences between the two traditions with respect to the potency of the hero loom large. The Eteonos version corroborates the impression that Sophocles has recodified a received narrative tradition and refocused it so as to emphasize the great benefit of Oedipus to Colonus and thus of Colonus to Athens.[40]

§3 The Code of Place[41]

Just as the mythical code is refocused on the death of Oedipus in Colonus, the political-geographical code is rewritten in such a way as to redefine

---

40. On the mythical background of *OC* see the forthcoming article by Calame.

41. Jones 1962:214-35 stresses the importance of place in *OC*. "[T]he local circumstances ... matter greatly, religiously. The essence of the matter is a kind of interdependence of man and place ..." (219). Kirkwood 1986, a study of the theme of place in *OC*, shows that the tragedy "is indeed a deeply patriotic vision, of an Athens, or an Attica, seen not primarily as an imperial state or a political power, but as a place of beauty and a strength that emanates from the land itself, a chthonic power" (109). The interpretation of Allison 1984 is similar to Kirkwood's: "The constant preoccupation is with Attica and its local people, and particularly with ... Kolonos itself ... . This preoccupation ... manifests itself to a greater or lesser degree in virtually every part of the drama, and contributes powerfully to the dramatic and thematic impact of the work as a whole." Winnington-Ingram 1980:339-40 surveys the references to place in *OC*.

and revalorize this deme (in contrast with the associations hypothesized in §1). A Colonus-Athens axis is established (cf. the use of theatrical space to this end); Colonus gains in importance in relation to the rest of Attica. Colonus also has its own map, which is redrawn to accommodate the new mythical code.

Prologue 1-116

The first two lines of the play, a question addressed to Antigone by Oedipus, pose a disjunction between *khôros* "place" and polis. Which have they reached, a place or a city? Antigone's answer preserves the disjunction: she can see the towers of a polis in the distance, but here is a sacred *khôros* (14-16). They both knew, having heard it from wayfarers that the polis was Athens; they still do not know the *khôros* (24-25); Antigone offers to go and inquire, using instead of *khôros* the word *topos* (26), a synonym.

As they talk, the place has also become something else: a ἕδρα "seat" for Oedipus. The word is first used, innocently, by the stranger from Colonus, who asks Oedipus to remove himself from his seat in the grove of the Eumenides (36-37). This place (*khôros*) is sacrosanct (37). What is the place (*khôros*), Oedipus asks (38). When he learns whose grove it is, he uses ἕδρα in a more pregnant sense: "I would never depart from my seat in this land" (45). The phrase "seat in this land" (ἕδρας γῆς τῆσδ') locates the precise point from which he speaks not in the *khôros* and not in relation to the polis, Athens, but in relation to a geographical category, "this land," that could embrace both *khôros* and city. The phrase in fact epitomizes the tragedy: Oedipus must get a particular spot in the grove of the Eumenides for his grave, which will then make Colonus truly the "bulwark of Attica" that the stranger boasts it is (58).[42]

And yet the question concerning the *khôros* remains unanswered and Oedipus has to ask it once again: "What is the place (*khôros*) that we have entered?" (52). The stranger then gives a rather full reply, which at first only describes the *khôros* without identifying it: the whole *khôros* is sacred, the stranger says. It is Poseidon's. There is also the Titan Prometheus (53-55a). The stranger then describes and identifies the particular *topos*, i.e., within the *khôros*, by putting it in relation to Athens, and thus by-passing the question of *khôros*. "The *topos* on which

---

42. Lloyd-Jones and Wilson 1990a read Musgrave's γε for γῆς for reasons given in Lloyd-Jones and Wilson 1990b:215. On the importance of the ἕδρα see Allison 1984:71-72.

you tread is called the bronze-stepped threshold of this land, the bulwark of Athens" (55b-58). This *topos*, as we know, is a grove of the Eumenides, which is named after its most remarkable feature, a set of bronze steps leading to the underworld (cf. 1591). The genitival construction used by the stranger, putting the particular place in relation to the broadest geographical category ("threshold of this land" [χθονὸς ... τῆσδε ... ὁδός]), is the same as the one already used by Oedipus ("seat in this land" 45). Therefore it is not surprising that, at the end of the play, as Oedipus goes to seek his grave, he goes to these steps.[43] They mark the place where he finds the seat for which he has, as it turns out, come to Colonus.

Only after these preliminary descriptions of the place, does the stranger provide the identification—and then not as definitely as Oedipus would like—that Oedipus has asked for. The neighboring fields consider the Knight Colonus their founder, and the people are named after him (58b-61). To the audience the place is now Colonus but it is not yet that for Oedipus. He has to ask: Do you mean that there are those who inhabit this place (*topoi* plur. 64, synonym of *khôros*)? And the stranger repeats: yes, named after Colonus (63). He points to a statue of the hero (demonstrative pronoun at 59 and at 65), which Oedipus, however, cannot see.

After the stranger departs, Oedipus addresses a prayer to the Eumenides, in which he reveals that, in the prophecy he had received from Apollo, many years before, he had also learned that he would end his life in a grove of the Eumenides. He refers to the place first as a "seat": "because yours is the first seat in this land where I have rested" (84-85; cf. the construction of 45). And then he uses a word for place not heard until now in the play: Apollo said that I would find rest after a long time "when I came to a last region (χώρα) where I would find a seat (ἕδρα) of the dread goddesses" (89-90). The seat, the goddesses', is now located in a "region." Hereafter in the play χώρα is used fourteen times, *khôros* four times.[44] Oedipus will use *khôros* only to distinguish Colonus from Athens (644) or to designate a place with Colonus (1520, 1540); the chorus uses the word once to refer vaguely to a particular part of Attica (1058).

---

43. His going is out of sight of the spectators, reported by the messenger, which only means that, at 55b-58, the stranger is using the metonymy I have pointed out: in the prologue, Oedipus is not standing at or on the steps, which are to be imagined as off stage somewhere. See Campbell 1879:282-83.

44. χώρα:145 (Oed.); 226 (Chorus); 296 (Oed.); 405 (Ismene); 637 (Theseus); 700 (Chorus); 727 (Chorus); 788 (Oed.); 909 (Theseus); 934 (Theseus); 1024 (Theseus); 1476 (Oed.); 1553 (Oed.); 1765 (Theseus).

How did Colonus, which, in answer to Oedipus' urgent question, had just become identified as a *khôros*, become a *khôra* "region"? The answer is that Apollo had defined it as such by his use of the term in his oracle. Perceiving the correspondence between the *khôros* and the prophecy, Oedipus will now, following the oracle, speak of the place as a *khôra*. A standard sense of this word is "the territory of a city,"[45] and it is implicit that Oedipus understands the oracular word in this sense, for he links the Eumenides of his final resting place, Colonus, with Athens in a short prayer of supplication that concludes the speech under discussion (84–110). Oedipus' original desire to get a "seat in this land" (45) has now become more specific: he must get a "seat in a last place (*khôra*)" (89–90).

The change, from the beginning of the play to the prayer just mentioned, in Oedipus' notion of the place in which he finds himself, is reinforced by his coming to know the political relations of Colonus to Athens. From the first, he had thought of the place, whatever it was, as politically organized (n.b. *astoi* 13), and his distinction in line 10, between sacred and profane, presupposes such organization, because a sacred precinct presupposes an organized community. He had learned from the stranger that Colonus was ruled from Athens, by Theseus, and he had asked the stranger to go to him with a message (66–70). But the stranger chose to refer to his fellow demesmen the question of Oedipus' staying or going (77–80; though the stranger's first impulse had been to consult the polis: 47). When the chorus appears, it is old demesmen of Colonus who have come as *episkopoi* (112; cf. *ephoroi* 145 [Oedipus' expression]). The official ring of this word already intimates their identity with the polis (cf. 184–87).[46] The Colonus-Athens axis is already assumed. What remains to be established is Oedipus' place in Colonus and the new relation of Colonus to Athens that Oedipus will bring about through the contribution of his grave to the defense of Attica.

Parodos / Kommos 117–253

The action on stage dramatizes the precariousness of Oedipus' place in Colonus, as he retreats deeper into the grove in fear of the chorus of Colonans, then little by little comes forward to a place where *nomos* permits them to speak with him (168).[47] The chorus exhorts him to act in

---

45. LSJ s.v. II.3; Ste. Croix 1981:9.
46. Cf. LSJ s.v. 3
47. Jebb 1928:xxxviii has a diagram of the action.

conformity with the preferences of the polis (184-87; this passage is discussed in §7).—Oedipus himself is *apoptolis* (207).—When they discover his identity they send him from the land, lest he pollute the city (*polis* 236). For them, their "land" is a city, an institution, a community (234-36). Oedipus must be received on terms agreeable to the city and he must repair his violation of the grove of the Eumenides in order, at the end of his life, to return into the grove and fulfill the oracle by occupying his promised "seat."

First Episode 254-667

After the chorus' verdict, Oedipus immediately refers to Athens' reputation for compassion (260) and he ends a long speech of self-exoneration with another reference to Athens' good name (282-83). Though the stranger had said that the local demesmen (δημόταις 78) would decide whether Oedipus stayed or left, Oedipus still expects to see the chief (288-90)—who is curiously unnamed, though Oedipus has already heard of Theseus (69)—and now the elders consent to turn the matter over to "the rulers of this land" (γῆς/ἄνακτας 294-95), i.e., Theseus. The chorus' form of expression acknowledges, in the most general terms (γῆ), the political unification of Attica and the superior jurisdiction of the Athenian king. The Colonan stranger's indecisiveness (47; cf. 77-80) is now resolved.

The chance arrival of Ismene, who reports new oracles concerning her father, gives Oedipus a more precise sense of his destiny and prepares him for his interview with Theseus. The oracles have said that the Thebans need Oedipus for their welfare (389-90). Kreon will come for him, in order that he may be buried "near Cadmean land (γῆς)" (399). Oedipus' refusal to be buried there and his continuing anger against Thebes bode ill for his native city (409-11) and especially for his sons (416-52). If they knew of the oracles, then they had all the more reason to bring him back; instead they pursue their own rivalry for the throne, and leave their father an exile.

Oedipus can now combine the oracle that he received in his youth, concerning a grove of the Eumenides as his final resting place (84-110), with the new oracle brought by Ismene. He sees that the efficacy of his burial place here in Colonus will affect Thebes in particular. If the men of Colonus are willing with the goddesses of their deme (δημούχοις 458) to help Oedipus, they will gain a great savior for their city (πόλει 459) and troubles for his (Theban) enemies.[48] As in the prayer already mentioned (106-110), Colonus and Athens are linked. Athens gets the benefit of Oedipus' presence in Colonus.

The men of Colonus now tell Oedipus how to make expiation to the Eumenides (461-64). He must pray to them to be received as a suppliant (488). While the old men question Oedipus about his crimes (Kommos 510-48), Ismene performs the necessary rites on her father's behalf.

Theseus appears on stage immediately after the kommos (549). He speaks for the polis (557) and is a model of graciousness and nobility. He learns of the boon that Oedipus has to offer. Toward the end of their interchange, Theseus specifies the reasons for his acceptance of Oedipus. First, there is a hereditary relationship of xenia (632-33; cf. §9). Second, "having come as a suppliant of the divinities (i.e., the Eumenides in Colonus), you return a not inconsiderable benefit to me and this land (γῇ τῇδε)" (634-45; cf. 487). Therefore "I shall never dismiss the goodwill of this man but shall settle him (κατοικιῶ 637) as ... in the territory (khôra 637)."[49] The offer of settlement in the territory opens two possibilities. Oedipus could stay at Colonus, or he could go with Theseus to Athens (638-41). Oedipus' choice was already implied in Theseus' characterization of him as a "suppliant of the divinities," i.e., Eumenides. It is only, Oedipus explains, by his staying in this place, i.e., near the Eumenides, that he will confer the benefit he has promised. Oedipus now uses khôros (644), in distinction to Theseus' khôra (637), as a way of indicating the particular place in which he wants to stay. But everything depends upon the fact that this particular place is not at all a separate geographic or political entity but belongs to the larger territory.

First Stasimon 668-719

The first stasimon, following upon the agreement of Oedipus and Theseus, now more surely establishes the Colonus-Athens axis that has

---

48. On δημούχοις see Kamerbeek 1984:82, who translates "who protect the deme," even though δῆμος occurs only once in tragedy (*TGF* 2nd ed., frag. adesp. 41). Jebb ad loc. rightly compares δημόταις 78, and says that "the word is tinged here [458] with the notion of 'deme'." How one decides to translate δημούχοις will ultimately depend upon one's view of the function of anachronism in the tragedy; cf. the discussion in the Introduction.

49. The ellipsis in my translation indicates a word (ἔμπαλιν) that may be corrupt. On Musgrave's emendation (ἔμπολιν) see Vidal-Naquet 1986:51-55.

been emerging and to which the presence of Oedipus gives new meaning. R. C. Jebb's summary neatly expresses this point: "The first strophe and antistrophe (668-80 = 681-93) praise Colonus: the second (694-706 = 707-19) praise Attica. But the local theme is skillfully knitted to the national theme. The narcissus and crocus of Colonus introduce the Attic olive (*2nd strophe*). The equestrian fame of Colonus suggests the Attic breed of horses, and this, in turn, suggests Poseidon's other gift to Athens,—the empire of the sea (*2nd antistrophe*)."[50] In other words, two kinds of organization are at work. One is, so to speak, logical: the first pair of strophes is mainly about Colonus; the second pair is about Attica. The other is chiastic: the very first word of the stasimon is εὐίππου (668); horses are one of the themes of the second antistrophe, where this word returns (711; cf. §1 above).

Second Episode 720-1043 (Lyrics 833-43 = 876-86)

Kreon appears. Oedipus delivers a prophetic curse on Kreon, Thebes, and his own sons, according to which their *khôra* will get exactly the opposite of what Attica gets from Oedipus (788 and context). The references to horses and horsemen (897-901 etc.) have been discussed above (§1). Oedipus' speech of self-defense (960-1013) is discussed below apropos of the conditions of Oedipus' forgiveness and acceptance (§10).

Second Stasimon 1044-95

The chorus evokes the clash between the Theban abductors and the Colonan/Athenian rescuers of Ismene and Antigone. They imagine two escape routes that the abductors might have taken, one to the northwest, in the direction of "the Pythian shores," i.e., the bay of Eleusis, and the other almost due north, by "Oea's snowy rock," apparently Mt. Aegaleos (cf. the discussion of the geography in Ch. 2). The chorus in effect gives a panorama of the northern frontier of Attica, all of which they regard as subject to the might of Theseus through his cavalry (cf. §1 above).

Third Episode 1096-1210

Theseus, Antigone, Ismene return. Polyneices is a suppliant at the altar of Poseidon where Theseus had been sacrificing (1157-59). Oedipus is persuaded to hear him out.

50. Jebb 1928:112.

Third Stasimon 1211-48

"Endure what life God gives and ask no longer span" (Yeats).[51] The antistrophe then sketches three phases of life: giddy youth; a middle period beset by "envy, factions, strife, battles, and murders" (φθόνος, στάσεις, ἔρις, μάχαι / καὶ φόνοι 1234-35; cf. the end of §1); friendless (ἄφιλον 1237) old age. To this generic picture of human life, the third phase of which the chorus associates both with themselves and with Oedipus, is linked in the epode the generic simile of a headland lashed by wind and waves from all four points of the compass. The antistrophe and the epode thus establish a polarity between man as a political creature, for the experiences of the middle phase occur in the polis, and man as an object in nature. In Oedipus' case, what has mediated between these extremes is philia, expressed in his daughters' tendance of him (§7). The chorus' generalization about "friendless old age" does not apply to him. But this mediation, as it turns out, was only temporary, serving him in the long period of wandering and suffering between his expulsion from Thebes and his arrival at Colonus. Now, at the end of his life, he is restored to the political through the highly complex mediation of Theseus' reception of him (§§4, 9) and through his cult-partnership with the Eumenides at Colonus (§11).

Fourth Episode 1249-1555

Polyneices entreats his father to give up his anger against him and to return with him to Thebes after he has defeated his brother Eteocles. Oedipus curses him (see §8 below). Polyneices exits, and thunder is heard, the sign of Oedipus' death (cf. 94-95).

Polyneices has two perspectives on Thebes, one positive and one negative. It is his "fatherland" (1291, 1330), and he believes that by primogeniture he has the right to the throne. He is indignant that his younger brother usurped his place "having persuaded the polis" (1298), i.e., having followed the procedure normal in a democracy like Athens. This is the only time that Polyneices ever refers to Thebes as a polis. His claim to return to his native city and to rule there derives directly from kinship. Toward the end of his long entreaty to his father, he implores Oedipus "by the fountains and by the gods of our race" to listen to him (1333). "Of our race (ὁμογνίων)" could apply to the fountains, too.[52] Thebes is thus

---

51. "A Man Young and Old" XI.
52. Lloyd-Jones and Wilson 1990b:255, against Dawe 1978:146-47.

reduced to the private fountains and shrines of the Labdacids. Polyneices is of course unaware that this form of supplication is now completely useless, because Oedipus has turned his back on Thebes. Polyneices was already mistaken at the outset, when he addressed his father as an exile (1255), and again when he equated his condition with his father's (1335-37). Oedipus has now been accepted in several ways as an inhabitant of Attica (§§4, 9-11). In Polyneices' negative perspective on Thebes, the city is simply a military objective (1305, 1312, 1319, 1325). Antigone pleads with him not to destroy the "polis" (1417), but there has been no sign that he can think of Thebes as a polis. She also, sensitive to her brother's point of view, pleads with him not to destroy his "fatherland" (πάτρα 1421, cf. 1291, 1330), but he only restates his principle of primogeniture (1422-23). As an old-style dynast, he has married into the royal family of Argos in order to form a military alliance with that city (1301ff.), and it is an Argive army that he leads against Thebes. Oedipus, for his part, has in effect formed a military alliance with Athens against Thebes (616-23,1533-34), but this is a defensive alliance based on an already existing relationship of xenia (§9).

Thunder sounds, the sign of Oedipus' death (Kommos 1447-56 = 1462-71, 1477-85 = 1491-99). Oedipus summons Theseus. He will show him the spot (khôron [acc.]1520, 1540; cf. topois [dat.] 1523, 1761) where he is to die. Word-order and versification express the link between polis and grave: πόλει / χῶρον (1519-20). It is the link that was prefigured in the phrase "seat in this land" (45). Oedipus' final speech ends with the wish that Theseus, his land (khôra 1553), and his followers may be blessed (cf. the same tripartite division of Athens in the last strophe of the kommos: 1496-99 [discussed in §9]).

Oedipus now walks without a guide, calling upon his daughters to follow him (1542). χωρεῖτε (1543), he commands them. The denominative χωρέω, from khôros, has a factitive sense: "make a place," i.e., "give way." In the context, it is clear that Oedipus refers to creating a space between him and them: "do not touch me, but let me by myself find the sacred tomb" (1543-44). He will use the same verb (which will be discussed below) to dismiss them for the last time, moments before his death (1640-41).

Fourth Stasimon 1556-78

In this stasimon, in which the chorus offers a prayer for Oedipus' safe journey to the underworld, the mythical geography of that place is recodified in the form of a katabasis of Oedipus (cf. Ch. 2). Because his starting-point on earth is the grove of the Eumenides, it is appropriate that they call upon the χθόνιαι θεαί and Cerberus (1568-69). The scholiast identifies the former with the Erinyes, by which he must mean the Eumenides of Colonus (cf. §11). These goddesses are perceived not in their horizontal relation to Athens but in their vertical relation to the underworld, a new geography that Oedipus will have to traverse—the gates guarded by the dog (1569), the plain of the dead (1564, 1577), and the Stygian house (1564). In the phrase, "son [whoever this person is] of Earth and Tartarus" (1574), Earth is hardly the earth (γῆ) so often used in a political sense in this play, as a synonym of *khôra*, but a personification of the physical earth with its life-giving and -receiving depths. The relationship that Oedipus has secured on the surface of the earth, a political one, in terms of places, Colonus, Athens, and Thebes, he must now confirm in another place, beneath the surface of the earth.

Exodos 1579-1779

The messenger who reports the miraculous death of Oedipus begins his speech: ἄνδρες πολῖται "citizens" or "men of the polis" (1579). The messenger speaks from the perspective of the city, as did the chorus at the time of the rescue of Ismene and Antigone from their Theban kidnappers (1095: the only other use of πολῖται in this play). Now that Oedipus is dead and the bargain is fulfilled, life returns to normal. It only remains for the messenger to describe what happened, and for the daughters to end their grief and return to Thebes.

Oedipus departed without a human guide, indeed as the guide of the others, himself led by Hermes and Persephone (1587-89, cf. 1544-48). His goal was the bronze-fitted threshold (1590) to the Underworld, after which, by metonymy, the *topos* on which Oedipus first tread, a grove of the Eumenides, was called "the bronze-stepped way of this land, the bulwark of Athens" (55b-58). When he reached the "sheer threshold" (1590), he stopped in one of the many branching byways nearby (κελεύθων ἐν πολυσχίστων μιᾷ ὁδός 1592). "We are reminded, perhaps designedly, of that σχιστὴ ὁδός in Phocis at which the misfortunes of his early manhood began (*OT* 733)."[53] This stopping-point rounds off not only the action of *Oedipus at Colonus* but of the life of Oedipus from the time of his parricide. He was now near the cup-shaped hollow, where there was a memorial of some sort (the text does not make it clear) to the

53. Jebb 1928:245.

pledges exchanged by Perithous and Theseus when they went down to Hades to carry off Persephone (1593-94). These landmarks, the hollow in the rock (whence Perithous and Theseus had descended?) and the memorial, then become the reference-point for a still more precise description of Oedipus' stopping place (στάς 1595, cf. ἔστη 1592). This place is coordinated with the "Thorician rock," "the hollow pear tree," and the "stone tomb" (1595).[54] The text, the syntax in any acceptable form of the text, and the topographical references all cause difficulty. As for the last of these, the scholiast despaired: "these things are known to the locals." Indeed, the great specificity of the messenger's description renders Oedipus' location vague to Sophocles' audience and to us, while the Colonan elders to whom the messenger speaks are implicitly represented as the ones who know exactly what he means.[55] The messenger's precise topography thus conceals the location of Oedipus' grave at the same time that it confirms Oedipus' death in Colonus.

The sentence under discussion concludes "he sat down" (καθέζετ' 1597). The simplex, ἕζομαι, is from the same root (*sed) as ἕδρα "seat." Oedipus has taken the "seat in this land" (45) that was destined for him. He never moves again. He summons Theseus to him (1630) and he sends his daughters away from (1640-41). And yet there comes a voice that bids him move. The messenger reports the mysterious voice of a god who called out to Oedipus: ὦ οὗτος οὗτος, Οἰδίπους, τί μέλλομεν / χωρεῖν; (1627-28). The denominative χωρέω here has the same facitive sense as above at 1543): "make a place (khôros)," i.e., "give way," "leave the place you are in." In order finally to occupy the place to the securing of which he has devoted so much effort, he must absent that place, as a geographical location, and go into the underworld. Likewise, in the geographical dimension in which they remain, the daughters must retire from that place, which it is not right for them to see. Oedipus says to them: χωρεῖν τόπων ἐκ τῶνδε (1641). But the verb has different meanings for the Oedipus and for his daughters. For the latter, to make a place is again to give their father a place by separating themselves laterally from him. For Oedipus, however, to make a place is physically to leave the surface of the earth but with the result that the very spot from which he departed becomes a new place that will have special powers precisely because Oedipus is not entirely absent from that place but will continue to act from it (perhaps to appear from it [cf. §2]).

---

54. For the sexual theme, see Nagy 1990a:231-32.
55. Cf. Jebb 1928:247.

Antigone and Ismene lament (Kommos 1670-1750). Theseus enters and reassures them (Anapests 1751-79).

∞ ∞ ∞ ∞ ∞ ∞

In the recodifying of the political-geographical map, there are three principal moments. One, on the international scale, is the redefinition of the relations between Thebes and Athens, which become hostile or potentially hostile, so that Oedipus' revulsion against his native city becomes another guarantee of his benefit to Athens. Thebes, in implicit contrast to Athens, is defined as the site of self-destructive dynastic quarrels into which the rest of Greece can be drawn, as Polyneices' alliance with Argos shows.[56] Another moment is the redrawing of the map of Colonus so that, remaining as a whole a cult center of Poseidon (with the Stranger's words at 54-55 cf. Thuc. 8.67.2), it is divided by the difference between a more limited sacred ground (the grove of the Eumenides) and a profane ground. *Oedipus at Colonus* is in fact the earliest evidence for a grove of the Eumenides at Colonus, which, if it already existed and was not invented by Sophocles, is given a new prominence.[57] While the bronze-fitted threshold retains what was probably its customary place in the old map, within the grove, it gains new validity from the nearby grave of Oedipus, a new point on the map. Because the grave of Oedipus is the crucial thing for Colonus as bulwark of Attica, the grove as point of entrance to the underworld must be stressed—thus, in addition to the threshold, the allusion to the katabasis of Perithous and Theseus and the invocation of the Eumenides as chthonic goddesses. The effect of the division of Colonus into sacred and profane ground, where sacred means above all the grove of the Eumenides, is to qualify the importance of the received designation of Colonus as a cult center of Poseidon, i.e., as the Knights' cult center. The third moment is the recodifying of the altar of Poseidon, which, in terms of theatrical space, is close by the part of Colonus represented by the stage. Though Colonus can boast that Poseidon first tamed horses here (713-15; a euphemistic recoding of the myth of Poseidon's begetting of the first horse at Colonus), the altar of Poseidon is not the focus of Knights' activity; rather, Theseus sacrifices at it with the whole people (887-99) and the author of synoikismos is assumed to be devoted to this god (cf. 1494). The altar serves as asylum

---

56. Cf. Zeitlin 1990.
57. See Segal 1981:371 n. 31 for discussion and bibliography; also Kearns (cited in §2 above).

for Polyneices (1158). In these ways, then, the political-geographical map that Sophocles expected that his spectators would bring with them to the theater is quite drastically redrawn and resemanticized.

The following seven sections of this monograph (§§4-10) show how, within the large-scale recoding of myth and place, the reception of Oedipus in Colonus is expressed by means of various legal and social codes. These are in some cases (exile; enktêsis; political dishonor; the right to support by sons) encoded in an abbreviated and anagrammatic fashion, because they are anachronistic in the representation of the heroic age that must be preserved and that must predominate. Further, the canon of tragic diction does not always admit the contemporary language of the code. In other cases, those of philia and xenia, the adoption of the code by the tragedy is much fuller. Indeed, certain aspects of philia are recodified in *Oedipus at Colonus* in such a way that its connection with the family is qualified and it is now located in two separate spheres, the physical and emotional (represented by Oedipus' physical reliance on and physical contact with his daughters; cf. Ch. 2 on the spatial representation thereof) and the political (represented by xenia as the form of a new philia between Oedipus and Theseus). The denial of obligatory philia within the family is represented not only by Oedipus' repudiation of genos-connections in his reply to Kreon (§6) but also in his curse on his sons. At this point, another code comes into play, which is awkwardly combined with the various political and social codes (cf. the remarks on Theseus in the Conclusion). In cursing his sons, Oedipus takes on the character of the avenging hero that he will become post mortem and his action is expressed in terms of a cultic code that links him with the Eumenides/Erinyes (§11). Curiously, the code of contemporary political rhetoric, in particular the promise of soteria, is melded with this encoding of the cult (§12).

In the deployment of several of these codes, intertextuality (as I have noted) has a role, as is hardly surprising, because they already had a long history in Greek literature when Sophocles composed *Oedipus at Colonus*. Indeed, this tragedy is densely intertextual, as Di Benedetto in particular has shown, and this aspect of its style is consonant with the kind of self-consciousness demonstrated in Chapter Two above. The effect of intertextuality in the contexts in which I have had occasion to refer to it is to corroborate the particular encoding and/or recoding. The contemporary reference of the code does not disappear in autotelic "poetic" allusion. (I assume that few readers would now take such a view of the matter in any case.) Thus intertextuality enhances the apologetic and conciliatory tendency of this tragedy.

§4 Exile and ἔγκτησις

In relation to his sons and his native city, Oedipus is an exile (443): 430, 444, 590 (Theseus, apropos of Oedipus and Thebes), 599-601, 1257 (Polyneices of Oedipus), 1335 (Polyneices of Oedipus and himself). In what way can Oedipus the Theban exile be received in Athens? Following the lead of Pierre Vidal-Naquet, I look to Athenian law providing for foreigners', including political exiles', ownership of land and houses in Attic territory.[58] The legal status of Oedipus in Athens, to which Vidal-Naquet devoted considerable study,[59] removing various misconceptions established in scholarship on the subject, will thus be strictly related to the concern with the location of Oedipus within Attica and the relation of Colonus to Athens.

The existence of the law or laws in question is inferred from the formula for the grant of ἔγκτησις found in many Attic inscriptions. The oldest of these permits the building of a shrine to Bendis (*IG* II².1283); most of the others are for private property. Of the four possible fifth-century examples of this grant, the second-oldest comes from 409/408, and thus belongs to the events assumed to be the background of *Oedipus at Colonus*. This inscription, amongst other things, rewards the assassins of Phrynichos (nineteen months after the assassination).[60] A certain Thrasyboulos (not the general and statesman) is singled out for several privileges; then in a rider he and his accomplices also receive the grant under discussion. The relevant lines run as follows:

> Let the secretary of the Boule have their names engraved as
> benefactors on a marble stele in the city. And let them have
> possession of the same things as the Athenians, lands and a
> dwelling, and let them have habitation in Athens, and let the Boule
> and the prytaneis who are in power at any given time have care of
> them, in order that they may not be treated unjustly.
>
> *IG* I².110+.28-34[61]

The formula as restored in this inscription differs somewhat from the one found in thirty-odd fourth-century inscriptions: γῆς καὶ οἰκίας ἔγκτησιν (the word-order varies). Ἀθένεσι(ν) is often found. *Epimeleia*, not in the

---

58. Vidal-Naquet 1986:59-63.
59. Vidal-Naquet 1986:49-63.
60. Meiggs-Lewis 1975:262-63 for the historical problems.
61. From Pečírka 1966:19. My generalizations about the grant are based on Pečírka, especially pp. 137-59.

text quoted above, is a typical award. Provision is often made for descendants. Political exiles, to repeat, are a category of recipient.

Though the canon of tragic diction does not allow the formula for the grant to appear as such in *Oedipus at Colonus*, Oedipus' various demands for settlement in Colonus amount to a periphrasis. One of Oedipus' first questions is whether the place is habitable (ἐξοικήσιμος 27), though at this point he wonders if there are inhabitants for Antigone to consult.[62] The oracle had told him that through his dwelling (οἰκήσαντα 92) there he would be a gain to those who received him (cf. 627). He wants a "seat in this land" (ἕδρας γῆς τῆσδ' 45).[63] The matter is finally decided when Theseus says that he will "settle" (κατοικιῶ 638) Oedipus in Attica. Oedipus is given the chance to go to the home of Theseus but chooses to remain in the particular place in Colonus that the oracle had predicted. Oedipus has thus received the equivalent of the grant of *enktêsis*, although it is for a grave, not a house, and in return not for services rendered but for services that he will render in the future. Oedipus in effect requests *epimeleia* when he says τὰ λοιπά μου / μέλου δικαίως (1137-38).

In sum, while the grant can hardly be expressed as such in tragic diction, it is, in various synonyms, encoded anagrammatically in the tragedy.

§5 ἀτιμία

As an exile (cf. beginning of preceding section), Oedipus can describe his experience in terms that Sophocles' contemporaries well knew. Oedipus curses his sons

οἵ γε τὸν φύσαντ' ἐμὲ
οὕτως ἀτίμως πατρίδος ἐξωθούμενον
οὐκ ἔσχον οὐδ' ἤμυναν, ἀλλ' ἀνάστατος
αὐτοῖν ἐπέμφθην κἀξεκηρύχθην φύγας.

427-30

---

62. As P. E. Easterling has pointed out to me.
63. Where the word means a permanent seat, not a temporary one, as in the Stranger's use (36; cf. the chorus at 176, 232). For Oedipus' use of ἕδρα cf. 84, 90. He also uses it of the suppliancy of Polyneices (1163, 1166); it is one of several parallels between him and his son that make the son's situation the inverse of his own.

Historical Place in Oedipus at Colonus 115

because, when I, the one who begot them,
was thrust in such dishonor[64] from the fatherland,
they did not stop me nor did they defend me, but uprooted,
for all they cared, I was sent away, and proclaimed an exile.

The language is political. All of the main terms (ἀτιμ- [cf. §1], ἐξωθέω, ἀνάστατος, ἐκκηρύσσω) are paralleled in Herodotus, Thucydides, and the orators. Oedipus will never return from exile to his native city, but, through the right to inhabit Attica (cf. preceding section) and through various other modes of acceptance (cf. §§7, 9-10 below), he ceases to be an exile.

But before the reparation of his diminished civil rights can take place through these mechanisms, Oedipus has to face another kind of *atimia*. In questioning the Stranger about the place that he and Antigone have reached, Oedipus begins

πρός νυν θεῶν, ὦ ξεῖνε, μή μ' ἀτιμάσῃς,
τοιόνδ' ἀλήτην, ὧν σε προστρέπω φράσαι.

49-50

For the gods' sake, stranger, deem me not unworthy,
beggar that I am, of the honor of the things that I beg you to tell.[65]

The dishonor that Oedipus fears is closely connected with his status as a beggar. He fears to be what epic calls an ἀτίμητος μετανάστης (*Il.* 9.648 = 16.59; cf. *OC* 174-75: ὦ ξεῖνοι μὴ ... ἀδικηθῶ[66] / ... μετανάστας "Strangers, let me not be wronged, removed [from my place]"). The Homeric model for Oedipus' situation is, however, Odysseus the *xenos* dishonored in his own house when he returns disguised as a beggar. The relation of the tragedy to the *Odyssey* is already signaled in the opening lines, as Vincenzo Di Benedetto has shown, stressing the shared themes of wandering and suffering.[67] The dishonoring of the beggar, whether feared or experienced, is another shared theme, and intertextuality is a way of recoding *atimia*, a widely used and abused contemporary punishment (cf. §1), as a heroic age experience.

---

64. English does not have a word with the same range of meanings as ἀτίμ-, viz. from loss of civil rights to scorn, etc. Here "dishonor" and verbal forms thereof are a stopgap.

65. For the syntax see Kamerbeek's note ad loc.

66. "The verb, known from Hdt. and Thuc., is a ἅπαξ in Tragedy": Kamerbeek ad loc. Cf. the political language of 427-30, quoted above.

67. Di Benedetto 1979 and 1983:217-19. Cf. *Vita Soph.* 20.

Both Odysseus and Oedipus are beggars who hide great power beneath their rags. Oedipus says to the chorus, begging not to be driven away:

μηδέ μου κάρα
τὸ δυσπρόσοπτον εἰσορῶν <u>ἀτιμάσῃς</u>.
ἥκω γὰρ ἱερὸς εὐσεβής τε καὶ φέρων
ὄνησιν ἀστοῖς τοῖσδ'

285-88

Nor
dishonor me beholding my face, horrid to look upon.
For I have come as one holy and pious and bearing
advantage to these people.

As in lines 49–50, quoted above, outward physical repulsiveness expects dishonor (cf. 1378–79). When Odysseus returns to Ithaca as a beggar, his appearance has this very effect. The swineherds dishonor him (ἀτιμάζουσι) because of his squalor and garments (14.506).[68] Odysseus' vengeance on the suitors involves his going to them as a "wretched beggar or old man" (16.273), and Telemachus must endure it if they dishonor (ἀτιμήσουσι) his father (16.274–77), as they have been doing (cf. 23.28). After the test of the bow, Odysseus says to his son:

Τηλέμαχ', οὔ σ' ὁ <u>ξεῖνος</u> ἐνὶ μεγάροισιν ἐλέγχει
ἥμενος, οὐδέ τι τοῦ σκοποῦ ἤμβροτον οὐδέ τι τόξον
δὴν ἔκαμον τανύων· ἔτι μοι μένος ἔμπεδόν ἐστιν,
οὐχ ὡς με μνηστῆρες <u>ἀτιμάζοντες</u> ὄνονται.

21.424-27

Telemachus, the stranger sitting in the hall does not disgrace
you, nor did he at all miss the mark nor toil long
stringing the bow. There is still strength within me,
not as the suitors scorned me, dishonoring me.

Moments later, he strips off his rags, and the slaughter begins (22.1ff.)

The ethico-religious principle violated by the suitors is clearly articulated by Eumaeus, when he says to Odysseus:

<u>ξεῖν'</u>, οὔ μοι θέμις ἔστ', οὐδ' εἰ κακίων σέθεν ἔλθοι,
<u>ξεῖνον</u> <u>ἀτιμῆσαι</u>· πρὸς γὰρ Διός εἰσιν ἅπαντες

---

68. Consider also 20.166–67, where "looking at" means accepting and is the opposite of "dishonoring."

ξεῖνοί τε πτωχοί τε· δόσις δ' ὀλίγη τε φίλη τε
γίγνεται ἡμετέρη

14.56-59

Stranger, it is not meet in my view, even if someone baser than
   you should come,
to dishonor a stranger. For from Zeus are all
strangers and beggars. My gift is "small but kindly."[69]

The Stranger in *Oedipus at Colonus*, beseeched as such by Oedipus in lines 49-50 (quoted above), knows the principle. He replies: σήμαινε, κοὐκ ἄτιμος ἔκ γ' ἐμοῦ φανεῖ "speak, and, as far as I am concerned, you will not be dishonored (of your request)" (51). Addressing the man of Colonus as *xeinos* (49), Oedipus by a speech act establishes the relationship to which he expects the man to conform.

This simple hospitality, protecting the stranger from dishonor, even if he is a beggar and physically repulsive, precedes, in *Oedipus at Colonus*, another kind of xenia that emerges as Theseus and Oedipus renew a traditional guest-friendship (see §9 below). The acceptance of Oedipus as he appears, with its mere concession of the right not to be dislodged, precedes his complex, highly overdetermined or overcoded installation as a politically sanctioned inhabitant of Attica (cf. the preceding section) and as a cult partner of the Eumenides (cf. §11 below). The wandering of the blind beggar onto the stage at the very beginning of the tragedy already dramatizes the various modes of his arrival (and thus points to the various conditions of his acceptance)—it is the wandering of the Odyssean beggar, of the political exile, and of the future cult hero.[70]

§6 Philia (1)

The kidnapping of Oedipus' daughters is, from one point of view, the chorus' (842, 879, 884) and Theseus' (911-23), an illegal act of plunder against a sovereign state. From another, Kreon's, it is an act of retaliation (ἀντιδρᾶν) for Oedipus' refusal to return to Thebes and for his curses on Kreon and his race (951-53). Though Kreon cannot take Oedipus by force, because Oedipus is protected by the Athenians (815), Kreon's sei-

---

69. "Kindly" (φίλη), i.e., "such as one would give to a *philos*." Cf. §§6-7 below on philia.
70. Edmunds 1981:229-30 on the wandering of heroes.

zure of Ismene and Antigone is justified, he believes, because they are his (830, 832)—he is their guardian.

Kreon characterizes what he takes to be Oedipus' disloyalty rather precisely in terms of philia. Oedipus ought to have replied differently to a *philos* like Kreon (813).[71] Oedipus has turned against his fatherland and his *philoi* (850). He has acted in despite of *philoi* (854). Indeed, as soon as Oedipus learned of the approach of Kreon, he called upon the chorus as φίλτατοι γέροντες (724), and, when Theseus came to the rescue, Oedipus addressed him as φίλτατ' (891, 1103). Oedipus has, in fact, abandoned old *philoi* and found new ones, just as Polyneices found "warrior *philoi* and a new kinship" in Argos (379). Oedipus is himself an example of those changes of spirit ἐν ἀνδράσιν / φίλοις (612-13) of which he had warned Theseus. If one leaves aside the question of justice,[72] Kreon's assessment of the situation is correct.

Another way to state the change in Oedipus' relation to Thebes is in terms of family. Kreon says that he was sent by the Thebans because he was expected as a relative (he was Oedipus' brother-in-law and uncle) to feel the most pity for him (γένει 738). Oedipus, Kreon says, is a shame for their whole family (γένος 754). Oedipus, however, rebukes Kreon for his insincerity. When Oedipus was content to live out his days in Thebes, then it was that Kreon expelled him. τὸ συγγενὲς τοῦτ' οὐδαμῶς τότ' ἦν φίλον "Then this kinship of which you speak was in no way dear" (770). Oedipus can now curse Kreon and Kreon's family (γένος 868) as if Oedipus did not belong to it (cf. 951-53, cited above). He distinguishes between the gods' possible anger at his family (γένος 965) as a cause of his misfortune and his own responsibility.

Oedipus' new philia in Athens thus represents a break with his *genos* that was initiated by Kreon (770) and that his sons did nothing to mend. Oedipus' experience has a close parallel in that of Orestes, who in the Euripidean tragedy of that name, is disappointed in his expectations of his uncle Menelaus and of course has nothing to expect from his grandfather Tyndareus now that he has killed his mother, Clytemnestra, Tyndareus' daughter. Moved by Pylades' expression of friendship (n.b. φίλος 802), Orestes says

τοῦτ' ἐκεῖνο, κτᾶσθ' ἑταίρους, μὴ τὸ συγγενὲς μόνον·

---

71. On the text of 813 see Mastronarde 1979:73, who argues plausibly that γε should be read. L-J-W 1990a read Musgrave's δέ for reasons given in L-J-W 1990b on 813.
72. For a good discussion of this question, see Blundell 1989:232-38.

ὡς ἀνὴρ ὅστις τρόποισι συντακῇ θυραῖος ὤν
μυρίων κρείσσων ὁμαίμων ἀνδρὶ κεκτῆσθαι φίλος.

804-806

That's it—get yourself comrades, not just kin.
Since the man who's fused to you by character, though an outsider,
is a better friend to have than ten thousand close relatives.

It is already clear by the mid-point of the play that Orestes' principle will culminate in a *hetaireia* (the word occurs at 1072 and 1079 for the only times in Euripides)—the gang of three consisting of himself, Pylades, and Electra.[73] Whereas Orestes corresponded to the Oedipus of *Oedipus at Colonus* in the first half of *Orestes*, he will now, as the gang begins to hatch its plot, correspond rather to Kreon.

In particular, the taking of a hostage by Orestes and his companions resembles Kreon's kidnapping of Oedipus' two daughters. Electra proposes that, in order to inhibit Menelaus' retaliation after they have killed Helen, they seize Hermione, Helen's and Menelaus' daughter (ὅμηρον 1189). While Ismene and Antigone are not, strictly speaking, hostages, because Kreon has no intention of returning them, they belong, equally with Hermione, to a plan of retaliation for the perceived betrayal of philia on the part of the girls' father. No one has doubted that the *hetaireia* of *Orestes* reflects contemporary Athenian politics. Because Kreon is in other respects (cf. §10) a contemporary politician, his kidnapping of Ismene and Antigone ought to be seen in the same light as the hostage-taking in *Orestes*.

Sophocles has, then, represented the conflict between Oedipus and Kreon by means of an established code of philia. According to this code, both are right. Kreon violated philia when he drove Oedipus into exile many years ago. From Kreon's point of view, Oedipus now violates it by refusing to return to Thebes. Kreon's assumption is that philia cannot be abrogated. Kreon is justified in his kidnapping of Ismene and Antigone because they are "his own." The same philia-based claims of the family on which he expected Oedipus peaceably to act justify his violence toward his nieces. In this way, Sophocles shows up internal contradictions in the code of philia, which as in *Orestes*, proves to be a poor guide to political action. But Sophocles also recodes philia in *Oedipus at Colonus* in the form of two positive models, to be discussed in the next

---

73. See Longo 1975 for an analysis of philia and *hetaireia* in this tragedy.

section, one the relation between Oedipus and Theseus, the other the relation between Oedipus and his daughters.

Addendum on kidnapping

Orestes himself was once a hostage.[74] Telephus, in the Euripidean tragedy of that name (438 B.C.E.), king of the Mysians, having entered the Greek camp in Argos in disguise, obtained a hearing by seizing the child Orestes and taking refuge at an altar. The scene had a grip on the mind of Aristophanes, who parodied it in *Acharnians* (425 B.C.E.) and a good many years later in *Thesmophoriazusae* (411 B.C.E.). A real-life precedent or parallel was Themistocles' suppliancy in the house of Admetos, king of the Molossians (Thuc. 1.136-37). Admetos' wife instructed Themistocles to take her child and sit at the hearth—this was, says Thucydides, the most urgent form of supplication (1.137.1). Though the child was not really a hostage, because no death-threat was attached to Themistocles' deed, which the child's mother had initiated, some connection with the *Telephus* has always been suggested—the historical event influenced the tragedy or the tragedy influenced the biographical tradition of Themistocles.

Further, the Aristophanic and the Themistoclean "hostages" have been compared with Hermione in *Orestes*, though Hermione is not an infant and Orestes and his companions are not suppliants. The comparison between *Orestes* and *Oedipus at Colonus* offered here, however, is based on the representation in these tragedies of a political phenomenon that appears rather often in Greek literature—the betrayal of philia. For hostage-taking as retaliation for such betrayal, no real-life comparandum is available, and yet it is certain that, under conditions of stasis, a superior third party might take hostages as a way of controlling one of the factions, i.e., that hostage-taking might be a form of action in a situation like the one in the second half of *Orestes*, which, as Oddone Longo has shown, conforms remarkably closely in several ways to the generalized account of stasis given by Thucydides (3.82-83).[75] In the summer of 412 B.C.E., the Athenians suppressed the revolt of Chios, for which city Thucydides gave an eloquent apologia (8.24.4-5). Blockaded by sea and devasted in its territory, some of the Chians attempted to bring the city over to the Athenians. The Chian archontes, perceiving the design, did

---

74. And in the fourth epeisodion of *Andromache* (802-1008) Orestes takes Hermione away from the house of her husband Neoptolemus.
75. Longo 1975. He does not mention Thuc. 8.24-38.

nothing themselves (ἡσύχασαν), but sent for the Spartan admiral Astyochos and considered with him "how they might most moderately (μετριώτατα) put an end to the (pro-Athenian) plot (ἐπιβουλήν), either by taking hostages (ὁμηρῶν λήψει) or in some other way" (8.31.1). Astyochos then proceeded to choose hostages (8.31.1). Later in the summer, the Spartans sent Pedaritos to Chios as magistrate (8.28.5). Whether because of changes in Chian politics or because of his own administrative style or both, he executed Tydeus the son of Ion and his faction on the charge of Atticism, and the rest of the Chians were subjected to an oligarchy by force (8.38.3).

§7 Philia (2)

In an influential article, Emile Benveniste took the relations between xenoi as a key to the understanding of philia.[76] To be sure, the relations of xenia between Oedipus and Theseus make them *philoi*[77] in this exclusive, aristocratic institution, and yet the chorus can envisage a broader form of these relations. As they try to coax Oedipus out of the grove of the Eumenides, they say:

τόλμα ξεῖνος ἐπὶ ξένης,
ὦ τλάμων, ὅ τι καὶ πόλις
τέτροφεν ἄφιλον ἀποστυγεῖν
καὶ τὸ φίλον σέβεσθαι.

184-87

Endure, stranger in a strange land,
o wretched one, to loathe
whatever the city holds in settled dislike
and to reverence what it holds dear.[78]

---

76. Benveniste 1969:341: "Nous ferons usage pour définir cette notion [of *philótēs*, which in later Greek is philia] d'un indice précieux que nous fournit la phraséologie homérique; c'est la liaison entre *phílos* et *xénos*, entre *phileîn* et *xenízein*. Formulons d'emblée ce que cette liaison enseigne dans nombre d'emplois: la notion de *phílos* énonce le comportement obligé d'un membre de la communauté à l'égard du *xénos*, de l' "hôte" étranger. Telle est la définition que nous proposons." A bibliography on philia can be found in the first note (unnumbered) of Robinson 1990, in which, however, Taillardat 1982 is omitted.
77. 607, 891, 1169, 1552, 1631. See also Giangiulio 1992.
78. My translation borrows phrases from Jebb's notes ad loc. For the attribution of these lines to the chorus see Jebb and Kamerbeek ad loc.

While the chorus consists of men of Colonus with considerable local pride, they speak for the polis, for all of Athens. The reference of their words is to Athenian nomos (cf. 168), with which Oedipus should conform. As a xenos, then, Oedipus is not someone who will enter into a privileged relation, as in the case of his xenia with Theseus; rather, he will defer to the "otherness" of the foreign city in which he finds himself. And yet this city's customs are presented in terms of philia, and Oedipus is invited to share the beliefs of the Athenians. This participation entails, of course, like any form of philia, a sharp distinction between *philon* and *aphilon*, with the corresponding emotional reactions.

The notion of a city's customs and beliefs as a form of philia in which all the citizens participate does not have many parallels. In one of the prooemial poems of the Theognidea, however, the Muses and Charites sing this "beautiful line" (16) at the wedding of Cadmus: "ὅττι καλὸν φίλον ἐστί, τὸ δ' οὐ καλὸν οὐ φίλον ἐστί" "'what is beautiful is *philon*, what is not beautiful is not *philon*'" (17). This marriage is one of the founding events of Thebes, and this line is tantamount to a charter for the city (leaving aside the question of its implications for Megara and the Theognidea). As in the chorus' words to Oedipus, the opposition between that which is and that which is not *philon* is fundamental. The city establishes the *philon* as the standard, and the citizens only have to know what that standard requires. (In Oedipus' case, it is only a particular rule concerning a particular locale.) The *philon* thus has the function of stabilizing and harmonizing the city.[79] Cadmus' wife is Harmonia. (Oedipus' behavior toward the Eumenides must conform to that of the Athenians.)

The ideal implicit in the chorus' words and advocated by the Muses and Charites is fundamentally unstable, because, as the very form of the expression of this ideal shows, philia entails the notion of opposition. In later attestations of the Muses' and Charites' "beautiful line," it is a proverb for pursuing one's own advantage or getting vengeance on one's enemies, and even within the Theognidea the city of Megara is represented as polarized into two groups, Theognis' friends and his enemies.[80] Benveniste's article provides a set of data which incidentally shows why philia always presupposes opposition, division, and hostility. Before he addresses the problem of the semantics of Homeric *philos*, Benveniste discusses a group of words derived from IE *keiwo-s*: Gothic *heiwa-* "familial group"; Sanskrit *śeva* "amicable, dear," referring to relations between groups; and Latin *civis* "citizen." He states: "there is, as it were,

---

79. Nagy 1985:27–28.
80. Cf. Edmunds 1985b:102–103.

a progression in three stages from the narrow group to the city." He proceeds to speak of the Greek *philos* as belonging to "this same category" of words.[81] And yet it is precisely in its restriction to groups within the city that *philos* is distinguished from the Latin *civis*. Only very rarely— the two places discussed above may be the only examples—does *philos* refer to the whole city, and citizenship is certainly outside its semantic range.

In *Oedipus at Colonus*, Oedipus' fulfillment of his destiny and his future benefit to Athens depend upon his personal relations of philia and xenia with Theseus in particular. At the outset, as Oedipus and the chorus await the arrival of Theseus, Oedipus links his goals to his expectation that Theseus will be motivated by one of the principles of philia:

ἀλλ' εὐτυχὴς ἵκοιτο τῇ θ' αὑτοῦ πόλει
ἐμοί τε· τίς γὰρ ἐσθλὸς οὐχ αὑτῷ φίλος;

308–309

Well, may he come with blessings to his city
and to me. For what noble man is not *philos* to himself?

As Jebb well explained, Oedipus does not complete the thought of the wish expressed in the first of these sentences, viz., that, if Theseus accepts Oedipus, he will have acquired a benefit for his city. Instead, Oedipus elliptically[82] adds a generalization about the nobleman, that he is a *philos* to himself, viz. that he will act in his own self-interest, which, in this case, will mean his acceptance of Oedipus with the consequent benefit to his city. Although the relationship of the two sentences is somewhat strained at the level of plain sense, the connecting thought is expressed in the versification by the parallelism of the final words of the two lines:

αὑτοῦ πόλει
αὑτῷ φίλος.[83]

Oedipus has, in effect, hypothesized a motive for Theseus' welcome of him that would accord with what may be the central ethical principle of philia: reciprocity. Hesiod says:

---

81. Benveniste 1969:337. Critique of Benveniste in Hooker 1987:57–63.
82. γὰρ: "(and I think he will come with blessings), for ..." Cf. Denniston 1966:60–62 (sections III.1–2).
83. Since φ was pronounced as *p* + aspiration, the parallelism of πόλει and φίλος was stronger acoustically than appears on the printed page.

τὸν φιλέοντα φιλεῖν καὶ τῷ προσιόντι προσεῖναι,
καὶ δόμεν ὅς κεν δῷ, καὶ μὴ δόμεν ὅς κεν μὴ δῷ.

OD 353-54

Be a *philos* to a *philos*, and give your company to him that seeks it,[84]
and give to the one who gives, and do not give to the one who does not give.

This fundamental principle of reciprocity is also the point of contact between philia and xenia, for the latter word comes from the etymon *$k^w sen(-w)$-* "to give one thing for another."[85]

When Oedipus has to argue, on the basis of the future disintegration of friendly relations between Thebes and Athens, for the value of his burial in Attica, it is remarkable that he assumes that Theseus is more familiar with philia than with international relations (cf. his pact with Peirithous: 1594). Oedipus says to Theseus:

φθίνει μὲν ἰσχὺς γῆς, φθίνει δὲ σώματος,
θνῄσκει δὲ πίστις, βλαστάνει δ' ἀπιστία,
καὶ πνεῦμα ταὐτὸν οὔποτ' ἐν ἀνδράσιν
φίλοις βέβηκεν οὔτε πρὸς πόλιν πόλει.

610-13

The strength of the earth dwindles, and the strength of the body,
and trust dies and distrust grows up,
and the same breeze does not prevail
between friends or between cities.

Oedipus' introduction of philia as the climactic illustration of change begins already in line 611, with his reference to trust succeeded by distrust. For in the traditional conception of philia, trust is the sine qua non.[86] Oedipus' assumptions concerning Theseus appear later in this same speech: before Theseus asserts the hereditary xenia (631ff.) discussed in section 9 below, Oedipus already tries to put his relations with Theseus on the basis of philia. Though he cannot, he says, reveal further secrets concerning his future benefit to Athens, he asks Theseus to guard his trustworthiness (πιστόν 626) toward Oedipus. In this context, in which the cycles of philia and trust have already been established as norms of

---

84. My translation is from West 1978 ad loc.
85. Schwartz 1982.
86. Taillardat 1982 proposed an etymological connection between πιστ- and φιλ-.

human behavior (in the passage just quoted), Theseus will have to understand that his general offer of assistance (560f.), which was not, however, an offer of philia, is now being accepted as precisely that. When, with meiosis, Oedipus says that Theseus will never say that he received him as a useless inhabitant of this place (626-28), Oedipus in effect avows that he is an aristocratic χρηστός "good, serviceable man" (cf. 1014) of the sort that Theseus knows, one who can help his friends, unlike the rich man scorned by Theognis, whose wealth is of use neither to himself or to his friends (philoi).[87]

Oedipus' request is, however, highly overdetermined (cf. conclusion of §5). As "inhabitant" not only will he receive the right of enktêsis (cf. §4 above), he will also be the traditional aristocratic philos; and he will also be the cultic "inhabitant" of the grove of the Eumenides (cf. §11 below).

Oedipus' relationship of philia with Theseus stands in contrast to another kind of philia, that of Oedipus and his daughters. While Oedipus' relations with his sons (negative) are often, and rightly, contrasted with his relations with his daughters (positive), the bond between Oedipus and Theseus (positive) is of a different sort from the father-daughter relationship (positive), even though both are repeatedly characterized in terms of philia. The former can be called political; the latter is familial. For Antigone, the basis of philia is the family. When the chorus, in dismay at Oedipus' invasion of the grove of the Eumenides, try to drive him from their land, Antigone intercedes, beseeching them in the name of whatever is philon to them, whether it is a child or ...[88] Child is the first item in Antigone's list of things that may be philon, and the relationship of child and parent is primary in her sense of philia. (Appropriately, the chorus reply to her as "child of Oedipus" [254].) Interceding, as a philos (cf. 1194) for Polyneices, she reminds Oedipus of what he had to suffer because of his parents: he should not be as bad as they were (1195ff.). In his reply, Oedipus addresses her as "child," and says that he will do what is philon to her and Polyneices (1204-1205). ὦ πάτερ, ὦ φίλος "o

---

87. Theognis 865-67. On the principle of usefulness, cf. Edmunds 1985b:98. In the aristocratic constitution of the Cretan city of Dreros (650-600 B.C.E.), a man who holds the office of kosmos for a second time within ten years will, amongst other things, be held ἄκρηστον (Meiggs-Lewis 2). The principle was appropriated by the Athenian democracy: Thuc. 2.40.2.

88. The text of 250-51 contains problems. It is at least certain that Antigone beseeches the chorus in the name of whatever is philon to them and that "child" was the first thing in her list.

father, o philos" (1700) she exclaims after the messenger has reported Oedipus' mysterious death.

The philia of Oedipus and Antigone takes the outward form of physical contact, which is seen from the moment they appear on stage because Antigone is leading her father (cf. 347). He is physically dependent on her (501-502). When Antigone leads him out of the grove to the point at which the chorus can negotiate with him, she says

βάσει βάσιν ἅρμοσαι,
γεραὸν ἐς χέρα σῶμα σὸν προκλίνας φιλίαν ἐμάν.

199-201

Join step to step,
leaning your aged body upon my *philian* hand.

The phrase ἐς χέρα ... φιλίαν ἐμάν reminds of the Homeric χεῖρα φίλην (*Od.* 21.433 etc.), and yet Antigone's hand is philos to her father, not to herself.[89] Her physical support of him is the direct expression of her philia.

As he is philos to her, she and Ismene are philoi to him as his supporters. When Theseus restores his daughters to him after they have been abducted by Kreon, Oedipus exclaims ὦ φίλτατ' ἔρνη "o shoots most philos" (1108) and ὦ σκῆπτρα φωτός "props of a mortal man" (1109). The two parallel exclamations bring together the notions of philia and of support, and show that his philia toward them reciprocates this support. Oedipus calls upon his daughters to press close to him on either side:

ἔχω τὰ φίλτατ', οὐδ' ἔτ' ἂν πανάθλιος
θανὼν ἂν εἴην σφῷν παρεστώσαιν ἐμοί.
ἐρείσατ', ὦ παῖ, πλευρὸν ἀμφιδέξιον
ἐμφύντε τῷ φύσαντι.

1110-13

I hold the things most philos to me, and I would not now be
  wholly wretched
if I should die, because you two stand beside me.
Press each of you your side to mine on either side
clinging to your sire.

Again physical contact is the expression of philia.

The messenger's speech reports the final words of Oedipus to his daughters. In the hour of Oedipus' death, after his daughters have bathed

---

89. The adjective can be active in the Homeric phrase: Robinson 1990:108 gives examples.

him and arrayed him in new clothes, he takes leave of them, in effect thanking them for their exertions on his behalf (1611-15a). He then offers them a consolation for these exertions:

ἀλλ' ἓν γὰρ μόνον
τὰ πάντα λύει ταῦτ' ἔπος μοχθήματα.
τὸ γὰρ φιλεῖν οὐκ ἔστιν ἐξ ὅτου πλέον
ἢ τοῦδε τἀνδρὸς ἔσχεθ'.

1615b-18

Yet one word alone
makes up for all these toils.
For *philein* you had from me more than from any other.

He repays them with philia. For their support, itself motivated by philia, they get in return his philia. To the exchange of benefits on which the philia of Oedipus and Theseus is based, there corresponds, in the philia of Oedipus and his daughters, a reciprocity of affect.[90] And thereafter they embrace for the last time (1620).[91]

At the conclusion of the messenger's speech, Antigone and Ismene appear on stage and join in a song of lamentation. The theme of philia returns in these words of Antigone:

πόθος ⟨τοι⟩ καὶ κακῶν ἄρ' ἦν τις.
καὶ γὰρ ὁ μηδαμὰ τὸ φίλον φίλον,
ὁπότε γε καὶ τὸν ἐν χεροῖν κατεῖχον.

1697-99

So there is a yearning even for ills.
For that which was never philon was philon,[92]
because then I had him, too,[93] in my hands.

That which is *kakon* could never be philon, and yet the toil that Antigone had to undergo now appears philon because then she had her father. Her "in my hands" epitomizes the philia that she felt. (Because this philia of Oedipus and his daughters entails physical contact, it is grimly appropri-

---

90. As Hooker 1987:46-47 observes, the "emotive" meaning of the *phil-* base is attested already in Linear B. It persists in Homer, Hooker shows, alongside the possessive and institutional uses.
91. Cf. the parting embrace of Polyneices, Antigone, and Ismene, clearly indicated in Polyneices' words at 1432-37.
92. Here I follow Kamerbeek's interpretation. See Jebb's apparatus for various emendations in line 1698.
93. I.e., in addition to the ills.

ate that Polyneices should describe the filth of his father's garment, which clings to and defiles his flesh, as *dusphiles* "hateful," i.e., the opposite of philos.) Philia, as recodified in this tragedy, is essentially connected, at one level, to physical contact and affect. The prohibition against mourning at the grave, as the normal function of philoi, stands for a break with the normal understanding of philia. This break has already been signaled, correctly, by Kreon. Upon his death, Oedipus "belongs to a polis, not to an oikos; to Athens, not to Thebes."[94]

§8 Livelihood and Curse

Oedipus' curse on his sons is at least as old as the *Thebaid*. Two fragments of this epic provide, in fact, two different scenarios for the curse; both differ in turn from that found in *Oedipus at Colonus*. In one scenario, Polyneices set the beautiful silver table of Cadmus beside Oedipus and filled him a golden cup of wine. When Oedipus perceived that these possessions of his father had been set beside him, he grew angry and cursed both his sons, with the Erinys paying heed (Athen. 465E = *Thebais* frag. 2 Bernabé). Though the fragment breaks off in the middle of the curse, it was apparently the same mutual destruction as in *Oedipus at Colonus*. The circumstances of Oedipus are quite different, however, in the epic. He is still in Thebes, and, as many scholars have suggested, he has some sacred status.[95] In the second scenario, the sons have sent their father a hip-joint that is unacceptable. The scholiast (on *OC* 1375 = *Thebais* frag. 3 Bernabé) who preserves this four-line fragment explains that customarily Eteocles and Polyneices sent Oedipus a piece of the shoulder from each sacrificial victim. Oedipus then (though there must be an ellipsis in the midst of the four lines) prays to Zeus the king and the other immortals that the two may go down into Hades by mutual destruction. In both scenarios, Oedipus is owed honor and tendance by his sons.

In *Oedipus at Colonus*, the error of the sons is one of complete omission with respect to tendance. It is no longer a question of the proper utensils and the honorific part of the victim. Oedipus is in exile, a beggar, and the sons have failed to provide their father with the food to keep him alive. His daughters have had to take on the role the sons should have played. The support of Oedipus (noun τροφή; verb τρέφειν) is a theme in the play.

94. Segal 1981:402.
95. For references, see the apparatus of Bernabé 1987.

The traditional obligation of sons to support fathers has often been pointed out as background to this theme.[96] In Athens, however, this obligation had taken the form of law from the time of Solon, who denied civil rights to anyone who failed to support his parents (D.L. 1.5: verb τρέφειν). The law was worked out in detail: Solon provided that a son who had not been taught a trade by his father did not owe him support (Plut. Sol. 22.1: same verb); nor did sons born of a concubine (op. cit. 22.4: same verb). Further details are spelled out in an oration of Isaeus.[97] This is the law on which Bdelycleon wants his father to rely in giving up his life as a juror and thus his independence (Ar. V. 736, 1003-1004). Another Aristophanic example is found in *Birds* where the father-beater wants to enter Nephelococcugia because he has heard that amongst birds sons are permitted to attack their fathers (757-59). But now he learns from Peisetaerus that the birds have another law, in fact the Athenian law from which the young man wanted to escape:

> Whenever the fatherstork has reared (verb τρέφειν)
> the young ones and taught them all to fly,
> the chicks must support (verb τρέφειν) their father in turn.
>
> 1355-57

Polyneices is therefore culpable under the Athenian law requiring sons to support fathers, which is encoded in this tragedy. In fact he damns himself out of his own mouth (1265-66). The anger that Oedipus feels against him and Eteocles is directly the opposite of the intense philia that he feels toward his daughters. The inversion of his sons' and daughters' roles has caused an emotional inversion in Oedipus, for he might have been expected to value the preservation of his line above all else and thus to have cared more for his sons. As P. E. Easterling has shown, Oedipus' curse on his sons cannot be understood, either psychologically or dramatically, as apart from his feelings toward his daughters.[98]

Though Oedipus' curse on his sons can thus be partly understood in terms of a particular legal code and also in terms of a recodified philia (§7), as a form of punishment it is of a completely different order. As Oedipus' anger, despite its family context, has something larger than

---

96. Perhaps the earliest reference is Hesiod *OD* 188, where the word θρεπτήρια is used. For this place and other early evidence, see Daly 1990:185 n. 2. For a general survey, see Lacey 1968:116-18. It is curious that at Xen. *Mem.* 2.2.13 Socrates uses the verb θεραπεύειν. In all other references to the Athenian law I have seen, the verb is τρέφειν.
97. 8.32. Cf. Aesch. 1.28; Dem. 24.107, 57.70.
98. Easterling 1967; Blundell 1989:228-29, 240ff.

130 Chapter 3

human about it,[99] so the voice that pronounces the curse is an ὀμφή (550, 1351), a divine voice (cf. 1428 verb θεσπίζειν). Indeed, the very efficacy of the curse, which is assumed by all concerned, issues not from some human capacity but from the new power that Oedipus will have as a cult partner of the Eumenides, those personified curses (see §11 below, and, for the collocation of curse, nourishment, and the Erinyes, cf. Aesch. *Sept.* 785ff.). The curse, in short, belongs to a different code altogether.

Polyneices' self-avowed crime and its punishment are therefore not in balance. His crime can be understood in, in fact is represented in, the context of Athenian law, while the punishment issues from a sub- or supra-political domain. This mixture pervades the play. While the advent of Oedipus activates various codes (xenia [§9 below], philia), Athenian laws (*enktêsis*, the Draco homicide law [§10 below]), and contemporary Athenian concerns (soteria [§12 below]), the benefit of Oedipus to Athens, which is the basis of his reception, depends upon his association with the Eumenides, upon his burial in their grove at Colonus. Offered the choice of going to Athens with Theseus or remaining in Colonus, Oedipus must choose the latter (636-41), and, in so doing, he reverts to the word χῶρος in order to indicate a particular place within Colonus (644; cf. §3 above). Though the political center of Attica is Athens, Oedipus benefits the whole χώρα to which he has come only by occupying a particular spot on the periphery, an "untrodden grove" (125) that cannot be entered. The benefit and that which is benefited are thus in the same mixture as the crime of Polyneices and its punishment.

§9 Xenia

The new philia of Oedipus with Athens can be seen as an aspect of a particular kind of ritualized friendship, namely xenia. Theseus gives two reasons for receiving Oedipus in Attica, of which the first is the following:

τίς δῆτ' ἂν ἀνδρὸς εὐμένειαν ἐκβάλοι
τοιοῦδ', ὅτῳ πρῶτον μὲν ἡ δορύξενος
κοινὴ παρ' ἡμῖν αἰέν ἐστιν ἑστία;

631-33

---

[99]. See Daly 1990:138 and n. 43 on the verb μηνίω.

Who, then, would cast out the favor of such a man,
for whom, first of all, a spear-friend's
hearth is shared for all time with us?

As Theseus' words to Polyneices in Euripides' *Suppliants* show (930), there existed an hereditary xenia between the king of Athens and the ruling family of Thebes. It is this xenia to which Theseus refers in the passage in *Oedipus at Colonus* just quoted.

This xenia is the mythical and dramatic representation of a historical institution that was both widespread and of many centuries' duration in ancient Greece. Xenia was a ritualized bond uniting elite members of different city-states and carrying solemn obligations of mutual assistance. Though it differs from philia in that *xenoi* are from different cities, it shares various features with philia and also with kinship.[100] Like philia within the city-state, ritualized friendship between citizens of different city-states antedates the political organization of the polis and remains implicitly or explicitly in opposition to the principle of community upon which polis government, of whatever sort it may be, rests.[101] The polis institution of proxeny, by which a citizen of another city was designated the polis' representative, and given various honors and privileges, can be regarded as the polis' appropriation of the forms of xenia.[102]

Theseus' second reason for receiving Oedipus shows that he understands Oedipus' promise of help as an expression of xenia.

> ἔπειτα δ' ἱκέτης δαιμόνων ἀφιγμένος
> γῇ τῇδε κἀμοὶ δασμὸν οὐ σμικρὸν τίνει.
> ἀγὼ σεβισθεὶς οὔποτ' ἐκβαλῶ χάριν
> τὴν τοῦδε.
>
> 634-37

And then having come as a suppliant of the divinities
he pays large tribute to me and to this land.
Reverencing these claims I shall never cast out the goodwill
of this man.

As Kamerbeek observes, Theseus' second reason is really two reasons. The first is the fact of Oedipus' supplication. The other is the promised

---

100. Herman 1988:16-31.
101. Herman 1988:78-80. See also "city: in conflict with ritualised friendships" in Index of Subjects.
102. Herman 1988:132-42.

benefit to Athens. (For the apologetic tendency of the tragedy to be maintained, the benefit must be not only a matter of private xenia—"to me"—but must also come to Athens—"to this land.")

Both can be seen to belong to the code of xenia. Because this code was never written down as such, it must be reconstructed from its attestation in many kinds of sources spanning a very long period. Within that period, however, and also from a cross-cultural perspective, as Gabriel Herman's *Ritualised Friendship and the Greek City* has shown, the code is remarkably consistent. His book provides an excellent model of xenia, with reference to which it will be seen that Theseus' final act as hereditary *xenos* of the Theban ruling family is, somewhat paradoxically, to accept a deposed king from that family in Attica and to grant him a final resting-place there. The principle of the geographical separation of *xenoi* is thus violated, and yet, for his part, Oedipus can fulfill his final benefaction as *xenos* only if he is buried in Attica. The duality of Oedipus' claims on Theseus corresponds, however, to a feature of ἔγκτησις: appointment as proxenos was one of the honors that often accompanied this grant.[103] If proxeny is indeed the extension into, and appropriation by, constitutional law of the older xenia, then one can suggest that this flexibility, by which one and the same person owns property in Attica and at the same time or later is proxenos of the Athenians in his native city, was traditional and that no contradiction was felt between the two kinds of honor.

There were three principal modes of entering into relations of xenia.[104] First, an impressive act of *euergesia* could put the recipient in a state of obligation in which he must display *charis*. Second, where it was in the mutual interest of two parties to do so, xenia could be initiated by pledges of loyalty (*pista*), by a handshake (*dexian didonai*, whence *dexia* neut. plur. "pledges," like *pista*), by exchanges of tokens (*symbola*) or gifts (*dôra*), oaths (*horkiai*), and libations (*spondai*). An example that Herman uses several times is the scene in *Iliad* 6 in which Glaucos and Diomedes discover that they are hereditary guest-friends (119-236). This example is especially pertinent to *Oedipus at Colonus* because Glaucos and Diomedes, like Theseus and Oedipus, are not initiating but renewing xenia. A third ritual leading to xenia is supplication. In the final stage of the ritual, no matter what form it took, a declaration of the new, or newly discovered, status ("I am your *xenos*," "I make you my *xenos*") and the exchange of objects were essential. A locution not discussed by

---

103. See the table in Pečírka 1966:137-59.
104. What follows is an analysis and summary of Herman 1988:41-72.

Herman is δέχομαι, which is used of the action of the host in the guest-friendship. Thus the host is a ξενοδόκος "one who receives strangers" (ξεν- + δοκ- < *dek-/dok-). If the guest-friendship is being renewed, the host says: ἀποδέχομαι "I accept you back."[105]

There are sixty-seven occurrences of words formed on the base ξεν-/ξειν- in Oedipus at Colonus,[106] and the reaffirmation of xenia is expressed in most of the ways that Herman's model predicts, i.e., xenia is highly overdetermined. First, although the *euergesia* of Oedipus lies in the future (cf. the comments on *enktêsis* above in §4), his benefit to Athens is, from the beginning of the play, the basis of his relations with Athens (90-92, cf. 1495-99, to be quoted below). Second, as for the gestural and objective manifestations of xenia, Oedipus offers himself as a "gift" (577, 647). Theseus is asked by Oedipus to give and keep a pledge (*piston* 626); in this way he will receive (δέξασθαι 627) a far from useless inhabitant of the land (the diction of *enktêsis* and of xenia appear in the same context). Oedipus will reciprocate with a pledge (1488). At first, neither a kiss (verb *philein*, i.e., the cementing of philia) nor a handshake is possible, because of Oedipus' pollution (1130-35). Later, there is a handshake between Theseus and Oedipus (1631ff.). Theseus puts himself under oath (*horkios* 1637) to keep his promise to Oedipus concerning protection of the daughters.[107] Third, Oedipus is a suppliant, indeed a "savior suppliant" (487, cf. 44, 284).[108]

The relationship of xenia is epitomized in the following words of the chorus, in which they summon Theseus, in order that Oedipus may, at the hour of his death, repay the benefits he has received:

ὁ γὰρ ξένος σε καὶ πόλισμα καὶ φίλους ἐπαξιοῖ
δικαίαν χάριν παρασχεῖν παθών.

1496-97

For the stranger deems you and the city and your friends worthy
to have offered them a just recompense for treatment received.[109]

---

105. Isocrates, *Letter* 7.13, quoted by Herman 1988:70.
106. The Ionic is for the most part restricted to the vocative: see Jebb on 1014; and Ellendt s.v.
107. Lines 1634-37 are replete with the terms of xenia.
108. See Ch. 2 for OC as a suppliant drama; also §12 below.
109. My translation follows the notes of Jebb. See also Kamerbeek's useful note on 1496-97.

134 Chapter 3

The giving and receiving of benefits is the dynamic of xenia. The chorus uses the word *charis*, which is a variant of *euergesia* in the various formulations of xenia discussed by Herman.[110] The chorus refers to Theseus and his *philoi* (cf. 1103), as is to be expected, because xenia is between individuals. And yet they include the polis, an intrusive element in their otherwise accurate restatement of Oedipus' request for the presence of Theseus (1489-90). Their formulation of Oedipus' xenia with Theseus corresponds in this respect precisely to Theseus' own, which has been quoted above ("he pays large tribute to me and to this land": 635). Finally, Oedipus himself articulates the threefold nature of the Athenian side of the xenia when he says, as he leaves the stage toward the end of the tragedy,

ἀλλά, φίλτατε ξένων,
αὐτός τε χώρα θ' ἥδε πρόσπολοί τε σοὶ
εὐδαίμονες γένοισθε.

1552-54

Dearest of xenoi,
may you yourself and this land and your attendants
prosper.

With "you, the city, and your *philoi*" (1496) compare "you, this land, and your attendants." Here, "this land" includes the city (cf. §3 on the semantics of χῶρος and χώρα), to which Oedipus brings great benefit. The apologetic tendency of the tragedy could not succeed if the dramatization of xenia were nothing but the reaffirmation of an old aristocratic custom.

§10 Oedipus' Self-Exoneration and the Homicide Law of Draco

The institution of xenia is not enough, however, to secure the reception of Oedipus in Athens. He is, after all, a parricide and is therefore polluted. If Sophocles had wished to archaize, he could have had Oedipus purified by Theseus. Purification was the normal hope of the murderer in exile (cf. Adrastus in Hdt. 1.35ff., who had killed his brother ἀέκων [1.35.3]) and was then purified by Croesus). The *Epigonoi* provides an example that inverts the roles that might have been expected in *Oedipus at Colonus*.

An Athenian is purified by Thebans: Kephalos killed his wife unintentionally (ἄκων) and was purified by the Cadmians (Phot. s.v. Τευμησία).[111] Oedipus, for his part, must exonerate himself before Athenians, first before the elders of Colonus (258-91) and then, speaking against Kreon, before the elders and Theseus (960-1013).

The second of these speeches follows Kreon's justification, to Theseus, of his abduction of Antigone and Ismene (940-43) and of his attempt to seize Oedipus: he knew that Athens would never receive someone polluted as Oedipus is with the crimes of parricide and incest (944-50). Furthermore, Oedipus had angered him by curses on him and his genos (951-53; cf. §7 on genos). Oedipus' reply to Kreon is a carefully constructed brief:

960-68 (8 lines) Introduction
969-77 (8 lines) Defense against charge of parricide
978-87 (9 lines) Defense against charge of incest
988-90 (3 lines) Summary
991-1002 (11 lines) Cross-examination of Kreon
1003-1013 (10 lines) Conclusion and prayer to Eumenides.

Oedipus' characterization of Kreon's attitude toward Theseus and Athens as θωπεῦσαι "wheedling" (1003) invokes the atmosphere of the Athenian law court, in which, says Aristophanes' Philocleon, the juror can hear every kind of wheedling (θώπευμ' V. 563). In rebuking Kreon for having forced him to speak of his mother, Kreon's sister, he assumes the convention of the Athenian law court according to which women who are owed respect may not be named.[112] (Here Jocasta is not in fact named, but Oedipus still feels that it is shameful of Kreon to have forced Oedipus to speak of Kreon's "female blood relative" [979]). Oedipus sums up his cross-examination of Kreon by saying that Kreon does not observe the distinction between what may and what may not be said (1000-1001), using a phrase found thrice in Demosthenes (18.122, 21.79, 22.61.)[113] The challenge with which Oedipus begins his defense against the charge

---

110. Herman 1988:48.
111. The evidence for archaic epic assembled by Gagarin 1981:6-10 does not, however, reflect a clear distinction between intentional and unintentional homicide.
112. Schaps 1977; Henderson 1987a:106.
113. I have the first two of these references from Jebb ad loc. and the third from Victor Bers.

of parricide—δίδαξον (969)—is also found in Demosthenes (35.49), and the verb was rather common in the law courts.[114]

The legal basis of Oedipus' self-defense is his lack of intent to commit the crimes he committed. The adjective ἄκων "unintentional" occurs four times in the speech (964, 977, 987 [bis]). The relevant Athenian law was to be found in Draco's code, which had, in fact, been republished in 409/8 B.C.E. as a decree of the newly restored democracy. As it happens, the first part of the republished law, which concerns unintentional homicide, is the best preserved.

First Axon

> Even if someone kills someone without premeditation, he shall be exiled. The Basileis are to adjudge responsible for homicide either ... or the one who instigated the killing. The Ephetai are to give the verdict. Pardon is to be granted, if there is a father or brother or sons, by all, or the one who opposes it shall prevail. And if these do not exist, pardon is to be granted by those as far as the degree of cousin's son and cousin, if all are willing to grant it; the one who opposes it shall prevail. And if there is not even one of these alive, and the killer did it unintentionally, and the Fifty-One, the Ephetai, decide that he did it unintentionally, then let ten members of the phratry admit him to the country, if they are willing. Let the Fifty-One choose these men according to their rank.[115]

IG I²115 (I³104).10-19

First, a general resemblance between Oedipus' situation in Athens and the provisions for pardon can be noted. Whether καί (line 11) refers to an earlier section on premeditated homicide ("and"), not republished in 409/8 B.C.E.,[116] or whether it is adverbial ("even if," as in the translation above), the murderer goes into exile (line 10). He then returns, and, if the necessary conditions are met, he is forgiven. Unintentional homicide thus involves a pattern of exile and return. Oedipus has fulfilled this pattern. He was an exile (430, 444, cf. 590, 599-601). Though he has not returned to his own city, he becomes an inhabitant of Attica, under the protection of Theseus, and his *atîmia* is canceled (cf. 49, 51, 286, 428).

Oedipus concludes the second part of his speech, the defense against charge of parricide, as follows: "If I came to blows with my father

---

114. Plato. *Apol.* 21b1; Lysias 7.3, 9.3, 10.15, 12.3, 12.62, 13.4, etc.
115. The translation is that of Stroud 1968:6.
116. As argued by Wallace 1989:17.

and killed him, knowing nothing[117] of what I was doing and against whom, how could you reasonably blame the unintentional (ἄκον) deed?" (975-77). The absence of intent is specifically linked to ignorance, which is analyzed into two parts: he did not know that he was killing the person with whom he was engaged in conflict; he did not know that that person was his father. The first part is inconsistent with the recollection of the parricide in *Oedipus the King* 807-13, especially with the last of these lines ("I killed them all"). The second part is surely honest. He did not know whom he was killing. Oedipus' case is thus the reverse of the one used by Aristotle to illustrate an unintentional act (ἄκοντα ποιῆσαι *Magna Moralia* 1189^{b}29-38), in which a woman knows the man to whom she administers a potion but does not know that the potion will kill him. In both cases, however, the absence of intent depends upon ignorance. In other words, the criterion of intent is knowledge.[118]

The republication of Draco's homicide law provides a model for Oedipus' self-defense.[119] *Oedipus at Colonus* thus continues a series of reaffirmations of ancestral law which had begun with the probouloi of 413 B.C.E., of whom Sophocles was probably one.[120] The Four Hundred established a board of syngrapheis to write a new constitution (Thuc. 8.57). The Five Thousand appointed nomothetai (Thuc. 8.97).[121] The restored democracy then undertook its own assertion of the true Athenian law,[122] sorting it out of the welter of laws and decrees to be found in

---

117. μηδὲν ξυνιείς, cf. 273 οὐδὲν εἰδώς; cf. *OT* 397: ὁ μηδὲν εἰδὼς Οἰδίπους.

118. This criterion would tend to explain why ἄκων and μὴ ἐκ προνοίας are "legally equivalent": Gagarin 1981:34; cf. Loomis 1972:94.

119. And gives a concrete sense to a commonplace of the literary criticism of *OC* and *OT*: the subjective innocence of Oedipus in the second tragedy. Cf. Seidensticker 1972:263 n. 1: "Im OT liegt die Betonung auf den objektiven Verfehlungen, im OK auf der subjektiven Schuldlosigkeit des Oidipus."

120. In the autumn of 413, after news of the final defeat in Sicily reached Athens, ten probouloi were appointed as the governing board of Athens (Thuc. 8.1.3; cf. Aristot. *Ath. Pol.* 29.2). A passage in Aristotle's *Rhetoric* suggests that Sophocles was one of them (1419a25-30). Though it has often been said that the man to whom Aristotle refers is some other Sophocles, I believe that there are several reasons for identifying him as the poet. It is a matter of Aristotle's way of referring to persons, as argued by Jameson 1971:542-46; cf. Calder 1971:172-74; Kirsten 1973:15 n. 19; Karavites 1976. Sandys 1877.1:263 denied this identification, as did Avery 1973, challenging Jameson. Cf. HCT 5.165; Rhodes 1981:373.

121. See Stroud 1968:22-24 on this group.

122. Cf. Ostwald 1986:405 on the sequence of committees. The ambition of the restored democracy to codify all Athenian law went beyond the scope of the previous committees and initiated a task that took longer than anyone expected: Hansen 1990:8-9.

138 Chapter 3

various inscriptions and copies in other media[123] and, as the Draco republication itself shows, harking back to the origins of Athenian law.[124] The republication even has a symbolic aspect if it is, as it seems to be, unedited and if the ephetai are an anachronism.[125] The medium was the message, and the message was: we represent the true, ancestral Athens. Sophocles then reenters this process with *Oedipus at Colonus*, and says to the democracy: Oedipus can be forgiven under the terms of your own laws.

But before Oedipus is welcomed by the king of Athens and before he argues the case for his pardon, he must be reconciled with the Eumenides and secure his place in Colonus. The particular relationship with the Eumenides is a crucial aspect of the role that Oedipus will play in Athens.

§11 Oedipus and the Eumenides

When Oedipus reaches Colonus, he unknowingly enters a sacred grove. When the Stranger of Colonus arrives on the scene, he refuses to answer Oedipus' question, even to let him finish asking the question, until Oedipus has removed himself from the grove. Oedipus then asks another question: to which deity is the grove sacred (38)? The Stranger replies: dread goddesses possess it, the daughters of Earth and Darkness (39–40). This parentage already suggests the Erinyes, who in Aeschylus are the daughters of mother Night (*Eum.* 416, 844) and in Hesiod of Earth, who has been impregnated by the blood from the severed genitals of Uranus (*Theog.* 184). Oedipus continues, asking for their awful (σεμνόν) name (41), a leading question, as will be seen. The Stranger replies: here they are called the all-seeing Eumenides; other names are in use elsewhere (42–43). The second part of this answer, on the variety of names, opens the door to further, more specific syncretism.[126] After the Stranger departs, Oedipus, now free to speak his mind, begins a prayer to the Eumenides with the words ὦ πότνιαι δεινῶπες (84). *Potniai*, here a

---

123. Stroud 1968:24.
124. Cf. Ostwald 1986:367ff. on preoccupation with the *patrios politeia*; Kagan 1987:256.
125. As argued by Wallace 1989:102–105.
126. What I am calling a "syncretism" of course rests on the fundamental ambivalence of the Eumenides-Erinyes, on which see Henrichs 1991:163–69, with reference especially to Aeschylus and with valuable doxography.

substantive, is an epithet of the Erinyes (Aesch. *Sept.* 887; *Eum.* 951) and the eponymous name of a Theban town where they were worshipped[127] and where, in Aeschylus' *Laius* or *Oedipus*, Oedipus killed Laius (frag. 173 N² = 387a Radt). *Deinopes* also recalls the Erinyes, whose faces were hideous.[128] A moment later, Oedipus refers to them as the "August Goddesses" (θεῶν / σεμνῶν 89-90), a title anticipated in the form of his question at line 41 and used again at line 458. The Semnai had been identified with the Erinyes in Aeschylus' *Eumenides*, and the cult of the Erinyes described in that tragedy is that of the Semnai near the Areopagus (cf. Paus. 1.28.6).[129] Much closer in time to the composition of *Oedipus at Colonus*, Euripides' *Orestes* (408 B.C.E.) refers to the Erinyes as Eumenides (38, 321, 836, 1650). Even a scholar like A. L. Brown, who resolutely denies the syncretism of Eumenides and Erinyes in *Oedipus at Colonus*, states that the effect of Oedipus' nomenclature is "to identify the goddesses of Colonus, who were probably fairly obscure to most Athenians, with the better known ones [i.e., the Erinyes] beneath the Areopagus."[130]

Sophocles has thus done much to suggest that the Eumenides/Semnai of Colonus are Erinyes. Why then did he not call them Erinyes?[131] Simply because they did not have this cult-name at Colonus, and, as Brown says, the cult was obscure in any case, just as the grave of Oedipus, if already established at Colonus, in Sophocles' time was probably also obscure (cf. §2). But Sophocles had reasons, which will now begin to appear, for wishing to create the identification just noted. These reasons have to do with Oedipus' future benefactions to Athens.

The name Erinys is heard in the tragedy for the first time at line 1299, where Polyneices blames his father for the strife between him and his brother that drove him out of Thebes: your Erinys (singular) is the cause. Polyneices states a similar thought to Antigone, using now the plural: the road he must take back to the army in Argos is ill-fated thanks "to this father and his Erinyes" (1434). But the two references to the Erinys/Erinyes are quite different: the first bears on the origin of the quarrel between the brothers, the second on the doom of the army that Polyneices has assembled in Argos. Polyneices is certain of this doom because Oedipus has not only refused to support him—when victory will

---

127. With Demeter and Kore. For references, see Wüst, *RE* Suppl. vol. 8, cols. 91, 130-31.
128. See Sommerstein 1989 on line 990.
129. Sommerstein 1989:10-11.
130. Brown 1984:277. For a critique of Brown, see Lloyd-Jones 1990.

go to whichever side he supports (1332-33)—but has cursed both his sons to death (1372-76, 1383-96). Polyneices' second reference to the Erinyes of Oedipus therefore has this curse as its background.[132]

Cursing is a function that the Erinyes and Oedipus have in common. The Erinyes can be called Curses (Aesch. *Eum.* 417), and in Homer they are most often the embodiment of the curse of a parent.[133] In Aeschylus' *Seven Against Thebes*, the beleaguered Eteocles calls upon "Curse and mighty Erinys of my father" (70). The connection is standard, from the *Thebaid* down to Euripides' *Phoenissae*.[134] In *Oedipus at Colonus*, Sophocles dramatizes the curse, and does not fail to coinvolve the Semnai/Eumenides/"Erinyes." When, in the presence of Polyneices, Oedipus curses his sons, he calls upon the "daimones of this place," along with Tartarus and Ares (1389-92). Oedipus has already cursed them earlier in the tragedy (421ff.) when he learns from Ismene that, despite their knowledge of Thebes' dependence on him for its safety, they had preferred to compete for the throne themselves rather than recall him. Oedipus refers to this imprecation when he curses Kreon: "May these daimones not make me voiceless of this further curse" (864-65).[135] This shared function of cursing is prepared for early in the play, as Albert Henrichs has shown, in the very phrase νήφων ἀοίνοις (100), which expresses "the close ritual reciprocity between the Semnai and their worshiper"[136] and perhaps also points to Oedipus' future status as a cult hero who will himself receive wineless offerings.[137] Theseus welcomes the εὐμένειαν (631) of Oedipus; the Eumenides, as their name shows, have this same quality as one of their aspects.

These curses of Oedipus identify him as the chthonic hero he will soon become,[138] and display the power that he will have to help his new city, even if the destruction of Eteocles and Polyneices does not benefit Athens in any way. The later (?) grave of Oedipus in the precinct of the Semnai near the Areopagus (Paus. 1.28.6) is a clear parallel to the situation at Colonus: the hero cooperates with the avenging daimones, but

---

131. To restate the question of Brown 1984:277.
132. See Jebb 1928 on line 1434.
133. Sommerstein 1989:7.
134. Cf. Edmunds 1981:225-26. On the relation of *OC* to the *Phoenissae*, see Di Benedetto 1983:223, 228-29.
135. See Jebb and Kamerbeek ad loc. Cf. Brown 1984:279 n. 120.
136. Henrichs 1983:95; also Henrichs 1991:171.
137. On the similarities between Oedipus and the Eumenides, see Segal 1981:375.
138. Edmunds 1981:229; see Henrichs 1983:95 n. 32 for references in scholarship on *OC* to "proleptic characterization."

always for the good of the city, respecting the prerogatives of human law, as in the "charter" provided in Aeschylus' *Eumenides*. The two kinds of claims, those represented by the Eumenides and those represented by the legal institutions of the city, are always in balance. Indeed the Areopagus is not forgotten in *Oedipus at Colonus*: Kreon justifies his attempt to seize Oedipus on the grounds that the Areopagus would not have permitted such a polluted man to remain in the polis (944-49); he does not know that Theseus, the basileus (67), has granted Oedipus the right to dwell in Attica (κατοικιῶ 637), implicitly pardoning him and thus prefiguring the role of the archon basileus, who presided over the Areopagus Council. The legal basis of Oedipus' acceptance is then more fully established in the speech analyzed in the preceding section of this book. Though Oedipus chooses to remain at Colonus and not to go with Theseus into the city proper precisely because of his foreordained resting place in a grove of the Eumenides (84-93, 644-46), from the beginning he pairs the Eumenides and Athens. The prayer already cited concludes: "Come, sweet daughters of ancient Darkness, come city most honored of all, Athens, who are called great Pallas', have pity" (106-109). Oedipus concludes the curse on his sons in 421ff. by calling on the elders of Colonus: "For if you, strangers, are willing, with these dread goddesses who are protectors of the land (δημούχοις), to aid me, you will get a great savior for this city (πόλει)" (457-60).[139] Oedipus concludes his speech of self-exoneration by calling upon the Eumenides "to come as helpers and allies, in order that you (Kreon) may learn by what sort of men this city (πόλις) is defended" (1012-13). It is his expectation that the Eumenides may support the effort of Theseus and the Athenians to rescue his daughters.

Oedipus' acceptance in Attica thus takes place on two distinct levels, one represented by the Eumenides, the other by Theseus, and these two levels have distinct codes. This duality is expressed in several words formed on the base οἰκ- which describe Oedipus' settlement in Colonus and which are shared by the distinct codes. When Theseus uses κατοικιῶ (637), the model, as argued above, is the institution of *enktêsis* and Theseus speaks with the voice of positive law. Oedipus, however, has referred to his dwelling οἰκήσαντα (92) in the grove of the Eumenides as the basis of his power to help those who have received him and to harm

---

139. I have not translated the first word or words of 458, which is or are corrupt. My point is not affected. Both Jebb and Kamerbeek take δημούχοις as referring to Colonus, though the same adjective at 1087 and 1348 clearly refers to all of Attica. In any case, in the passage under discussion, Oedipus links the Eumenides and Athens.

those who exiled him, using the word "dwelling" in its cultic sense.[140] The ambiguity of Oedipus' "settlement" is pervasive. Furthermore, the purification of Oedipus that might have come at the hands of Theseus (cf. the beginning of the preceding section) is replaced by Oedipus' expiation of the Eumenides, into whose inviolable grove he has unknowingly entered: it is a commonplace of literary criticism on this tragedy that the expiation, a ritual described in greater detail than any other in ancient literature,[141] somehow conveys a larger atonement for blood-guilt and defilement.[142]

But its value to Athens is unambiguous, and in this respect Sophocles' version of the "burial" of Oedipus at Colonus differs both from the Atthidographer Androtion's and also from the Eteonos tradition (see §2). The future cult of Oedipus at Colonus also differs considerably from the cult founded by the Aegids of Sparta to appease the Erinyes of Laius and Oedipus (Hdt. 4.149.2; cf. Paus. 9.5.14-15). The intent of that cult was to put an end to a particular affliction, the stillbirths or early deaths of Aegid children; the Oedipus of this cult corresponds to the Oedipus of Sophocles' *Oedipus the King*, whose presence in Thebes has caused a plague one symptom of which is stillbirths.[143] The positive value to a city, Athens, of Oedipus' association with the Erinyes (to the extent that the Eumenides/Semnai of Colonus are characterized as Erinyes), and of a cult of Oedipus, are an innovation of Sophocles, for which the apparition of Oedipus would have been the warrant (see §2).

§12 Soteria

In the summer of 413, after the news of the defeat of their expeditionary force in Sicily, the Athenians, with no ships, no crews, and no money in the treasury, "lost hope that they could survive (verb σῴζω)" (Thuc. 8.1.2). Nevertheless, they resolved to do what they could under the circumstances, and, as one of their emergency measures, they chose a board of elderly men "to plan and propose measures (verb προβουλεύω), as necessary" (Thuc. 8.1.3). In 411, the board of probouloi was still in existence,[144] and the issue of safety was still alive. Aristophanes' Lysistrata

140. Edmunds 1981:223 and n. 8.
141. Burkert 1985:8.
142. Seidensticker 1972:263 and n. 3 for bibliography.
143. Edmunds 1981:226-27.
144. On Sophocles as proboulos, see §10 n. 10.

organizes an international sex strike as a way to bring peace and thus secure the soteria of all of Greece (*Lys.* 29-30 and context). She has another plan, too: she and her accomplices have occupied the Acropolis and seized the Athenian treasury in order to cut off military funding. She justifies her action in a long debate with a proboulos (476-613). As for the money, the women will manage it, just as they manage household money.

> PROBOULOS: It's not the same.
> LYSISTRATA: Why not?
> PROBOULOS: The war depends on this money.
> LYSISTRATA: We shouldn't have a war in the first place.
> PROBOULOS: How else can we be saved (verb σῴζω)?
> LYSISTRATA: We will save (verb σῴζω) you.
> PROBOULOS: You?
> LYSISTRATA: Us.
> PROBOULOS: That's disgusting.
> LYSISTRATA: You're going to be saved (verb σῴζω), even if you don't want to be.
> PROBOULOS: That's bizarre.
> LYSISTRATA: You're annoyed, but we have to do it.
> PROBOULOS: By Demeter, it's wrong.
> LYSISTRATA: My friend, you must be saved (verb σῴζω).
>
> 496-501

The soteria of the city, which depended on money and supplies, was, then, a theme of Athenian politics and public discourse from 413, and was to provide an issue that those wishing to restore Alcibiades and to introduce oligarchic modifications of the constitution could appropriate.[145]

In the winter of 412/11, neither Athenians nor Spartans could claim an advantage in the naval conflict in the eastern Mediterranean. Everything depended on the support of Tissaphernes, who, on Alcibiades' advice, was going to let the opposing powers wear each other down (Thuc. 8.46). Alcibiades, for his part, planned to use his perceived influence with Tissaphernes as a lever to open his return to Athens. He let the trierarchs of the Athenian fleet stationed at Samos know that he would make Tissaphernes their ally if they would abolish the democracy in Athens and establish an oligarchy (Thuc. 8.47). Under these conditions, he could return from exile. Despite the misgivings of Phrynichos, a conspiracy

---

145. I doubt that it is accurate to speak of soteria as an oligarchic "slogan," as does Bieler 1951. Consider Rhodes 1972:231-35. Bibliography on soteria in Raaflaub 1992:32 n. 79.

formed, and prepared to send Peisander to Athens (Thuc. 8.48-49). At some point after his arrival in Athens in the second half of December, perhaps after the performance of *Lysistrata* at the Lenaea,[146] Peisander bluntly told the Athenian demos that Persian support and victory over Sparta could be obtained if the democracy were modified and Alcibiades were recalled (Thuc. 8.53.1). When this proposal met vehement resistance, Peisander asked each of the objectors one by one if he had any hope of "safety for the city" (σωτηρίας τῇ πόλει) without the support of the Persian king (Thuc. 8.53.2). Everyone said no. Peisander then stated that this support was impossible unless the Athenians governed themselves "more prudently" and restricted offices to the few, and unless they ceased to be more concerned about the constitution than about safety (σωτηρίας) (Thuc. 8.53.3). The people were resigned to the fact that there was no other safety (σωτηρίαν) for them (Thuc. 8.54.1). Peisander had focused on the issue, soteria, that he knew was uppermost in the minds of the Athenians.

The Assembly approved a decree requiring the people to choose, in addition to the existing ten probouloi, twenty others, who were to draft legislation for whatever they considered best for the city concerning its safety (περὶ τῆς σωτηρίας Ath. Pol. 29.2).[147] This new board made itself heard for the first time at a special meeting of the Assembly at Colonus in early June 411.[148] Their first resolution was that the prytaneis put to the vote whatever anyone said "about safety" (περὶ τῆς σωτηρίας Ath. Pol. 29.4). It was at this meeting that, along with the adoption of various emergency measures, the existing constitution was abrogated and replaced by a governing body of four hundred (Thuc. 8.67.3), who were later to choose five thousand *dunatōtatoi*, who would be the new government of Athens (*Ath. Pol.* 29.5; cf. Thuc. 8.65.3). Soteria was the oligarchs' justification of the new regime to the fleet at Samos (Thuc. 8.86.3).

Sometime in the five years following the collapse of the oligarchic revolution, Sophocles, who was probably one of the ten probouloi,[149] and who had something to do with the creation of the Four Hundred,[150]

---

146. In the first half of February; on the chronology see *HCT* 5.117, 131, 186-87; Henderson 1987b:xxi.
147. On the discrepancy between Thucydides and Aristotle with respect to this board, see *HCT* 5.164-65; Rhodes 1981:363, 373.
148. On the date see *HCT* 5.187, 234-37.
149. Cf. §10 n. 10.
150. *HCT* 5.165.

wrote a tragedy in which the protagonist presented himself as the savior (σωτήρ) of Athens. Upon learning from Ismene that, despite oracles concerning the importance of his grave to Thebes, his sons had set their own rivalry for the tyranny before any thought of recalling their father, Oedipus gives a long speech damning his sons and affirming his desire to remain in Athens. He concludes the speech, addressing the chorus, with these words:

> If you, strangers, are willing,
> with these reverend goddesses who sustain your people,
>   to defend me, for this city
> you will get a great savior (noun σωτήρ), and troubles for my
>   enemies.
>
>   457-60

The goddesses are the Eumenides. The chorus replies with commiseration (461-62a) and with an offer to advise him of the best course of action, because he has presented himself as a "savior (σωτήρ') of this land" (462b-64). Their advice will concern Oedipus' relations with the Eumenides. In the course of their detailed instructions for a ritual of purification, they tell Oedipus to pray that "as we call them Eumenides [i.e., kindly ones], they receive the suppliant savior (adj. σωτήριον)[151] from kindly hearts" (486-87).

The oligarchs' promise of soteria, which was the ostensible agenda at the special meeting of the Assembly at Colonus in 411, is now fulfilled by an exiled Theban king. It is his grave at Colonus that will bring soteria. Colonus is not a separate χῶρος but belongs to the Athenian χώρα. For this reason, Oedipus can speak of his bringing soteria to the polis. The efficacy of Oedipus' gift is closely linked with the Eumenides (cf. §11). As their cult-partner, he will reinforce and amplify the function of protecting the deme (δημούχοις 458) that they already have.[152]

In the context of recent Athenian political history, which saw something like a vendetta against the oligarchs and those associated with them, Oedipus' claims seem to us inopportune, to say the least. If, however, we broaden the context of reception to include earlier tragedy, we can see that such claims were not unheard of. Euripides' *Heracleidai*, usually dated to the first years of the Peloponnesian War, provides a rather strik-

---

151. I follow the reading of the mss., with Jebb, Kamerbeek, and Burian 1974:414 n. 12 taking the adj. as active in sense. For the objections, see Ellendt 1872 s.v. σωτήριος; L-J-W 1990b on 487. L-J-W 1990a print Bake's σωτηρίους.
152. On the meaning of δημούχοις see §3 n. 48.

146 Chapter 3

ing precedent. This tragedy belongs, like *Oedipus at Colonus*, to the category of suppliant drama. The children of Heracles, persecuted by Eurystheus, take refuge at the altar of Zeus at Marathon. To defend them, the Athenian king, Demophon, the counterpart of Theseus, must defeat the army of Eurystheus, who is taken prisoner. Eurystheus now requires protection of the Athenians, while Alcmene, the mother of Heracles, demands his death. A bargain is concluded: Eurystheus is to be handed over to the implacable Alcmene for execution, but the Athenians will receive his corpse for burial (1022-25). According to ancient oracle of Apollo, the Athenians will bury him in the deme Pallene before a shrine of Athena (1026-31). Eurystheus tells the chorus of Marathonians:

> Well-disposed to you and savior to the city (πόλει
> σωτήριος)
> I'll lie forever a foreign resident (μέτοικος)[153] in your land,
> most war-like against the descendants of these persons
>   (Alcmene and the Argives)
> whenever they come here with a mighty force.
>
>   1032-35

In sum, through his burial in Attica, he will help the Athenians hurt the Argives (1044). The notion of "safety for the city" (πόλει σωτηρίαν 1045) is repeated by Alcmene, as if to impress on the audience the significance of the strange bargain concerning Eurystheus.

The parallelism between the functions of Eurystheus and Oedipus and between the two plays as wholes is extensive.[154] Though Oedipus, and Colonus through Oedipus, makes a new promise of the soteria already promised at Colonus in 411 and unfilled by the oligarchic regime, Oedipus' soteria did not have to be taken as a naked political statement but could be received within existing traditions of Athenian cult and Athenian tragedy.

§13 Oedipus in Pindar, *Pythian* 4.263-69

Pindar's *Fourth Pythian* (462 B.C.E.) celebrates the victory of Arcesilas of Cyrene in the chariot race. The epilogue of this ode asks Arcesilas to

---

153. With which contrast the legal status of Oedipus in *Oedipus at Colonus*. Cf. §4 and the references there to Vidal-Naquet.
154. Note that two of the fragments preserved by Stobaeus (frags. 852-853 N) concern obligations to parents. Cf. §8 above on *trophē*.

restore the exiled Damophilos to Cyrene. At the very point at which the central myth of the ode comes to an end and the epilogue begins, Pindar addresses Arcesilas:

γνῶθι νῦν τὰν Οἰδιπόδα σοφίαν· εἰ γάρ τις ὄζους
ὀξυτόμῳ πελέκει
ἐξερείψειεν μεγάλας δρυός, αἰσχύνοι δέ οἱ θαητὸν εἶδος,
καὶ φθινόκαρπος ἐοῖσα διδοῖ ψᾶφον περ' αὐτᾶς,
εἴ ποτε χειμέριον πῦρ ἐξίκηται λοίσθιον,
ἢ σὺν ὀρθαῖς κιόνεσσι δεσποσύναισιν ἐρειδομένα
μόχθον ἄλλοις ἀμφέπῃ δύστανον ἐν τείχεσιν,
ἑὸν ἐρημώσαισα χῶρον.

Pindar, Pyth. 4.263-69

Know the parable[155] concerning[156] Oedipus. For if someone with a sharp-cutting ax
should strike off the branches of a great oak and dishonor its wondrous form,
even with its fruitfulness gone it puts its own case to the vote,[157]
if ever in the future it reaches a winter's fire,
or fixed with upright pillars as its masters[158]
it tends a wretched toil in other walls
abandoning its own place.

According to one of the main lines of interpretation of this passage, which goes back to the scholiast, the parable refers to Damophilos.[159] The parable, then, would concern Damophilos in the same way as it concerns Oedipus. If so, the first question is what the parable says about Oedipus. The answer seems quite clear. Oedipus was like an old oak tree that, even after it had been cut down and moved away from its roots, could still be of use in new circumstances. In the context of the Oedipus myth, the parable must refer to the reduced condition of Oedipus, to his exile from

---

155. I have taken this word from the note ad loc. of Gildersleeve 1899, with whom I agree that the sentence as a whole cannot mean: "Be as wise as Oedipus." The scholiast speaks of τὸ αἴνιγμα. Sophia here is an encoded message, the product of poetic skill: cf. Nagy 1985 and, for other discussions, the index in Figueira and Nagy 1985 s.v. sophos.

156. I do not think that the genitive here (Οἰδιπόδα) corresponds exactly to the genitive in line 277 ('Ομήρου), which is possessive, although it is possible that Pindar is referring to a parable that Oedipus used of himself in some poem, in which case I should translate "Oedipus' parable."

157. "It puts its own case to the vote" is the translation of Gildersleeve 1899 ad loc.
158. Taking δεσποσύναισιν as a substantive.
159. For the doxography, see Carey 1980:145.

Thebes, and to his potential benefit to a new place. The parallel with *Oedipus at Colonus* is not far to seek.[160] The second question is what the parable says about Damophilos. Since he is a young man and hopes to return to his native city (293-95), to which he can be of great use (281-87), exile is the only similarity between him and Oedipus. For this reason, the parable, as applied to Damophilos, is in the nature of a warning to Arcesilas: do not let the exile of Damophilos become like the exile of Oedipus, which deprived his native city of his benefit. This interpretation of the parable is corroborated by another mythical exemplum, that of Atlas, in lines 289-90: "He (Damophilos), another Atlas, struggles with heaven, far from his native land and belongings." As Gildersleeve pointed out, Atlas recalls the image of the columns in the parable of Oedipus. With Atlas, Pindar contrasts the Titans, whom Zeus freed (291). Even though they had rebelled against him, as Damophilos had participated in an insurrection against Arcesilas (a hint in 272), Zeus forgave them. Pindar's advice is: Damophilos should be treated like the Titans, not like Atlas.[161]

The epilogue of the *Fourth Pythian* contains many difficulties. The purpose of the present discussion is only to show that, on one plausible interpretation of the parable, Oedipus is already, in 462 B.C.E., long before the composition of *Oedipus at Colonus*, known as an exile who, having left his own place (χῶρον 269; cf. the importance of place in *Oedipus at Colonus*), brings benefits to another.

---

160. See Gildersleeve 1899:302.
161. Cf. Giannini 1979:60-62 and Segal 1986: 84-85, 106-108 for further dimensions of the relationship between Damophilos and Arcesilas.

Conclusion

Part 1 of this book began by establishing a theoretical basis for a semiotic reading of *Oedipus at Colonus* that would concentrate on theatrical space. This reading discovered a high degree of metatheater in the tragedy, which had the effect of putting dramatic representation itself into question. In short, the tragedy proved to be partly about tragedy. Part 2 discovered an apologetic tendency related to the restoration of the democracy after 411 B.C.E., the same period, I have assumed, in which the tragedy was composed. The tragedy, then, was also about the political and social situation in Athens. (It is, of course, about still other things, too, that were not discussed in this book.) In conclusion, I return to the metatheatricality of the tragedy.

In the first place, the metatheatrical aspect of the tragedy is perhaps no less historical than the matters discussed in Part 2. Euripides' *Bacchae*, composed at the same time, is analogous in this respect, and, in general, self-conscious mannerism is a tendency of Greek drama at the end of the fifth century. Nevertheless, as indicated in the Introduction, the semiotic reading, though posing as historical and staying within the bounds of what is known (or of what I know) about the Theater of Dionysus, proved to have been infected by its semiotic starting point. For this reading went beyond metatheater to discover a problematics, which is sometimes referred to as the "crisis of representation," typical of the late twentieth century. A most convenient way of restating the findings concerning the theatrical sign in *Oedipus at Colonus* is thus in terms of différance. Because différance can be substituted for deconstruction[1] and because deconstruction is often considered pernicious, I must begin with some disclaimers. First, my intent is not to "deconstruct" *Oedipus at*

---

1. Derrida 1991:275.

150 *Conclusion*

Colonus, if to "deconstruct" means to "destroy" or to "treat with irreverence." (These colloquial senses of to "deconstruct" are common.) Second, on my understanding of the matter, deconstruction is not focused on the replacement of hierarchical and binary structures with indeterminacy.[2] (This drastic simplification is common.) Deconstruction discovers, amongst other things, the productive or "originary" movement of différance. For reasons that will become clear, it is the productive aspect on which I shall focus. Third, in order to avoid confusion about such expressions as "Derrida," "Derridean," and "deconstruction," I have limited my frame of reference to a single, rather straight-forward essay by Derrida called "Différance."[3]

I begin with a metaphor that occurs in one of Derrida's definitions of différance in the aforementioned essay: "Différance is what brings it about that the movement of signification is possible only if each so-called 'present' element, appearing on the stage of presence, is related to something other than itself, keeping in itself the mark of the past element and already allowing itself to be hollowed out by the marks of its relation to a future element, the trace ... constituting the so-called present by this very relation to that which it is not ... ."[4] The metaphor, "the stage of presence," can, as Chapter One has already suggested, be reversed, and one can as well speak of the presence of the stage, i.e., of the specific dramatic presence or even hyper-presence that comes about in performance ("Me voici tout présent"). The question can then be asked: in this presence of the stage do theatrical signs undergo the process of différance. (In order to avoid an excessive number of quotation marks, I shall say at the outset that I am well aware that many of the words I shall have to use are inadmissible in a paraphrase of Derrida.)

Différance combines the two senses of the verb *différer*. One is to defer. Derrida glosses: "to put off until later, to take into account, to take account of time and of the forces in an operation that implies an economic calculation, a detour, a delay, a being late, a reserve, a representation," terms that he sums up in "temporization." For now, suffice it to observe that, in Oedipus' case, it is his promised support of Attica that is deferred to the future, that is held in reserve, etc., so that the representation of the support is also deferred, with the result that the tragedy is about that deferral. The other sense of *différer* is: "to not be identical, to

2. Cf. Derrida 1988:126-27.
3. Derrida 1972. The translations are mine. I have used the notes in the excellent translation by Alan Bass (Derrida 1982).
4. Derrida 1972:13.

Conclusion 151

be other, to be discernible (*discernable*)." This sense is summed up in the word "spacing."[5] Oedipus' promise is linked to his grave, which is separated in space from any place that others can visit, except Theseus, and it is not clear that even Theseus had a clear view of the spot whence Oedipus disappeared from the earth.

In order to show how the two senses of *différer* are joined, Derrida turns to semiotics (I take the liberty of thus translating his *sémiologie*) and linguistics, and, in particular, to Ferdinand de Saussure. It will thus be all the easier to discuss the relation of différance to the theatrical sign as it has been analyzed in *Oedipus at Colonus*. To anticipate the conclusion of this stage of my discussion, it will be seen that the theatrical sign on "the stage of presence" as problematized in this tragedy has to some extent prefigured the formal definition of the sign in différance and that this anticipation in Sophocles (with which compare, for example, the *pharmakon* in Plato's *Phaedrus*, which became part of Derrida's conceptual apparatus[6]) is especially a matter of the productive effects of différance. From Saussure's principles of the arbitrariness of the sign and its differential character, Derrida draws the consequence that the signified concept is never present in itself but is inscribed in a chain or system in which it refers to other concepts "by a systematic play of differences."[7] Having defined the differences in language as "effects" in distinction to predetermined meanings, Derrida adds that différance "will be then the movement of play that 'produces' ... these differences, these effects of difference. This does not mean that the différance which produced these differences is before them, in a present that is simple and unmodified in itself, in-different. Différance is the non-full, non-simple 'origin,' the structured and differentiating (*différante*) origin of differences. Thus the name 'origin' is no longer appropriate."[8] Proceeding, then, from Saussure's differential sign, Derrida reaches an apparent impasse. If differences are produced effects but have no cause, how can they be produced, how can they be effects? In place of cause, Derrida uses the "trace," which is neither a cause nor an effect. "Trace" is defined in the first of the quotations from Derrida in this Conclusion, in which the metaphor "the stage of presence" occurred. In that passage, Derrida stresses the temporal aspect of the trace. He elaborates thus: "An interval must separate the

---

5. Derrida 1972:8.
6. Derrida 1981.
7. Derrida 1972:11. Cf. Kristeva 1969: 205 n. 21: Derrida "substitue ... le terme de *différance* à la notion chargée d'idéalismes de *signe*."
8. Derrida 1972:12.

152 Conclusion

present from that which it is not in order that it may be itself, but this interval that constitutes it in present must at the same time divide the present in itself .... This interval dynamically constituting itself, dividing itself, is what one can call *spacing*, the becoming-space of time or the becoming-time of space (*temporization*)."[9] Thus the two sense of *différer* are brought together in the notion of the present constituted by a fleeting "synthesis" of backward- and forward-looking traces.[10]

Before pursuing the production of differences in *Oedipus at Colonus*, I pause on what we might call the historical dimension of différance. At the end of his discussion of Saussure, Derrida extends to the sign in general what Saussure had said of the relation of *parole* (speech) to *langue* (language as system), viz., that whereas *langue* is necessary in order that *parole* be understood, historically the latter always precedes the former.[11] At this point, history, in a qualified sense, enters the definition of différance, which, Derrida now says, is "the movement by which *langue* or any code, any system of referral in general constitutes itself 'historically' as a web of differences."[12] (Derrida has to put the word "historically" in quotation marks because of its complicity with metaphysically based notions like the opposition between history and structure, notions replaced by différance.) This "historical" aspect of différance provides a way of bringing together two phenomena that have been heretofore unconnected in the discussion of *Oedipus at Colonus*, intertextuality and metatheater. The first of these has been left more or less undiscussed in this book for the reason that it has been thoroughly covered in earlier scholarship.[13] At this point, it is only necessary to repeat that *Oedipus at Colonus* is a densely intertextual play. Its intertextuality can be understood as the "historical" mode in which the semiotic system of the play constitutes itself, simply because, in the first place, intertextuality by any definition is a form of reference to earlier

---

9. Derrida 1972:13-14.
10. One searches for metaphors to express the notion of the trace or interval. Saussure's use of a chess game as a metaphor for linguistic change is suggestive and, in particular, his statement about moving a piece, which "is something entirely different from the preceding state of the board and also from the state of the board which results. The change which has taken place belongs to neither" (Saussure 1986:88).
11. Thus historical change takes place not at the level of the system (*langue*) but at the level of its individual elements, i.e. at the level of speech: Saussure 1986:ch. 3.
12. Derrida 1972:12-13.
13. Again, Di Benedetto 1983. Cf. Jebb on 1116 and 1242. If the fragment discussed by Eucken 1979 (frag. 730d Kannicht) antedates Sophocles, whether or not it is by Sophocles, then, on Eucken's demonstration, it seems that *OC* 1044ff. must be an echo.

works. *Oedipus at Colonus* is, from this point of view, a play (in the Derridean sense) of differences from other, earlier works and also from other performances of other tragedies (although the history of performance is even more imponderable than some of the other semiotic problems discussed in Chapter Two.) Further, intertextuality functions in the same way as metatheater. Manfred Schmeling has theorized the relation of the two as follows: theater in theater, to which intertextuality is often attached (cf. the Polyneices scene in *Oedipus at Colonus*), constitutes a literary history internal to the work itself. The autoreflexive forms of theater appear, he says, when a particular tradition has become predictable to the point of boredom (I have spoken of the tragedy's own frustration in the case of *Oedipus at Colonus*) and when extra-theatrical developments, social, economic, etc., have overtaken the tradition.[14] These conditions are arguably those of *Oedipus at Colonus*. In any case, metatheater and intertextuality are "historical" ways in which the tragedy can express its difference from its genre by opening up difference within itself, self-difference.

But, to return to my main argument, metatheater can also be understood in other ways. The theatrical code insists on its presence, on the immediacy of its representation, and thus the present of the stage may become a laboratory for the investigation of this insistence. As I have suggested, it was to some extent such a laboratory for Sophocles. Indeed, *Oedipus at Colonus* discovers various scissions in this presence. First, on the side of temporization, the tragedy begins with a fact that I have suggested was known to its spectators, the presence of Oedipus at Colonus (cf. 3§2). They may also have known of a recent manifestation of the power of his grave—his apparition at a cavalry skirmish in which Boeotian troops led by Agis were repulsed. Oedipus is *now* at Colonus. *Oedipus at Colonus*, set in the heroic age, dramatizes Oedipus' arrival at Colonus and his acceptance there *then*. The tragedy opens with Oedipus' wandering into Colonus and sitting down there. The tragedy is thus an explanation and confirmation of his presence at Colonus. The representation by the theatrical sign of the pregiven sign (the known grave of Oedipus at Colonus) thus takes the pregiven sign out of the present, discovers its reserve in the past, divides it between the present and the past.

Within the play, however, temporization of the theatrical sign moves in the opposite direction, from the heroic past toward the present of the spectators. The reserve of Oedipus' mana, which has been relocated in

14. Schmeling 1982.

the past as the sign of a sign, is continually deferred to a future time, to the future time when the hidden, sleeping corpse of Oedipus will drink warm Theban blood (621-22) (which, as said, may be the time of the spectators). Likewise, the curse on Polyneices and Eteocles will take effect later, after the time represented in the tragedy. The plot itself moves by deferral. Oedipus' seated posture is one of deferral (of others) and of waiting. He waits for Theseus (twice). He waits for his daughters to be restored to him. He waits for his death. This movement of deferral from the present to the future is then, with the off-stage death of Oedipus and its report by a messenger, exchanged for a deferral from the past to the present. When the death of Oedipus finally "appears," it is already in the past, and has to be represented to the chorus by the messenger. Thus the present of the stage is again divided. The grave of Oedipus is a trace, an interval between one state and another.

On the side of spacing, the sign is again divided. From the outset, the Oedipus seen on stage is not self-identical. Even in his opening words, in his first reference to himself, he divides himself into a first and a third person. What the spectators see is not the true Oedipus. The other characters (and the spectators) have to learn how to see Oedipus. He is, to use one of Derrida's synonyms for the aspect of différance now under discussion, *discernable*, i.e., visible but distinguishable from his appearance (for the implications of *discernable* cf. French *discernement*). The sign is distinguishable, different from itself. Likewise, the grave of Oedipus, on which, from the point of view of plot, everything depends, is at an interval, continuous with the stage space but removed from it and forbidden to everyone but Theseus and his successors, one in each generation. The grave thus conforms to Derrida's requirement that spacing be produced "with a certain perseverance in repetition, interval, distance."[15] For the location of the grave is repeatedly maintained in its separateness through the succession of unique witnesses and the enforcement of exclusivity. (As might have been expected, the grave, as trace, is both spacing and temporization.) As hostile to Athens' enemies and to Thebans in particular, the grave also curiously conforms to Derrida's comment on spacing as a matter of *different(t)(d)s*, "a word that one can write, as one wishes, with a final *t* or *d*, depending on whether it is a question of dissimilar alterity or of alterity of allergy and polemic."[16] The grave of Oedipus is indeed polemical; it is a differend. It is "allergic" in that, from an

---

15. Derrida 1972:8.
16. ibid.

incursion into Attic territory, it will suffer "another effect" (thus the etymological sense of "allergy"), i.e., a hostile, reactive one.

The various effects of the sign observed in Chapter Two are, then, those of différance, which provides a most convenient way of formalizing the results of the semiotic reading of the tragedy. I have suggested that there is even in *Oedipus at Colonus* an anticipation of the productive effect of différance. Because the trace is the "cause" of différance and the trace is what replaces the author, self-consciousness on Sophocles' part concerning these matters is likely to be connected to the absence of the author specific to the genre of tragedy (Plato *Rep.* 392D-394D; Arist. *Poet.* 3.48a20-24). Already in antiquity, drama was defined as the form of poetry in which the poet does not speak in his own person. In semiotic terms, the signs speak for him. In fact, *Oedipus at Colonus* contains a quite explicit reflection on the production of signs, one that amounts to a formulation of différance, at 1627-28, where the voice of a god summons Oedipus. To translate the god's τί μέλλομεν/χωρεῖν; into Derridean terms, "Why," he asks, "do we temporize spacing?" (cf. on the denominative χωρεῖν in Ch. 3§3). Rhetorically, in the framework of the plot, the god's "we" means "you," but the question, i.e., why are we an effect of différance, applies to both of them. As rhetorical, the question expects no answer; it is just a way of chiding Oedipus. As a formulation of différance, it is its own answer: we (Oedipus, the god, and, for that matter, anything in the tragedy) can be nothing but effects of différance. Our apparent immediacy, our presentness on stage is already a deferral and a delay. The god's explanation for his chiding question ("You have delayed for a long time") belongs to the formulation of différance. It also answers his own question and is tautological with that question. In the sentence just quoted, Oedipus is not "you" but τἀπὸ σοῦ "action on your part," "action coming from you," so that the source of the action is separated from the action and the envisaged action is deferred, temporized at the same time that, at the rhetorical level, Oedipus is blamed for delay. Further, the god's voice, the utterance itself that formulated différance, already participates in différance. The voice came "many times from many places" (1626). It was temporally and spatially divided. The voice of the god, who "stages" the death of Oedipus, to the extent that it has an agent, is thus heard in precisely the way, the only way, that the tragedian's voice can be heard on stage, i.e., divided into a plurality of voices.

One can compare the function of the two gods, Hermes and Persephone, who lead Oedipus from the stage at the end of the fourth episode, so that he can lead the others (1542-48). These gods "stage" the exit. At precisely the moment in which Oedipus changes roles with his daughters, who have had to lead him up until now, and becomes a dramatic agent in his own right, he disappears from the stage, proposing to "hide" himself in the house of Hades. At the moment, then, in which Oedipus gains parity with the other characters as an actor, as a "doer" (cf. Chapter Two sub fin.), he departs "already hollowed out," we might say, paraphrasing Derrida's definition of différance, "by the marks of his relation to a future element," i.e., the future element of his grave. The three gods, then, Hermes, Persephone, and the unnamed one, are another of Sophocles' ways of reflecting on the trace in the production of the theatrical sign.

Everything that has been said here concerning the relation of *Oedipus at Colonus* to différance could also have been said with reference to Derrida's essay *Memoirs of the Blind: The Self-Portrait and Other Ruins*, though this essay strangely repudiates Oedipus.[17] Certainly Derrida's notion that the figure of the draftsman is projected onto the figure of the blindman corresponds to my analysis of the metatheatricality of Oedipus, the blind man who manages to determine the space that can be seen by the other characters in the tragedy. Furthermore, Derrida's deconstructive analysis of the *trait* (the line that has been drawn by the draftsman) as withdrawal and differential inappearance corresponds to what I have said of the theatrical sign. But it is just at the point of this analysis that Derrida observes that he has fallen back on "the language of negative theology or of those discourses concerned with naming the withdrawal [*retrait*] of the invisible or hidden god."[18] The direction that his essay takes is indeed theological, and, for this reason, would be a more appropriate companion to a reading of *Oedipus at Colonus* that focused on the religious themes of the tragedy, e.g., faith, piety, sacrifice, lamentation, and weeping, which are all related to the withdrawal of the hidden and invisible hero.

The task remains of reconciling the Derridean formalization of the results of Chapter Two with the historical interpretation of the tragedy offered in Chapter Three. The concept of the trace is again the tool. The social and political codes that are recoded in the tragedy do not dissolve in the theatrical sign but bear the traces of their former, and their future, life. These traces are all, in the dramatic setting, anachronisms: they project things belonging to the spectators' time back into the time, the heroic age, represented on stage. As anachronisms, they relate the present of the stage, of stage-time, to something other than itself, hollowing out the

17. Derrida 1993b:17–18, 20.
18. Derrida 1993b:54.

present instance of discourse, the present sign, with the trace of its relation to the future. The present is constituted "by this very relation to what it is not." The present of the stage in *Oedipus at Colonus* is a past constituted by a future. The movement of signification can thus in itself be a lesson. The anachronistic recoding of signs moves them into the past but in so doing brings them into the future, i.e., into the spectators' present, in their (edifying) recoded form. Indeed, the traces of these signs move in the same system and thus in the same vectors as the traces of Oedipus and his grave, that non-simple, non-full, always deferred and thus unrepresentable origin. What might appear to us negative for Sophocles' medium is thus positive for his message.

If Chapters Two and Three and their relation can thus be construed in terms of différance, the question remains of the extent to which Sophocles might have anticipated Derrida's concept of the sign. Because my discussion to this point has in fact assumed some degree of anticipation, I should like to begin by broadening the context of reference in order to establish the probability that a fifth-century concept of the sign very close to the one that, on the basis of Derrida, I have been exposing in *Oedipus at Colonus* was indeed available. I shall use two examples. The first is the well-known saying of Heraclitus concerning Apollo: "The lord, whose oracle is at Delphi, neither makes a statement nor conceals but gives signs" (frag 93 D-K). The meaning of Apollo's words is neither present, as a stated intention, a meaning-to-say,[19] nor absent (hidden), but, as a sign, in play as difference. The other example also has to do with prophecy. Socrates' famous inner voice, his daimonion, was, he believed, prophetic (Pl. *Ap.* 40a; Xen. *Ap.* 13), and Xenophon says that, on the basis of his daimonion, he counseled many of his friends. "For, Socrates used to say, the daimonion gave him signs" (*Mem.* 1.1.4). Socrates often spoke of his daimonion as a sign.[20] It manifested itself as a voice.[21] It was thus a vocal and presumably verbal sign. An explanation of the prophetic power of his daimonion is imposed upon Socrates in a conversation with Euthydemus, on divine benefits to mankind, reported by Xenophon. When Socrates comes to the fourteenth of his examples, divination or prophecy, Euthydemus breaks in and says: "Socrates, the gods seem to have treated you in a friendlier fashion than others, if indeed without even being asked by you they tell you by signs what to do and

---

19. Cf. Derrida 1972:17.
20. Riddell 1867:101–109 quotes the main passages.
21. Pl. *Ap.* 31c–d; *Phdr.* 242b; *Theag.* 128d–e, 129b–c; Xen. *Ap.* 12 ("voice of a god").

what not to do." Socrates' lengthy reply begins: "Yes, and that I'm telling the truth [about my daimonion] you too will perceive if you do not wait until you see the shapes of the gods but if it suffices you seeing their deeds to reverence and honor the gods" (*Mem.* 4.3.12–13). Euthydemus must defer his desire for sight of the shapes of the gods and accept a representation (their deeds). Such is Socrates' explanation of the signs to which Euthydemus had referred. Signs are, then, as in the Heraclitus fragment, a default of presence, a deferral, a delay.

The "theory" of the sign that one can infer from these examples suggests that the notion of the play of the sign did not lie outside Sophocles' horizon and that the apparent aptness of the Derridean construal of the problem of representation in *Oedipus at Colonus* was not accidental. These examples also point to the limits of Sophoclean or any fifth-century différance. For the signs of which Socrates and Heraclitus speak come from and are determined by deities, who are present even if they are invisible and who are the origin of the signs they send "in a present that is simple and unmodified in itself, in-different," i.e., contrary to Derrida's notion of différance, these signs have a predetermined meaning even if it is opaque.[22] These gods already belong to the metaphysical tradition which Derrida would define as a "metaphysics of presence" and to which différance is opposed as the opposite of presence (to speak in traditional metaphysical terms). The gods are a "transcendental signified" that guarantees the truth of their signs, whether or not mortals can interpret them. Likewise, within the same metaphysical framework, the tragic poet, whether as educator of the city[23] or as the maker of plots (as he would be defined in the *Poetics*), had no reason to doubt that he was the controlling source of his words.

Thus, even if tragedy is the genre in which the author is absent, he is still present outside his work as the origin of his work. For this reason, the problematizing of dramatic representation, which within our horizon of expectation, precisely because of différance, seems to indicate a fifth-century "crisis of representation," might have had the opposite implications. The return of Theseus from an extra-theatrical space in which he witnessed an unrepresentable event might imply the power of the tragic poet to overcome the generic limitations that, earlier in the tragedy, were adumbrated in several ways. Indeed, in the return of Theseus in the exodos, the problems of representation, on the one hand, and the problems of

---

22. On the sign as intervention of the divine into the human sphere, see Manetti 1987:29–33.
23. Taplin 1983a.

Conclusion 159

Athens, for which Oedipus is to be a savior, come together and are resolved together. Theseus returns as the witness to the death of Oedipus, with knowledge of the location of the grave. The return of Theseus is a reaffirmation of the potentiality of the dramatic, which is summed up in Guildenstern's remark in *Rosencrantz and Guildenstern Are Dead*: "Somebody might come in. It's what we're counting on. Ultimately."[24] The entrance is a way, I think, of construing the apriori of the actor's body and the empty space.[25] It is the fundamental action of the actor. Because the death and the grave of Oedipus have been "represented" as extra-theatrical, the entrance of Theseus both reaffirms the theatrical or dramatic and, at the level of narrative, bearing witness to the grave, bears witness to Colonus as bulwark of Athens. The grave is there if somebody can return from the grave to the stage. As the discussion above of the god's voice suggested, the aspect of différance that Sophocles brings to the fore, in the very deferring of the death and grave of Oedipus, is its productiveness. Likewise, the movement of anachronistic, contemporary traces in the tragedy could be seen as a positive recirculation, reinforcing an edifying effect. To dwell within the problematics of the sign was not a plight but a mercy, for "the gods send signs to those who are in their grace" (*Mem.* 1.1.9).

It is thus quite possible to restore the semiotics of *Oedipus at Colonus* to a fifth-century context in which the theatrical sign has a primary source and meaning outside the play and in which the tragic poet, as hierophant of the sign, is the citizen-poet, the teacher of the polis. But if the results of the semiotic analysis conducted in Chapter Two are as radical as they seem, one is left with doubts about this reassuring picture of the Greek tragedian. By exposing the production of significance on stage, Sophocles may imply that significance is nothing but produced, nothing but a production; that there is no source of meaning more remote than the poet; that theatrical signs are inadequate to a representation of presence even if there were some presence to be represented. Such a conclusion would of course go diametrically against the received picture of the pious Sophocles (assuming that the piety of Sophocles is to be understood on the model of belief in divinities that are transcendent, eternal, etc.). Further, the apologetic tendency traced in Chapter Three, itself just as much a produced meaning and no longer grounded in some belief in a fixed meaning of Colonus, becomes less sincere and

---

24. Used by Niall Slater as the epigraph to a review of a book called *Exits and Entrances in Menander* (*Arion* 1.3 [1992] 195).
25. Cf. the quotations from Fischer-Lichte and Brook above, p. 23.

less attractive to us. Sophocles the apologist for Colonus becomes a politician.

For me, a dilemma remains. In any case, différance has viewed the two parts of this book as related readings of the same sign system. Anachronisms are traces and so are theatrical signs. From the hermeneutic point of view, however, the two readings have different meanings, which demand to be understood in terms of change, i.e., of difference. In the Introduction, I quoted Jauss' challenge: "The reconstruction of the original horizon of expectations would ... fall back into historicism if the historical interpretation could not in turn serve to transform the question, "'What did the text say?' into the question, 'What does the text say to me, and what do I say to it?'." What the text said, according to Chapter Three, bore a particular relation to the situation of the restored democracy (though, to repeat, this reading does not pretend to exhaust the historical meaning of the tragedy). In expressing this meaning, the text speaks to me as a scholar long interested in the history and literature of Athens in the second half of the fifth century; it also speaks to an "interpretive community" that shares my interest. The results of Chapter Three might even in some small way contribute to, say, a history of the crisis of democracy at the end of the fifth century. This history would have whatever value is assigned to the understanding of the past and of the Athenian past in particular. Jauss demands, however, a transformation of the historical questions into present ones, and, indeed, into the question of what the text says to me.

The text says more to me about itself and its own working than about Colonus and Athens. The particular historical issues that I have identified are of no greater personal meaning to me than are the details for the ritual of atonement to the Eumenides (details that we can assume were of great interest to the play's first audiences). Such things are of interest to me, as said, only as a scholar of Athenian literature and history. The historical issues could become more meaningful in another context, that of the crisis of democracy and the decline of Athens. In the Introduction, I referred to an article by Kurt Raaflaub that, while it does not discuss *Oedipus at Colonus*, goes a long way to establishing a context in which the historical resonance of that tragedy could be more than historical. Nevertheless, the tragedy *as dramatic text* speaks to me from the semiotic reading conducted in Chapter Two, partly because of the orientation established in Chapter One through the comparison of Aristotle and Artaud and partly because of what might be called the atmosphere of différance in which I live. Différance is inevitably what I say to the tragedy. Différance with a difference is what the tragedy finally says to me, because it forces me to wonder how the play of the sign might have appeared to someone else.

Appendix

Life of Sophocles and Reception of *Oedipus at Colonus*

The non-factuality of most of the ancient testimonia concerning the life of Sophocles is now generally accepted.[1] These testimonia, like the ones for other poets' lives, tend to derive from the poet's own works.[2] This view of the matter is also generally accepted. It should follow, then, that the Sophoclean testimonia provide facts concerning the ancient reception of the tragedian's works, if not in his own time, at least in subsequent generations. In the following discussion, some of the Sophoclean testimonia will be studied from this point of view in relation to *Oedipus at Colonus*. The question will be asked: judging from the testimonia, how did certain ancient readers read *Oedipus at Colonus*?

I shall begin, however, with an event in the life of Sophocles that I consider factual. At any rate, it cannot be derived from his poetry. That is his reception of Asclepius, who came to Athens in 420 (*IG* II²4960.17–19). "Sophocles received the god in his house and established an altar to him" (*Et. Mag.* 256.10ff. [s.v. Δεξίων] = T69; cf. Plut. *Num.* 4.6 = T67). Asclepius would have stayed with Sophocles during the period in which the land on which the Asclepieion was eventually built was under dispute (*IG* II²4960.20–23).[3] Plutarch refers to an epiphany of the god experienced by Sophocles and others (*Mor.* 1103A = T68). Sophocles was held to have composed a paean in his honor (*IG* II²4510 = Soph. frag. 4 Diehl; cf. T73). Sophocles was also the priest of an obscure hero, Halon or

---

1. See Lefkowitz 1981; Lloyd-Jones and Wilson 1990a:xiv–xv.
2. For other kinds of error, see Fairweather 1983.
3. Ferguson 1944:89–90.

164 Appendix

Alon, who was raised by Cheiron with Asclepius (*Vita* 11).[4] Sophocles' affinities for heroes (he is also said to have founded a cult of Heracles Menutos: *Vita* 12) and for Asclepius go together: though Asclepius is worshipped as a god, he has heroic aspects,[5] and the celebration of Heroa are associated with the Asclepieion at Athens (*IG* II²974.11). Luigi Beschi brings this latter fact into relation with the series of reliefs with funeral banquets found in the area of the Asclepieion: the figures depicted in these reliefs, he argues, are heroes.[6]

Sophocles' reception of Asclepius, the object of a new cult in Athens, bears a certain relation to the central event of *Oedipus at Colonus*, which is the reception of Oedipus in Attica, also the object of a new cult. Because Sophocles was the one who had received Asclepius, he was called Δεξίων "Receiver" after his death (*Et. Mag.* s.v.). His action as host of Asclepius corresponds to that of Theseus, who receives (verb δέχομαι 627, cf. 4, 44, 487, 945) Oedipus. Sophocles was host to Asclepius in his own house; Theseus invites Oedipus to his house (643). The cult of Asclepius is at first private, and then becomes public; Asclepius is φιλόπολις (Ar. *Plut.* 726). The cult of Oedipus is privately maintained by the king of Athens and his successors but for the public good: Oedipus has come to benefit the polis (*OC* 459, 1519, 1533). Oedipus has two daughters; Asclepius has three (and a fourth is added by the Athenians). Oedipus supports himself with a staff (cf. *OT* 456); Asclepius is represented as walking with a staff, as on the Telemachus monument.[7]

These limited similarities between Oedipus and Asclepius are not, however, the point of my comparison. The structure of reception, the founding of a new cult, is what *Oedipus at Colonus* "repeats" from Sophocles' own life. In this very general way, the tragedy was autobiographical. But after the death of Sophocles, it became—and here I return to the thesis announced at the beginning of this section—biographical. Sophocles, who had received Asclepius, was called Dexion and had his own hero shrine (*Et. Mag.*, cited above). It was in or contiguous with the

---

4. The mss. vary between Ἅλων and Ἄλων (the latter has better authority). If the breathing of the former reading were correct, and if the accent were changed to perispomenon, to yield Ἁλῶν (a far simpler emendation than the others that have been proposed), the name could be connected with ἀλάομαι "wander," if an earlier active root is posited. The name of this hero would be parallel to Ἀλήτης 'Wanderer', another hero (Pind. *Ol.* 13.14). I am grateful to Roger Woodard for advice about the etymology of the name.
5. Burkert 1985:214.
6. Beschi 1967–68:422–23.
7. At the bottom of the main relief: clear in the drawing in Beschi 1967–68:411.

Asclepieion, whose orgeones are those of "Amynos, Asclepius, and Dexion" (*IG* II²1252). The parallelism of their reception of Sophocles and his of Asclepius could not be clearer. If Beschi is correct in interpreting the obverse relief on the Telemachus monument as a depiction of Sophocles as Dexion, then this monument is a most concrete expression of the parallelism.

But *Oedipus at Colonus*, with its autobiographical structural similarity to the reception of Asclepius, stands between that reception and the orgeones' reception of Sophocles.[8] In the relief just mentioned, a lyre is the differential characteristic that separates this funeral banquet from the others found in the area of the Asclepieion and identifies the central figure as Sophocles.[9] (There was a painting of Sophocles with a lyre in the Stoa Poikile, commemorating Sophocles' performance on the lyre in his *Thamyris* [*Vita* 5].)[10] Dexion is the heroization not only of Sophocles the receiver of Asclepius but also of Sophocles the poet, and his *Oedipus at Colonus*, in ways I have already suggested, could have provided a model for his own reception as a hero. Whereas, however, as the receiver of a new hero or god in his own lifetime, Sophocles corresponded to Theseus in *Oedipus at Colonus*, he now, being received by the orgeones of Amynos and Asclepius as himself a hero, corresponds to Oedipus in that tragedy.[11]

With the tradition concerning Sophocles as Dexion must be compared the one concerning his death and "real" burial, which again can be related to *Oedipus at Colonus*. As for his death, even before the first performance of *Oedipus at Colonus*, Phrynichus in *Muses* (405 B.C.E.) called Sophocles "blessed" (μάκαρ) and said "he died well" (arg. II *OC* = frag. 31 K = T105).[12] This was a "fact" that could easily have been coordinated with the Sophocles = Oedipus equation after the appearance of the tragedy, for Oedipus's death was also remarkable, without pain (1663–65). Furthermore, at the time of Sophocles' death, he could not be buried near his ancestors, whose tomb was eleven stades outside the city, on the road to Deceleia, since the Spartans occupied that place. Dionysus, the

---

8. Ferguson 1944:87 n. 35.
9. Beschi 1967–68:424.
10. Cf. Fairweather 1983:323, abandoning the scepticism about the painting expressed in Fairweather 1974:252–53.
11. Cf. Lefkowitz 1981:84: "Behind the idea of Sophocles being worshipped as the hero Dexion lies the plot of the *Oedipus at Colonus*." Segal 1981:389 on the basis of his reading of *Oedipus at Colonus* states: "[S]o the position of Oedipus ... reflects the position of the poet himself"; cf. 406–408.
12. There are also various anecdotes reporting bizarre causes of death (TT85–91).

god of the theater, appeared to Lycurgus, the Spartan commander, and bade him allow the burial (*Vita* 15; TT92-94). In the case of Oedipus, then, an epiphany confirmed a presence and provided reason for a (secret) grave (cf. §2); in the case of Sophocles, an epiphany sanctioned a burial.

In one account of the epiphany, Lycurgus was ordered to give proper burial to "the new Siren" (Paus. 1.21.1 = T94). This story may have derived from the figure of a Siren on Sophocles' tombstone (cf. *Vita* 15). In any case, in the burial of the poet on the road to Deceleia, there is a transfiguration of the deceased, just as, in the cult of Dexion in the Asclepieion, the former receiver becomes the "Receiver." In both versions of Sophocles' posthumous existence, the same impulse toward transfiguration is apparent.

In corroboration of the hypothesis that *Oedipus at Colonus* contributed to this conception of Sophocles, one can point to another aspect of the play that was quite probably taken as autobiographical in antiquity. This is the Polyneices scene, behind which a quarrel between the poet and his son Iophon was thought to lie. The report of this quarrel in the *Vita*, the principal source, seems to me to fall into three parts, which are labeled A, B, and C in the following translation:

> (A) You can find in many authors the lawsuit that he once had with his son Iophon. For he had Iophon from Nikostrate, while (the other son) Ariston was from the Sicyonian Theoris; he was fonder of the latter's son, Sophocles by name. (B) And once he [the subject is no longer Sophocles; apparently the name of a comic poet has dropped out of the text] in a play introduced Iophon showing indignation against Sophocles and charging his father with senile dementia before the members of their phratry; but they penalized Iophon. (C) Satyrus says that he said: "If I am Sophocles, I am not out of my mind; if I am out of mind, I am not Sophocles," and then he read the *Oedipus* [*Coloneus*].[13]

Vita Soph. 13

Despite their justifiable scepticism concerning the *Vita*, scholars have always tried to find a logical sequence from A to C. But, given the crazy-quilt composition of the *Vita* as a whole, there is no reason to expect consistency in a passage like the one just quoted. In fact, B does not necessarily follow from the conditions in A. A legal proceeding before the

---

13. For the reading of *OC*: Cic. *de sen.* 7.22; Plut. *Mor.* 785A-B; Apul. *de magia* 298; Lucian *Makrobioi* 24.

phratry would have required some concrete manifestation of the poet's affection for his like-named grandson, and it would have to have been something within the competence of the phratry. B suggested to Carl Robert an attempt on Sophocles' part to present his grandson to the phratry for registration as a citizen, the boy's father, Ariston, being now deceased.[14] (But how could such a proceeding have been characterized as senile dementia on Sophocles' part?) A suggested to Wilhelm Schmid a lawsuit concerning inheritance.[15] Whatever the merits of these reconstructions, they at least show how A and B could refer to completely different affairs. The author of the *Vita* obviously thought that C followed from B, that Satyros was talking about the comedy, but it is difficult to imagine an Old Comedy in which the reading of *Oedipus at Colonus* would have had the effect of demolishing Iophon, as in B. In the comedies of Aristophanes, tragedians' quotations of their own works are in the nature of self-parody; in comic contexts, such quotations are rendered laughable in one way or another. (Not to mention the fact that Satyros's quotation of Sophocles is not metrical.)

Though a recitation of *Oedipus at Colonus* cannot be connected with B, as the author of the *Vita* thought, it might be connected with a historical lawsuit prompted by the conditions outlined in A or lying behind the comedy mentioned in B. As for the latter possibility, i.e., a trial that inspired a comedy, Aristotle refers to an eighty year-old, trembling Sophocles on the witness-stand (*Rhet.* 1416a14–17), though nothing suggests that the trial had anything to do with Iophon. Michael H. Jameson has proposed that this passage in Aristotle's *Rhetoric* and two others in which Sophocles is mentioned refer to an eisangelia at which Peisander had to defend himself against the charge of having caused the death of a certain Euctemon[16] and Sophocles, one of his accusers, was trembling under cross-examination. One can speculate that the appearance of the dottering tragedian at this eisangelia was somehow the basis of the comedy and that Iophon as accuser was a comic elaboration of the idea.

If it is assumed that the biographical tradition concerning conflict between father and son arose from the comedy (so that A is derived from B), then the recitation of *Oedipus at Colonus* is not hard to explain. It is prompted by a certain parallelism between the tragedy and the supposed event in the life of the tragedian. Iophon's charge against his father had

---

14. Robert 1915:477–78.
15. Schmid-Stählin 321–22.
16. Jameson 1971.

something to do with his father's old age.[17] The son asserts his right against his father. The hero of *Oedipus at Colonus* is an old man who has not received the obligatory support from his son. The father asserts his right against his son. The tragedy is easily read as a retaliation by the author against his son. In order to make the point crystal clear, the biographical tradition has Sophocles read the tragedy aloud in the courtroom in which he successfully defends himself against his son. In some of the testimonia, it is of course the stasimon in praise of Colonus that the tragedian recites, as would be expected of Sophocles the native of Colonus.[18]

To conclude, the ancient biographical tradition gives us a way to read *Oedipus at Colonus* as "autobiography" (the founding of a cult) and a way to understand the founding of the cult of Sophocles himself as a biographical "reading" of the tragedy, just as the conflict between Oedipus and Polyneices in the tragedy was understood to reflect a conflict between Sophocles and his son Iophon. As the expected background of the cult of Sophocles, his death was unusually blessed, like that of Oedipus, and Sophocles attains something like the special status of the hero of the tragedy. In both of Sophocles' "burials," furthermore, this special status is linked to his poetry. An epiphany of Dionysus permits the burial on the road to Deceleia, where Sophocles is the "new Siren." If Beschi is right, the lyre on the Telemachus monument says the same thing. In this respect, Sophocles seems to differ from the Oedipus I am positing as a sort of model for later generations' understanding of Sophocles. But they have in common a special power of language: to the poetry of Sophocles corresponds Oedipus' command of prayer, entreaty, persuasion, and, above all, curses (not only in *Oedipus at Colonus* but also in *Oedipus the King*). In sum, both have a special status as cult heroes, the result of unique or unusual lives and unusual deaths, and both have a special power of language.

---

17. Cf. Cic. *de sen.* 7.22 (T81): Sophocles ad summam senectutem tragoedias fecit; quod propter studium cum rem neglegere familiarem videretur, a filiis in iudicium vocatus est, ut, quem ad modum nostro more male rem gerentibus patribus bonis interdici solet, sic illum quasi desipientem a re familiari removerent iudices. Tum senex dicitur eam fabulam quam in manibus habebat et proxime scripserat, Oedipum Coloneum, recitasse iudicibus quaesisseque num illud carmen desipientis videretur, quo recitato sententiis iudicum est liberatus. TT81–84 show differences in the accuser ("sons" or "son" or "Iophon") and in specificity as regards the part of *OC* that Sophocles read in court.

18. On the demotic as it appears in *Vita* 1 see Fairweather 1983:343–44.

List of Works Cited

Aichele, Klaus 1971. "Das Epeisodion." In Jens 1971, pp. 47-83.
Allison, R. H. 1984. "'This is the place': Why is Oidipous at Kolonos?" *Prudentia* 16:67-91.
Arnott, P. D. 1962. *Greek Scenic Conventions in the Fifth Century B.C.* Clarendon Press: Oxford.
Artaud, Antonin 1958. *The Theater and Its Double*, trans. M. C. Richards. Grove Press: New York. From: *Le Théâtre et son double* (Paris: Gallimard, 1938)
Aston, Elaine and George Savona 1991. *Theatre as Sign-System: A Semiotics of Text and Performance.* Routledge: London and New York.
Avery, Harry 1973. "Sophocles' Political Career." *Historia* 22:509-14.
Bachelard, Gaston 1969. *The Poetics of Space*, trans. Maria Jolas. Beacon Press: Boston.
Benston, Kimberly W. 1992. "Being There: Performance as Mise-en-Scène. Abscene, Obscene, and Other Scene." *PMLA* 107.3:434-49.
Benveniste, Émile 1966. "La nature des pronoms." In *Problèmes de linguistique générale* (Gallimard: Paris), pp. 251-57.
———. 1969. *Le vocabulaire des institutions indo-européennes*, vol. 1. Les Éditions de Minuit: Paris.
Bernabé, Albert, ed. 1987. *Poetarum Epicorum Fragmenta*, part 1. Teubner: Leipzig.
Beschi, Luigi 1967-68. "Il monumento di Telemachos, fondatore dell' Asklepieion ateniese." *Annuario della Scuola Archeologica di Atene e delle Missioni italiane in Oriente* 45-46/NS 29-30: 421-36.
Bieler, Ludwig 1951. "A Political Slogan in Ancient Athens." *AJP* 72:181-84.

Blundell, M. W. 1989. *Helping Friends and Harming Enemies: A Study in Sophocles and Greek Ethics*. Cambridge University Press: Cambridge.

———. 1993 "The Ideal of Athens in *Oedipus at Colonus*." In Alan H. Sommerstein et al., ed. *Tragedy, Comedy and the Polis* (Levante: Bari), pp. 287-306.

Braun, E. 1982. *The Director and the Stage*. Methuen: London.

Brecht, Bertolt 1964. *Brecht on Theatre*, trans. and ed. John Willett. Hill and Wang: New York.

Brook, Peter 1978. *The Empty Space*. Atheneum: New York. First published 1968.

Brown, A. L. 1984. "Eumenides in Greek Tragedy." *CQ* 34:260-81.

Burian, Peter 1974. "Suppliant and Saviour: Oedipus at Colonus." *Phoenix* 28:408-29

Burkert, Walter 1979. *Structure and History in Greek Mythology and Ritual*. University of California Press: Berkeley and Los Angeles.

———. 1985. "Opferritual bei Sophokles: Pragmatik-Symbolik-Theater." *Die Altsprachliche Unterricht* 28.2:5-20.

Burnett, Anne Pippen 1971. *Catastrophe Survived: Euripides' Plays of Mixed Reversal*. Clarendon Press: Oxford.

Burton, R. W. B. 1980. *The Chorus in Sophocles' Tragedies*. Clarendon Press: Oxford.

Busolt, Georg 1904. *Griechische Geschichte bis zur Schlacht bei Chaeronea*, vol. 3. F. A. Perthes Aktiengesellschaft: Gotha.

Buxton, R. G. A. 1984. *Sophocles*. Greece & Rome: New Surveys in the Classics 16. Clarendon Press: Oxford.

Calame, Claude forthcoming (1997). "Mort héroïque et culte à mystères dans l'Oedipe à Colone de Sophocle: actes rituels au service de la recréation mythique." In F. Graf, ed. *Ansichten griechischer Rituale* (Teubner: Stuttgart and Leipzig).

Calder, W. M., III 1971. "Sophoclean Apologia:Philoctetes." *GRBS* 12:153-74.

Campbell, Lewis 1879. *Sophocles*, vol. 1, 2nd ed. Clarendon Press: Oxford.

———. 1906. "Colonus Hippius." *CR* 20:3-5.

Carey, Christopher 1980. "The Epilogue of Pindar's Fourth Pythian." *Maia* NS 32:143-52.

Cerbo, Ester 1989. "La scena di riconoscimento in Euripide: dall'amebeo alla monodia." *QUCC* NS 33:39-47.

Compagnon, Antoine 1979. *La seconde main, ou le travail de la citation*. Éditions du Seuil: Paris.

Cook, A. B. 1925. *Zeus*, vol. 2, part 2. Cambridge University Press: Cambridge.
Craik, E. M. 1980. "Arist. *Poetics* 1455a27: Karkinos' *Amphiaraos*." *Maia* 32:167-69.
———. ed. 1988. *Euripides' Phoenician Women*. Aris and Phillips: Warminster.
———. ed. 1990. *'Owls to Athens': Essays on Classical Subjects Presented to Sir Kenneth Dover*. Clarendon Press. Oxford.
Daly, James 1990. *Horizontal Resonance as a Principle of Composition in the Plays of Sophocles*. Garland Publishing: New York.
Dawe, R. D. 1978. *Studies on the Text of Sophocles*, vol. 3. E. J. Brill: Leiden.
De Finis, Lia, ed. 1989. *Scena e spettacolo nell' antichità: Atti del Convegno Internazionale di Studio* (Trento, March 28-30, 1988). L. S. Olschki: Florence.
de Lacy, Phillip H. and Benedict Einarson, trans. 1959. *Plutarch's Moralia*, vol. 7. Harvard University Press: Cambridge MA and London.
Denniston, J. D. 1966. *The Greek Particles*, 2nd ed. Clarendon Press: Oxford.
Derrida, Jacques 1972. "Différance," in *Marges de la philosophie* (Editions de Minuit: Paris), pp. 3-29.
———. 1978. *Writing and Difference*, trans. Alan Bass. University of Chicago Press: Chicago.
———. 1981. "Plato's Pharmacy," in *Dissemination*, trans. Barbara Johnson (University of Chicago Press: Chicago), pp. 63-171.
———. 1982. "Différance," in *Margins of Philosophy*, trans. Alan Bass (University of Chicago Press: Chicago), pp. 3-27.
———. 1988. *Limited Inc*. Northwestern University Press: Evanston IL.
———. 1991. *A Derrida Reader: Between the Blinds*, ed. Peggy Kamuf. Columbia University Press: New York.
———. 1993a. *Khôra*. Editions Galilée: Paris. Originally published in *Poikilia: Etudes offerts à Jean-Pierre Vernant* (Paris, 1987).
———. 1993b. *Memoirs of the Blind: The Self-Portrait and Other Ruins*, trans. P.-A. Brault and Michael Naas. University of Chicago Press: Chicago and London.
Di Benedetto, V. 1979. "Da Odisseo a Edipo: Soph. O. C. 1231. *Riv. di Fil.* 107:15-22.
———. 1983. *Sofocle*. La Nuova Italia: Florence.
Dingel, Joachim 1971. "Requisit und szenisches Bild in der griechischen Tragödie." In Jens 1971, pp. 347-67.

Dodds, E. R. 1960. *Euripides: Bacchae*. Clarendon Press: Oxford.
Donadi, Franceso 1970-71. "Nota al cap. VI della Poetica di Aristotele: il problema dell' ὄψις." *Atti e Memorie dell'Accademia Patavina di Scienze Lettere Arti* 83.3:413-51.
Dover, K. J. 1968. *Lysias and the Corpus Lysiacum*. University of California Press: Berkeley and Los Angeles.
Ducrot, Oswald and Tzvetan Todorov 1972. *Dictionnaire encyclopédique des sciences du langage*. Éditions du Seuil: Paris.
Dunn, Francis M. 1992. "Introduction: Beginning at Colonus." *YCS* 29:1-12.
Dupont-Roc, Roselyne and Jean Lallot, ed. 1980. *Aristote: La Poétique*. Éditions du Seuil: Paris.
Eagleton, Terry 1983. *Literary Theory: An Introduction*. University of Minnesota Press: Minneapolis.
Easterling, P. E. 1967. "Oedipus and Polyneices." *PCPS* 13:1-13.
———. 1985. "Anachronism in Greek Tragedy." *JHS* 105:1-10.
Edmunds, Lowell 1981. "The Cults and the Legend of Oedipus." *HSCP* 8:221-38.
———. 1985a. *Oedipus: The Ancient Legend and its Later Analogues*. The Johns Hopkins University Press: Baltimore and London.
———. 1985b. "The Genre of Theognidean Poetry." In Figueira and Nagy 1985, pp. 96-111.
———. 1987. *Cleon, Knights, and Aristophanes' Politics*, University Press of America: Lanham, MD.
———. 1991. "Oedipus in the Twentieth Century: Principal Dates." *Classical and Modern Literature* 11:317-24
———. 1993. "Thucydides in the Act of Writing." In *Tradizione e innovazione nella cultura greca da Omero all' età ellenistica: Scritti in onore di Bruno Gentili*, ed. Roberto Pretagostini, vol. 2 (GEI: Rome), pp. 831-52.
Elam, Keir 1980. *The Semiotics of Theater and Drama*. Methuen: London and New York.
Ellendt, F. 1872. *Lexicon Sophocleum*, 2nd ed. Repr. Georg Olms: Hildesheim, 1965.
Else, Gerald F. 1967. *Aristotle's Poetics*. Harvard University Press: Cambridge.
Eucken, Christoph 1979. "Das anonyme Theseus-Drama und der Oedipus Coloneus." *MH* 36:136-41.
Fairweather, Janet 1974. "Fiction in the Biographies of Ancient Writers." *Ancient Society* 5:231-75.
———. 1983. "Traditional Narrative, Inference, and Truth in the *Lives* of the Greek Poets." *Papers of the Liverpool Latin Seminar* 4:315-69.

Fantuzzi, Marco 1991. "Ora e luogo nella tragedia greca." *MD* 24:9-30.
Ferguson, W. S. 1944. "The Attic Orgeones." *Harvard Theological Review* 37:61-140.
Figueira, Thomas 1991. *Athens and Aigina in the Age of Imperial Colonization*. The Johns Hopkins: University Press: Baltimore and London.
Figueira, Thomas and Gregory Nagy, ed. 1985. *Theognis of Megara*. The Johns Hopkins University Press: Baltimore and London.
Fischer-Lichte, Erika 1983. *Semiotik des Theaters*, vol. 1 (*Das System der theatralischen Zeichen*); vol. 2 (*Vom "künstlichen" zum "natürlichen" Zeichen—Theater des Barock und der Aufklärung*); vol. 3 (*Die Aufführung als Text*). G. Narr: Tübingen.
———. 1992. *The Semiotics of Theater*, trans. Jeremy Gaines and D. L. Jones. Indiana University Press: Bloomington and Indianapolis.
Flashar, Helmut 1984. "Die Poetik des Aristoteles und die griechische Tragödie." *Poetica* 16:1-23.
Foley, Helene 1980. "The Masque of Dionysus." *TAPA* 110:107-33.
———. 1985. *Ritual Irony: Poetry and Sacrifice in Euripides*. Cornell University Press: Ithaca.
Gagarin, Michael 1981. *Drakon and Early Athenian Homicide Law*. Yale University Press: New Haven and London.
Giangiulio, Maurizio 1992. "La φιλότης tra Sibariti e Serdaioi (Meiggs-Lewis, 10)." *ZPE* 93:31-44.
Giannini, Pietro 1979. "Interpretazione della *Pitica* 4 di Pindaro." *QUCC* NS 2:36-63.
Gide, André 1942. *Théâtre*. Gallimard: Paris.
Gildersleeve, Basil L. 1899. Pindar: *The Olympian and Pythian Odes*. Harper: New York. Repr. Arno Press: New York, 1979.
Goldhill, Simon 1989. "Reading Performance Criticism." *G&R* 36:172-82.
Gould, J. P. 1973. "Hiketeia." *JHS* 93:74-103.
———. 1985. "Tragedy in Performance." In *The Cambridge History of Classical Literature*, vol. 1, *Greek Literature*, ed. P. E. Easterling and B. M. W. Knox (Cambridge University Press: Cambridge), pp. 263-80.
Grande, Maurizio 1989. "Spazio teatrale e scrittura di scena." *Dionisio* 59:353-60.
Green, J. R. 1990. "Carcinus and the Temple: A Lesson in the Staging of Tragedy." *GRBS* 31:281-85.
Greimas, A.-J. and J. Cortés, 1982. *Semiotics and Language: An Analytical Dictionary*, trans. Larry Crist et al. Indiana University Press: Bloomington.

174 Works Cited

———. 1986. *Sémiotique: Dictionnaire raisonné de la théorie du langage,* II. Hachette: Paris.
Halliwell, Stephen 1986. *Aristotle's Poetics.* University of North Carolina Press: Chapel Hill.
Hamilton, Richard 1978. "Announced Entrances in Greek Tragedy." *HSCP* 82:63-82.
Hammond, N. G. L. 1972. "The Conditions of Dramatic Production to the Death of Aeschylus." *GRBS* 13:387-450.
Hansen, Hardy 1990. *Aspects of the Athenian Law Code of 410/409- 400/399 B.C.* Garland Press: New York.
HCT = Gomme, A. W., Andrewes, A. and Dover, K. J. 1944-81. *A Historical Commentary on Thucydides.* Oxford University Press: Oxford.
Heath, Malcolm 1989. *Unity in Greek Poetics.* Clarendon Press: Oxford.
Henderson, Jeffrey 1987a. "Older Women in Attic Comedy." *TAPA* 117:105-29.
———. 1987b. *Aristophanes: Lysistrata.* Clarendon Press: Oxford.
Henrichs, Albert 1983. "The 'Sobriety' of Oedipus: Sophocles *OC* 100 Misunderstood." *HSCP* 87:87-100.
———. 1991. "Namenlosigkeit und Euphemismus: Zur Ambivalenz der chthonischen Mächte im attischen Drama." In *Fragmenta Dramatica: Beiträge zur Interpretation der griechischen Tragikerfragmente und ihrer Wirkungsgeschichte,* ed. Heinz Hofmann (Vandenhoeck & Ruprecht: Göttingen), pp. 161-201.
Herman, Gabriel 1987. *Ritualised Friendship and the Greek State.* Cambridge University Press: Cambridge.
Hignett, C. 1952. *A History of the Athenian Constitution.* Oxford University Press: Oxford.
Honzl, Jindřich 1976. "The Hierarchy of Dramatic Devices." In Matejka and Titunik 1976, pp. 118-27.
Hooker, James 1987. "Homeric φίλος." *Glotta* 65:44-65.
Issacharoff, Michael 1981. "Space and Reference in Drama." *Poetics Today* 2: 211-24. Repr. in *Discourse as Performance,* ch. 5.
———. 1988. "Stage Codes." In Issacharoff and Jones, ed. 1988, pp. 59-74.
———. 1989. *Discourse as Performance.* Stanford University Press: Stanford. From: *Le spectacle du discours* (Paris: Librairie José Corti, 1985).
Issacharoff, Michael and R. F. Jones, ed. 1988. *Performing Texts.* University of Pennsylvania Press: Philadelphia.
Jameson, Michael H. 1971. "Sophocles and the Four Hundred." *Historia* 20:541-68.

Jauss, Hans Robert 1982. "The Poetic Text within the Change of Horizons of Reading: The Example of Baudelaire's 'Spleen II'," in *Toward an Aesthetic of Reception*, trans. Timothy Bahti, Theory and History of Literature, vol. 2, pp. 139-85. University of Minnesota Press: Minneapolis.

Jebb, R. C. 1928. *Sophocles: The Plays and Fragments*. Part II. *The Oedipus Coloneus*. Cambridge University Press: Cambridge. Repr. Adolf M. Hakkert: Amsterdam, 1969.

Jens, Walter, ed. 1971. *Die Bauformen der griechischen Tragödie*. Wilhelm Fink: Munich.

Johnson, Barbara 1988. *The Critical Difference*. The Johns Hopkins University Press: Baltimore.

Jones, John 1962. *On Aristotle and Greek Tragedy*. Oxford University Press: New York.

Jones, W. H. S. trans. 1918. *Pausanias: Description of Greece*. Harvard University Press: Cambridge MA and London.

Kagan, Donald 1987. *The Fall of the Athenian Empire*. Cornell University Press: Ithaca and London.

Kaimio, Maarit 1970. *The Chorus of Greek Tragedy within the Light of the Person and Number Used*. Commentationes Humanarum Litterarum, 46. Societas Scientiarum Fennica. Helsinki.

———. 1988. *Physical Contact in Greek Tragedy: A Study of Stage Conventions*. Annales Academiae Scientarum Fennicae Ser. B, vol. 244. Helsinki.

Kamerbeek, J. C. 1984. *The Plays of Sophocles*. Part VII: *The Oedipus Coloneus*. E. J. Brill: Leiden.

Karavites, Peter 1976. "Tradition, Skepticism, and Sophocles' Political Career." *Klio* 58:359-65.

Kearns, Emily 1989. *The Heroes of Attica*. BICS Suppl. 57.

Kindermann, Heinz 1979. *Das Theaterpublikum der Antike*. Otto Müller: Salzburg.

———. 1990. *Il teatro greco e il suo pubblico*, ed. Angela Andrisano. Usher: Florence. Trans. of Kindermann 1979.

Kirkwood, G. M. 1986. "From Melos to Colonus: τίνας χώρους ἀφίγμεθ'." *TAPA* 116:99-117.

Kirsten, Ernst 1973. "Ur-Athen und die Heimat des Sophokles." *WS* NF 7:5-26.

Kitto, H. D. F. 1956. *Form and Meaning in Drama: A Study of Six Greek Plays and of Hamlet*. Methuen: London.

Klaus, Joerden 1971. "Zur Bedeutung des Außer- und Hinterszenischen." In Jens 1971, pp. 369-412.

Kopperschmidt, Josef 1971. "Hikesie als dramatische Form." In Jens 1971, pp. 321-46.
Kowzan, Tadeusz 1985. "From Written Text to Performance—From Performance to Written Text." In Fischer-Lichte, et al. 1985, pp. 1-11.
Kranz, Walther 1933. *Stasimon*. Weidmann: Berlin.
———. 1949. "Parodos." *RE* 36th half vol.: cols. 1684-94.
Kremer, Gerd 1971. "Die Struktur des Tragödienschlusses." In Jens 1971, pp. 117-41.
Kristeva, Julia 1969. "Pour une sémiologie des paragrammes" (1966), in Σημειωτική: *Recherches pour une sémanalyse* (Éditions du Seuil: Paris), pp. 174-207.
L-J-W = Lloyd-Jones and Wilson.
Lacey, W. K. 1968. *The Family in Classical Greece*. Cornell University Press: Ithaca.
Lanza, Diego ed. 1987. *Aristotele: Poetica*. Rizzoli: Milan.
Lardinois, André 1992. "Greek Myths for Athenian Rituals: Religion and Politics in Aeschylus' *Eumenides* and Sophocles' *Oedipus Coloneus*." *GRBS* 33:313-27.
Lawlor, Lillian B. 1964. *The Dance of the Ancient Greek Theatre*. University of Iowa Press: Iowa City.
Lefebvre, Henri 1986. *La production de l'espace*, 3rd ed. Éditions anthropos: Paris.
Lefkowitz, Mary R. 1981. *The Lives of the Greek Poets*. The Johns Hopkins University Press: Baltimore.
Lesky, Albin 1966. *A History of Greek Literature*, trans. James Willis and Cornelis de Heer. Thomas Y. Crowell Co: New York.
Lloyd-Jones, H. and N. Wilson 1990a. *Sophoclis Fabulae*. Clarendon Press: Oxford.
———. 1990b. *Sophoclea: Studies on the Text of Sophocles*. Clarendon Press: Oxford.
Lloyd-Jones, Hugh 1990. "Erinyes, Semnai Theai, Eumenides." In E. M. Craik, ed. 1990, pp. 203-11.
Longo, Odone 1975. "Proposte di lettura per l'Oreste di Euripide." *Maia* 27:265-87.
Loomis, W. T. 1972. "The Nature of Premeditation in Athenian Homicide Law." JHS 92:86-95.
Lotman, Jurij 1981. "Semiotica della scena" (con una postfazione di Simonetta Salvestroni). *Strumenti critici* 44:1-45.
Lucas, D. W. 1968. *Aristotle: Poetics*. Clarendon Press: Oxford.
Lyons, Charles R. 1987. "Character and Theatrical Space." In Redmond 1987, pp. 27-44.

Manetti, Giovanni 1987. *Le teorie del segno nell'antichità classica.* Bompiani: Milan.
Marzullo, Benedetto 1980. "Die visuelle Dimension des Theaters bei Aristoteles." *Philologus* 124:189-200.
Mastronarde, Donald J. 1979. *Contact and Discontinuity: Some Conventions of Speech and Action on the Greek Tragic Stage.* University of California Publications: Classical Studies 21. University of California Press: Berkeley, Los Angeles, and London.
Matejka, Ladislav 1976. "Postscript. Prague School Semiotics." In Matejka and Titunik 1976, pp. 265-90.
Matejka, Ladislav and Irwin R. Titunik, ed. 1976. *Semiotics of Art: Prague School Contributions.* MIT Press: Cambridge, MA and London.
Meiggs-Lewis = Meiggs, Russell and David Lewis 1975. *A Selection of Greek Historical Inscriptions To the End of the Fifth Century B.C.* Oxford University Press: Oxford.
Nagy, Gregory 1985. "Theognis and Megara: A Poet's Vision of His City." In Figueira and Nagy 1985, pp. 22-81.
———. 1990a. *Greek Mythology and Poetics.* Cornell University Press: Ithaca and London.
———. 1990b. *Pindar's Homer: The Lyric Possession of an Epic Past.* The Johns Hopkins University Press: Baltimore and London.
Nemeth, G. 1983. "On Dating Sophocles' Death." *Homonoia* 5:115-28.
Neumann, Gerhard 1965. *Gesten und Gebärden in der griechischen Kunst.* Walter de Gruyter: Berlin.
Newiger, Hans-Joachim 1979. "Drama und Theater." In *Das griechische Drama,* ed. G. A. Seeck (Wissenschaftliche Buchgesellschaft: Darmstadt), pp. 434-503.
Ostwald, Martin 1986. *From Popular Sovereignty to the Sovereignty of Law.* University of California Press: Berkeley, Los Angeles, and London.
Padel, Ruth 1990. "Making Space Speak." In Winkler and Zeitlin, ed. 1990, pp. 336-65.
Pavis, Patrice 1982. *Languages of the Stage: Essays in the Semiology of the Theatre.* Performing Arts Journal Publications: New York.
Pavese, Cesare 1947. *Dialoghi con Leucò.* Einaudi: Turin.
Pečirka, Jan 1966. *The Formula for the Grant of Enktesis in Attic Inscriptions.* Acta Universitatis Carolinae Philosophica et Historica, Monographia 15. Prague.
Pickard-Cambridge, A. W. 1946. *The Theatre of Dionysus at Athens.* Clarendon Press: Oxford.

178 *Works Cited*

———. 1968. *The Dramatic Festivals of Athens*, 2nd ed., rev. J. Gould and D. M. Lewis. Clarendon Press: Oxford.
Poe, Joe Park 1992. "Entrance-Announcements and Entrance-Speeches in Greek Tragedy." *HSCP* 94:121-56.
Raaflaub, Kurt 1992. "Politisches Denken und Krise der Polis: Athen im Verfassungskonflikt des späten 5. Jahrhunderts v. Chr." *Historische Zeitschrift* 225: 1-59.
Renehan, Robert 1992. "The New Oxford Sophocles." *CP* 87:335-75.
Rhodes, P. J. 1972. *The Athenian Boule*. Clarendon Press: Oxford.
———. 1981. *A Commentary on the Aristotelian Athenaion Politeia*. Clarendon Press: Oxford.
Riddell, James 1867. *The Apology of Plato*. Clarendon Press: Oxford.
Ritchie, W. 1964. *The Authenticity of the Rhesus of Euripides*. Cambridge University Press: Cambridge.
Robert, Carl 1915. *Oidipus: Geschichte eines poetischen Stoffs im griechischen Altertum*, 2 vols. Weidmann: Berlin.
Robinson, David 1990. "Homeric φίλος: Love of Life and Limbs, and Friendship with One's θυμός." In Craik, ed. 1990, pp. 97-108.
Rode, Jürgen 1971. "Das Chorlied." In Jens 1971, pp. 85-115.
Rossi, Luigi Enrico 1989. "Livelli di lingua, gestualità, rapporti di spazio e situazione drammatica sulla scena attica." In *de Finis* 1989, pp. 63-78.
Sandys, J. E. 1877. *The Rhetoric of Aristotle with a Commentary*. 3 vols. Cambridge University Press: Cambridge.
Saussure, Ferdinand de 1986. *Course in General Linguistics*, trans. Roy Harris. Open Court: La Salle IL.
Schaps, D. 1977. "The Woman Least Mentioned: Etiquette and Women's Names." *CQ* 27:323-30.
Schmeling, Manfred 1982. *Métathéâtre et intertexte: Aspects du théâtre dans le théâtre*. Archives des Lettres Modernes 204. Lettres Modernes: Paris.
Schmid-Stählin = Schmid, Wilhelm and Otto Stählin 1934. *Geschichte der griechischen Literatur*, First Part, Vol. 2. C. H. Beck: Munich.
Schneidewin, F. W. and A. Nauck 1909. *Sophokles*, vol. 3 (Oidipus auf Kolonos), 9th ed. (by Ludwig Radermacher). Weidmann: Berlin.
Schulze, Wilhelm 1918. "Beiträge zur Wort- und Sittengeschichte, II." *Sitzungsberichte der preussischen Akademie der Wissenschaften*, first half-vol., pp. 481-511. Berlin.
Schwartz, M. 1982. "The Indo-European Vocabulary of Exchange, Hopitality, and Intimacy." *Proceedings of the Berkeley Linguistics Society* 8:188-204.

Schwinge, E.-R. 1990. "Aristoteles und die Gattungsdifferenz von Epos und Drama." *Poetica: Zeitschrift für Sprach- und Literaturwissenschaft* 22:1-20.
Scolnicov, Hanna 1987. "Theatre Space, Theatrical Space, and the Theatrical Space Without." In Redmond 1987, pp. 11-26.
Seale, D. 1982. *Vision and Stagecraft in Sophocles.* University of Chicago Press: Chicago and London.
Segal, Charles 1981. *Tragedy and Civilization: An Interpretation of Sophocles.* Harvard University Press: Cambridge, MA and London.
———. 1982. *Dionysiac Poetics.* Princeton University Press: Princeton.
———. 1986. *Pindar's Mythmaking: The Fourth Pythian Ode.* Princeton University Press: Princeton.
Seidensticker, Bernd 1971. "Die Stichomythie." In Jens 1971, pp. 183-220.
———. 1972. "Beziehungen zwischen den beiden Oidipusdramen des Sophokles." *Hermes* 100:255-74.
Siewert, P. 1979. "Poseidon Hippios am Kolonos und die athenischen Hippeis." In Glen W. Bowersock, Michael C. J. Putnam, and Walter Burkert, ed. *Arktouros: Hellenic Studies Presented to Bernard M. W. Knox on the Occasion of His Sixty-Fifth Birthday* (Berlin and New York), pp. 280-89.
Slater, Niall 1993. "From Ancient Performance to New Historicism." *DRAMA* 2:1-14.
Slatkin, Laura 1986. "*Oedipus at Colonus*: Exile and Integration." In J. P. Euben, ed., *Greek Tragedy and Political Theory* (University of California Press: Berkeley and Los Angeles), pp. 210-21.
Smethurst, Mae J. 1989. *The Artistry of Aeschylus and Zeami: A Comparative Study of Greek Tragedy and No.* Princeton University Press: Princeton.
Solomon, Jon 1987. "Sophoclean Clusters of Dual Personal Pronouns." *Glotta* 65:72-80.
Sommerstein, Alan H., ed. 1989. *Aeschylus: Eumenides.* Cambridge University Press: Cambridge.
Ste. Croix, G. E. M. de 1981. *The Class Struggle in the Ancient Greek World.* Cornell University Press: Ithaca.
Stroud, Ronald S. 1968. *Drakon's Law on Homicide.* University of California Publications: Classical Studies, vol. 3. University of California Press: Berkeley and Los Angeles.
Taillardat, J. 1982. "ΦΙΛΟΤΗΣ, ΠΙΣΤΙΣ et FOEDUS." *REG* 95:1-14.
Tanner, R. G. 1966. "The Composition of the *Oedipus Coloneus*." In Maurice Kelly, ed. *For Service to Classical Studies: Essays in*

Honour of Francis Letters (F. W. Chesire: Melbourne, Canberra and Sydney), pp. 153-92.
Taplin, Oliver 1971. "Significant Actions in Sophocles' *Philoctetes*." *GRBS* 12:25-44.
———. 1977. *The Stagecraft of Aeschylus: The Dramatic Uses of Exits and Entrances in Greek Tragedy*. Clarendon Press: Oxford.
———. 1983a. "Tragedy and Trugedy." *CQ* 33:331-4.
———. 1983b. "Sophocles in his Theatre." In *Sophocle* (Fondation Hardt Entretiens 29), pp. 155-83.
———. 1986. "Tragedy and Comedy: A *Synkrisis*." *JHS* 106:163-74.
TD = Artaud 1958.
Ubersfeld, Anne 1978. *Lire le théâtre*. Editions Sociales: Paris.
———. 1991. *L'école du spectateur: Lire le théâtre 2*. Éditions Sociales: Paris.
Valk, v. d. M. 1985. *Studies in Euripides' Phoenissae and Andromache*. Hakkert: Amsterdam.
Vanderpool, Eugene 1952. "Kleophon." *Hesperia* 21:114-15.
Veltrusky, Jiří 1985. "Drama as Literature and Performance." In Fischer-Lichte, et al. 1985, pp. 12-21.
Vidal-Naquet, Pierre 1986. "Oedipe entre deux cités." *MHTIΣ* 1:37-69. Eng. trans. in J.-P. Vernant and id., *Myth and Tragedy in Ancient Greece* (Zone Books: New York, 1988), pp. 329-59.
Wallace, Robert 1989. *The Areopagus Council, to 307 B.C.* The Johns Hopkins University Press: Baltimore and London.
West, M. L. 1978. *Hesiod: Works and Days*. Clarendon Press: Oxford.
Wiles, David 1987. "Reading Greek Performance." *G&R* 34:136-51.
———. 1990-91. "Les *Sept contre Thèbes* d'Eschyle: Approche structuraliste vers l'espace théâtral." *CGITA* 6:145-60.
Winkler, John J. and Froma Zeitlin, ed. 1990. *Nothing To Do With Dionysus?* Princeton University Press: Princeton.
Winnington-Ingram, R. P. 1980. *Sophocles: An Interpretation*. Cambridge University Press: Cambridge.
Woodbury, Leonard 1970. "Sophocles Among the Generals." *Phoenix* 24:209-24.
Woodward, A. M. 1963. "Financial Documents from the Athenian Agora." *Hesperia* 32:144-86.
Zeitlin, Froma 1990. "Thebes: Theater of Self and Society in Athenian Drama." In Winkler and Zeitlin 1990, pp. 130-67.

Index Locorum

Oedipus at Colonus is indexed neither for Ch. 2 nor for Ch. 3§3, both of which are continuous readings of the tragedy in which nearly every line is cited.

Aeschylus, *Agamemnon*, 25; *Eumenides*, 77; 139; *189*, 90; *416*, 138; *417*, 140; *844*, 138; *951*, 139; *Laius* or *Oedipus* frag. *173 N² = 387a* Radt, *139*; *Seven Against Thebes*, 73, 74 n. 101; *785ff.*, 130; *887*, 139; *914*, *1004*, 95
Aeschines: *1.28*, 129 n. 97; *2.76*, *3.150*, 90 n. 11; scholium on: *1.125*, 91
Andocides: *1 (De Mysteriis)* : *65*, 91; *73, 77-79*, 90; *75-76*, 89; *2 (De reditu)* : *12, 13-16, 19-22, 23, 26*, 89
Androtion, 58, 142; *FGrH 324F62*, 95
Apollodorus: *3.14.1*, 92-93
Apuleius: *de Magia*: *298*, 166 n. 13
Aristeides: *Hyper ton tettarôn* : scholium on: 172, 96
Aristophanes: *Acharnians*, 120; *Birds* : *757-59, 1355-57*, 129; scholium on: *998*, 91; *Frogs*, 79, 87; *687-88, 689-91, 692, 693-94, 700-2, 706-15, 716-36*, 90; *Knights*, xi; *225, 227*, 93; *257, 314, 452, 461-63*, 92; *551-67*, 91, 92 n. 20; *Lysistrata* : *29-30*, 143; *476-613*, 143; *496-501*, 143; *Thesmophoriazusae*, 120; *Wasps* : *563*, 135; *736, 1003-4*, 129; *Wealth 66*, 69 n. 85; *726*, 164
Aristotle: *Constitution of the Athenians* : *28.3*, 90 n. 11; *29.2*, 137 n. 120, 144; *29.4*, 144; *29.5*, 144; *34.1*, 90 n. 11; *Magna Moralia* : *1189ᵇ29-38*, 137; *On Poets*, 26; *Poetics*, 1, 22, 158; *3.48a20-24*, 155; *1.47a13-16*, 23; *1.47b2ff.*, 19 n. 19; *1.47b14*, 19 n. 19; *3.48b17*, 50 n. 31; *6.49b24-27*, 65, 78; *6.49b27-28*, 17; *6.50a35*, 19 n. 19; *6.50a38*, 20; *6.50b7*, 19 n. 19;

181

182 Index Locorum

6.50b15-20, 15 n. 1, 15 n. 2, 18, 27; 9.51b27-28, 19; 12.52b20, 60; 13.53b17-23, 17; 14.53b28, 19 n. 19; 14.53b29, 19 n. 19; 16.55a19, 18, 18 n. 18; 17.54b15-18, 26; 17.55a22ff., 20 n. 24; 17.55a23-29, 26-27; 17.55a29-30, 20; 17.55a29-30, 20 n. 24; 18.56a11, 19 n. 19; 19.56b8ff., 20 n. 24; 22.58b22, 19 n. 19; 24.59b27, 19 n. 19; 24.60a3, 19 n. 19; 25.60b23, 19 n. 19; 25.61a28, 19 n. 19; 26.62a11-13, 15 n. 1, 18; Rhetoric : 1409a20, 19 n. 21; 1416a14-17, 167; 1419a25-30, 137 n. 120
Athenaeus: 465E = Thebais frag. 2 Bernabé, 128; 631C, 57 n. 48

Cicero: de Senectute : 7.22, 87, 166 n. 13, 168 n. 17
Cratinus: frag. 195K, 60 n. 56

Diogenes Laertius: 1.5, 129
Diodorus Siculus: 13.53.2, 90 n. 11; 13.72.3-73.2, 96, 96 n. 28
Demosthenes: 18.122, 135; 21.79, 135; 22.61, 135; 24.107, 129 n. 97; 35.49, 136; 57.70, 129 n. 97

Epigonoi, 134
Etymologicum Magnum, 163, 164, 16
Euripides: Andromache : 802-1008, 120 n. 74; Bacchae, 149; 1078-90, 88; 1277,

4 n. 7; Heracleidai, 145; Ion, 6; Iphigeneia on Taurus : 577-83, 18; Medea : 824-25, 58; Orestes, 120, 90 n. 13, 91 n. 15; 38, 139; 321, 139; 836, 139; 866-956, 90; 904, 90; 1650, 139; Phoenician Women, 73, 140, 140 n. 134; 1703-7, 98; Suppliants, 10 n. 18; 930, 131; Telephus, 120; scholia on: Orestes, 772, 903, 138; Vita Euripidis : 2 Schwartz, 77; frags. of uncertain tragedies: 852-53K, 146 n. 154

Harpocration, 88
Herodotus: 1.35ff., 134; 1.67.3ff., 97; 4.149.2, 142; 8.55, 58, 92; 9.13.1, 9 n. 16
Hecataeus: FGrH 1 F1, 41
Heraclitus: frag. 93 D-K, 157
Hesiod: Works and Days : 188, 129 n. 96; 353-54, 123-24; Theogony : 184, 138
Homer: Iliad : 6.119-236,132; 9.648 = 16.59, 115; 23.679, 95; scholia on: Iliad 23.679 (= Hesiod frag. 192 M-W), 95; Odyssey : 11.280, 73; 14.56-59, 117; 14.506, 116; 16.273, 116; 16.274-77, 116; 20.166-67, 116 n. 68; 22.1ff., 116; 21.424-27, 116; 21.433, 126; 23.28, 116

Inscriptions: Meiggs-Lewis 2, 125 n. 87; IG I².110+.28-34, 113; IG I²115 (I³104).10-19, 136; IG I³38.8, 9 n. 16; IG I³83.4-5, 9 n. 16; IG II²105.25-26,

Index Locorum 183

29-30, 9 n. 16; *IG II².1283*, 113; *IG II²974.11*, 164; *IG II²1252*, 165; *IG II²4510* = Soph. frag. 4 Diehl, 163; *IG II²4960.17-19, 20-23*, 163
Isaeus: *8.32*, 129 n. 97: 129
Isocrates: *Letters* : *7.13*, 133 n. 105

Lucian: *Makrobioi* : *24*, 166 n. 13
Lysias: *7.3*, 136 n. 114; *9.3*, 136 n. 114; *10.15*, 136 n. 114; *12.3*, 136 n. 114; *12.62*, 136 n. 114; *12.67*, 94; *13.4*, 136 n. 114; *13.7-12*, 90 n. 11; *20 (For Polystratos)*, 88; *20.6, 9, 10, 11, 14, 16, 17, 18, 22*, 89; *19.48*, 90 n. 11; *20.22*, 88; *25.25-26*, 89; *30.12*, 90 n. 11
Lysimachus, 100; *FGrH 382F2*, 99

Metagenes: frag. *14.1K* (vol. 1, p. 708), 60

Oxyrhynchus historian: *VI.2-3*, 90 n. 12

Pausanias: *1.15*, 96; *1.21.1*, 166; *1.26.5*, 58; *1.28.6*, 139, 140; *1.28.6-7*, 98; *1.30.2*, 58; *1.30.4*, 94 n. 22, 98; *2.2.2*, 97; *9.5.14-15*, 142
Pherecrates: frag. *134K*, 91
Philochorus, 58
Photius, 135
Phrynichus, *Muses*, 165
Pindar: *Olympian* : *13.14*, 165 n. 4; *Pythian* : *4.263-69*, 147; *272*, 148; *277*, 147 n. 156; *281-87*, 148; *289-90*, 148; *291*, 148; *293-95*, 148

Plato: *Apology* : *21b1*, 136 n. 114; *31c-d*, 157 n. 21; *40a*, 157; *Phaedrus*, 151; *242b*, 157 n. 21; *Republic* : *392d-394d*, 155; *Symposium*: *194*, 77; *Theagenes* : *128d-e, 129b-c*, 157 n. 21
Plutarch: *A Pleasant Life is Impossible* : *1103A*, 163; *de Genio Socratis* : *578B*, 97; *Cimon* : *8.3ff.*, 97; *Life of Numa* : *4.6*, 163; *Life of Solon* : *22.1, 22.4*, 129; *Lives of the Ten Orators* : *833E-F, 834A-B*, 94; *Old Men in Public Affairs* : *785A-B*, 166 n. 13; *Table-Talk* : *747B, 747E*, 57 n. 48
Pollux: *4.115*, 15 n. 2

Sappho: frag. *1.19-20 L-P*, 9
Sophocles: *Ajax*, 77; *Antigone*, 73, 87 n. 3; *53-54*, 95; *626-30*, 68 n. 81; *Inachus* : frag. 273 Pearson = 273 Radt, 60 nn. 54-55; *Oedipus at Colonus* : *4*, 164; *27*, 114; *36*, 114 n. 63; *39-40*, 138; *41*, 138; *42-43*, 138; *44*, 133, 164; *45*, 114; *49-50*, 115, 116, 117; *49*, 117, 136; *51*, 117, 136; *55*, 93 n. 21; *58*, 99; *62-63*, 98; *67*, 141; *70*, 140; *84*, 114 n. 63, 138; *84-93*, 141; *84-110*, 100; *89-90*, 139; *90*, 114 n. 63; *90-92*, 133; *92*, 114, 141; *100*, 140; *106-9*, 141; *125*, 130; *158*, 93 n. 21; *168*, 122; *174-75*, 115; *176*, 114 n. 63; *184-87*, 121; *199-201*, 126; *205*, 95

184 Index Locorum

n. 24; *226ff.*, 100; *232*, 114
n. 63; *250-51*, 125 n. 88;
254, 125; *258-91*, 135; *269*,
148; *273*, 137 n. 117; *285-
88*, 116; *286*, 136; *308-9*,
123; *347*, 126; *379*, 118;
421ff., 140, 141; *427-30*,
114; *428*, 136; *430*, 113, 136;
443, 113; *444*, 113, 136;
457-60, 141, 145; *458*, 139,
141 n. 139, 145; *459*, 164;
460, 96; *461-62a*, 145;
462b-64, 145; *486-87*, 145;
487, 133, 164; *501-2*, 126;
550, 130; *560f.*, 125; *577*,
96, 133; *590*, 113, 136; *599-
601*, 113, 136; *607*, 121
n. 77; *610-13*, 124; *611*,
124; *612-13*, 118; *621-22*,
96, 154; *622-22*, 99; *626-
28*, 125; *626*, 124, 133; *627*,
133, 164; *629-30*, 96; *631*,
140; *631ff.*, 124; *631-33*,
130; *634-37*, 13; *635*, 134;
636-41, 130; *637*, 141; *638*,
114; *643*, 164; *644*, 130;
646, 141; *647*, 133; *707-19*,
92, 92 n. 20; *720-1043*, 93;
724, 118; *738*, 118; *754*,
118; *770*, 118; *802*, 118;
804-6, 119; *813*, 118, 118
n. 71; *815*, 117; *830*, 9, 118;
832, 118; *837*, 9; *841*, 93;
842, 117; *844*, 9; *850*, 118;
854, 118; *859*, 9; *864-65*,
140; *868*, 118; *879*, 117;
884, 93, 117; *887-89*, 91
n. 16, 93; *891*, 118, 121
n. 77; *893*, 9; *897-901*, 93;
911-23, 117; *927*, 9; *944-
49*, 141; *944-50*, 135; *945*,
164; *951-53*, 117, 118, 135;
960-68, 135; *960-1013*, 135;
964, 136; *965*, 118; *969*, 136;
969-77, 135; *975-77*, 137;
977, 136; *978-87*, 135; *979*,
135; *987*, 136; *988-90*, 135;
991-1002, 135; *1000-1*, 135;
1003, 135; *1003-13*, 135;
1012-13, 141; *1014*, 125;
1022-25, 146; *1026-31*,
146; *1032-35*, 146; *1044*,
146; *1044ff.*, 152 n. 13; *1045*,
146; *1062*, 94; *1065-66*, 94;
1070-71, 98 n. 35; *1070-73*,
94; *1072*, 119; *1079*, 119;
1087, 141 n. 139; *1095*, 94;
1102-3, 94; *1103*, 118, 134;
1108, 126; *1109*, 126; *1110-
13*, 126; *1116*, 152 n. 13;
1125-27, 10; *1130-35*, 133;
1137-38, 114; *1163*, 114
n. 63; *1166*, 114 n. 63; *1169*,
121 n. 77; *1189*, 119; *1194*,
125; *1195ff.*, 125; *1204-5*,
125; *1211-48*, 94; *1231*, 95
n. 24; *1234-35*, 94; *1242*,
152 n. 13; *1257*, 113; *1265-
66*, 129; *1299*, 139; *1332-33*,
140; *1335*, 113; *1348*, 141
n. 139; *1351*, 130; *1357*, 94;
1372-76, 140; *1378-79*, 116;
1383-96, 140; *1389-92*, 140;
1428, 130; *1432-37*, 127
n. 91; *1434*, 139; *1488*, 133;
1489-90, 134; *1494*, 93;
1496-97, 133; *1496*, 134;
1519, 164; *1533*, 164; *1542-
48*, 155; *1552*, 121 n. 77;
1552-54, 134; *1590-655*, 98;
1594, 124; *1600*, 100; *1611-
15a*, 127; *1615b-18*, 127;

Index Locorum 185

1620, 127; *1621-29*, 88; *1626*, 155; *1627-28*, 155; *1631*, 121 n. 77; *1631ff.*, 133; *1634-37*, 133 n. 107; *1637*, 133; *1663-65*, 165; *1697-99*, 127; *1700*, 126; arg. *II*, 91; 165; scholia on: *698*, 58; *1375* = Thebais frag. 3 Bernabé, 128; *Oedipus the King*, 87, 142, 164, 168, 456; *397*, 137 n. 117; *807-13*, 137; *Philoctetes*, 88; *Thamyris*, 165; frag. *730d* Kannicht, 152 n. 13; *Vita Sophoclis* : *1*, 168 n. 18; *5*, 165; *11*, 164; *12*, 164; *13*, 166; *15*, 166; *20*, 115 n. 67
Stobaeus: 146 n. 154

Thebaid, 140; *frags. 2-3* Bernabé, 73; *frag. 2* Bernabé = Athen. *465E*, 128; *frag. 3* Bernabé = scholiast *OC 1375*, 128
Theognis: *16*, 122; *17*, 122; *865-67*, 125 n. 87

Thucydides, 41 n. 9; *1.22.2*, 78 n. 110; *1.136-37*, 120; *1.137.1*, 120; *2.40.2*, 125 n. 87; *3.82-83*, 120; *5.47.2*, 9 n. 16; *8.1.2*, 142; *8.1.3*, 137 n. 120, 142; *8.24-38*, 120 n. 75; *8.24.4-5*, 120; *8.28.5*, 121; *8.31.1*, 121; *8.38.3*, 121; *8.46*, 143; *8.47*, 143; *8.48-49*, 144; *8.53.1*, 144; *8.53.2*, 144; *8.53.3*, 144; *8.54.1*, 144; *8.57*, 137; *8.65.3*, 144; *8.67*, 91, 92; *8.67.2*, 91, 92 n. 19, 111; *8.67.3*, 144; *8.68.2*, 94; *8.86.3*, 144; *8.92.6*, 91; *8.97*, 137

Valerius Maximus: *5.3.3*, 98

Xenophon: *Apology* : *12*, 157 n. 21; *13*, 157; *Hellenica* : *1.1.33*, 96, 96 n. 28; *1.2.13*, 91; *1.7.35*, 90 n. 11; *Memorabilia* : *1.1.4*, 157; *1.1.9*, 159; *2.2.13*, 129 n. 96; *4.3.12-13*, 158

General Index

Admetos, 120
Aegispotamoi, battle of, 90
Alcibiades son of Cleinias, 143, 144
Alcibiades, the cousin of Alcibiades son of Cleinias, 90, 91
Alon (or Halon), 164
Amynos: see Asclepius
Anachronism, 8-10, 112, 156-57, 160
Andocides, 89
Antiphon, 89
Arcesilas of Cyrene, 146-47
Archeptolemus, 89
Archon Basileus, 141
Areopagus, 141; Council of, 141
Arginusae, battle of, 90
Aristarchus, 91
Ariston, son of Sophocles, 166
Aristotle, 15-23, 26-27, 31, 34
Artaud, Antonin, 2, 15-18, 20-21, 22, 23, 26, 28, 36
Asclepius, 11, 163-64, 165, 166; orgeones of, and of Amynos, 11, 165
Asclepieion, 163-64, 165
Assembly, 89, 144

Astyochos, 121
Atîmia, 114-17

Balinese theater, 21
Beckett, Samuel: *Rockaby*, 28, 31, 83; *Mother Courage*, 31
Bendis, 113
Benveniste, Émil, 32, 121, 122
Beschi, Luigi, 164, 165, 168
Boule, 89, 113
Brecht, Berthold, 15; Gestus, 43, 47
Bronteion, 75
Brook, Peter, 23
Brown, A. L., 139
Buxton, R. G. A., 7

Cheiron, *164*
Cheironomia, 57
Chios, 121; revolt of, 120
Cimon, 97
Cleigenes, 90
Cleisthenes, 89
Cleophon, 90
Curse, 128-30; cursing and the Erinyes, 140
Cyzicus, battle of, 89

Damophilos, 147, 148

187

188 General Index

Decelean War, 96
Deceleia, 165-66
Deconstruction: see Différance
Deixis, 57
Demophanes, 89
Derrida, Jacques, 16-17; "Différance," an essay, 150-52, 154-57, 158; Memoirs of the Blind: The Self-Portrait and Other Ruins, 156
Dexion, 11, 164
Di Benedetto, Vincenzo, 115
Différance, 150-61
Draco, homicide law of, 134-38

"Escapist" motifs, 65
Eagleton, Terry, 5
Easterling, P. E., 9, 129
Else, Gerald F., 20, 29
Enktêsis, 113-14, 132
Epeisodos, 60, 83
Epeisodion, 60
Epigenes, 89
Epimeleia, 113
Erechtheum, 92
Eteonos, town in Boeotia, 95, 96, 99, 100, 142
Euctemon, 167
Eumenides, 138-42; see also Semnai

Fischer-Lichte, Erika, 23, 67
Five Thousand, the, 88, 89, 137
Four Hundred, the, 88, 89, 91, 137, 144

Gadamer, Hans Georg, 7
Gide, André: Œdipe, 32-33
Gildersleeve, Basil, 148
Gospel at Colonus, The, 11

Greimas, A. J., 37

Halon: see Alon
Heracles Menutos, 164
Herman, Gabriel, 132-33
Hermeneutic circle, 35-38, 63
Honzl, Jindřich, 29, 62; Honzl's law, 29-30, 67, 69, 72, 76, 81

Intertextuality, 112, 153
Ionesco, Eugène: Les Chaises, 27
Iophon, son of Sophocles, 166, 167
Issacharoff, Michael, 3, 24-26, 27, 31, 34

Jameson, Michael H., 167
Jauss, Hans Robert, 1, 5, 160
Jebb, R. C., 106, 123

Kamerbeek, J. C., 77, 131
Katabasis, 77, 108, 111
Katalogeus, 88
Keos, town in Boeotia, 99
Kidnapping, 120-21
Kitto, H. D. F., 7
Knights, 92
Kwakiutl drama, 4

Lacan, Jacques, 80
Lanza, Diego, 19
Livelihood, 128-30
Longo, Oddone, 90, 120
Loraux, Nicole, 6
Lycurgus, Athenian statesman, 22
Lycurgus, Spartan commander, 166
Lyons, Charles R., 27

Marathon, battle of, 96

General Index 189

Mask, 33-34
Menippus, decree of, 89
Metatheatricality, 3-4, 9, 32, 43, 74, 153, 156

Neleus, 97
Nikostrate, wife of Sophocles, 166
Nomothetai, 137

Odeon, 77

Patrocleides, Decree of, 90
Paulhan, Jean, 21
Pavis, Patrice, 23
Pedaritos, 121
Peisander, 89, 144, 167
Persona muta, 69, 76
Philia, 117-28
Phrynichos, 89, 90, 91, 113, 143
Pickard-Cambridge, Arthur, 69
Piraeus, 91
Polystratos, 88-89
Poseidon, 92-94; Poseidon Hippios, 91
Potniai, 138; as name of Theban town, 139
Prague School, 29
Proagon, 76
Probouloi, 137, 144

Raaflaub, Kurt, 160
Robert, Carl, 167

Samos, 143
Saussure, Ferdinand de, 151
Satyrus, 166, 167
Schmeling, Manfred, 153
Schmid, Wilhelm, 167
Semiotics, 1-3, 8-10, 24-34, 149-51, 155

Semnai, cult of on Areopagus, 139, 140; *see also* Eumenides
Shakespeare: *King Lear*, 25
Sisyphus, 97
Siwidi, hero of Kwakiutl drama, 4
Soteria, 142-46
Steidle, Wolf, 2
Stoa Poikilê, 165
[Stoppard, Tom]: *Rosencrantz and Guildenstern Are Dead*, 159
Supplication, 51-53; suppliant drama, 53, 146
Synoikismos, 111

Taplin, Oliver, 2, 6
Telemachus monument, 164, 165, 168
Theramenes, 91
Thrasyboulos, 113
Thrasyllus, 90
Ta'ziyah, Shi'ite drama, 24
Theater of Dionysus, 4, 15, 25, 35, 149; Long Hall, 39; *skênê*, 39
Themistocles, 120
Theoris, wife of Sophocles, 166
Tissaphernes, 143

Übersfeld, Anne, 36-38

Vidal-Naquet, Pierre, 113

Wewanagila Dance Company of Vancouver, British Columbia, 4. *See also* Kwakiutl drama; Siwidi, hero of Kwakiutl drama

Xenia, 130-34

About the Author

Lowell Edmunds is Professor of Classics at Rutgers University. With Alan Dundes, he has edited *Oedipus: A Folklore Casebook* (Garland Publishing Inc., 1983; reprinted, with new introduction and new bibliographical essay, University of Wisconsin Press, 1995). His *Oedipus: The Ancient Legend and its Later Analogues* (The Johns Hopkins University Press, 1985) will be reprinted in 1997. He has contributed the chapter "Myth in Homer," to the *New Companion to Homer*, ed. Barry Powell and Ian Morris (forthcoming, Brill). With Robert Wallace, he has edited *Poet, Public, and Performance: Essays in Ancient Greek Literature and Literary History* (to be published by The Johns Hopkins University Press, 1997). This collection includes an article by him on the "seal" of Theognis.